To Marie
with
Owen Lee

A Prisoner in Paradise

by Owen Lee

The true story of an illicit love affair with a piece of Mexican real estate

A few names have been changed to protect the innocent and a few sequences have been altered for the sake of brevity.

Other books by Owen Lee:

The Complete Illustrated Guide to Snorkel & Deep Diving, Doubleday & Co

The Skin Diver's Bible, Doubleday & Co

The Skin Diver's Bible, Revised Edition, Doubleday & Co

Owen's English Language Guide to Zihuatanejo/Ixtapa, Seahorse Productions

Promises, A Novel, Fawcett

Mother Nature, Seahorse Productions

On DVD or VHS:

The Sea in Your Future (50 minutes)

The Nature Study Center (30 minutes)

The Endless Sea (50 minutes)

Mother Nature & My Nature (30 minutes)

The Bay, Reef and Jungle Tour (10 minutes)

Cover photo by Owen Lee
Back cover portrait by David Zaitz
Cover layout by Robby Whithead

Seahorse Productions

Library of Congress Control Number: 2007906657
Publisher: BookSurge
North Charleston, South Carolina

1. True Adventure. 2. Autobiography. 3. Diving for Treasures. 4. Captain Jacques Yves Cousteau. 5. Mexico's Golden Beaches. 6. The Nature Study Center & Camp de Mar. 7. The shattered dream.

ISBN 1-4196-7664-4

Acknowledgements

I would like to thank all of my friends and colleagues who in one way or another, over the years, contributed to the content and the context of this book. Special thanks go to Captain Jacques and Madame Simone Cousteau as well as Ruth and Jimmy Dugan for the initial ideas and inspiration that prompted me to write it. My friend, Mark Provo was a great help in revising and refining its theme and contents. As before, Lani Bertino was indispensable in finalizing and formatting the finished product. Finally, I could not have done it without the loving care and hospitality of Trudy Licht, who nursed me through three consecutive knee operations during the process of its creation.

Contents

Introduction

"Nothing is so powerful as an idea whose time has come."
— Jorge Santayana

When I was a teenager in the suburbs of Saint Louis, Missouri, television was still a thing of the future. Then, as now, radio filled the air with the Top Ten and a barrage mindless chatter. About the most exciting adventure available was a ride on an old Mississippi paddle wheel steamboat called *The Admiral*. Reading and movies provided the principal means of escape from the hum-drum life of the Midwestern suburbs. I devoured stories of far-flung adventures and spent weekends watching twenty-five-cent double features at the Brentwood Cinema. They imbued me with a restless yearning to see the world, and a short hitch with the U.S. military occupation of post-war Japan only whet my appetite for more travel. Between semesters, I rode the freight trains to the west coast and worked in the salmon canneries in Wrangel, Alaska.

On the G.I. Bill, a post-war scholarship awarded for U.S. military veterans, I pursued a curriculum in journalism at the University of Missouri. However, a chance encounter with Professor John G. Neidhardt changed my plans.

John Neidhardt was an acclaimed poet and a compassionate crusader for Native Americans' rights. A tiny but robust little man, his heart was a big as the wild mane of white hair that framed his weathered face. He taught me the beauty of words, the meaning of style and the power of conviction. Detecting my innate thirst for travel and adventure, he opened my young eyes to new horizons.

"Your G.I. Bill gives you the opportunity to study wherever you choose," he observed. "If I were you, I would use part of it to study in some foreign country, to get to know another culture, perhaps learn another language." Thus, my unsuspecting mentor launched me on a new career and a life, that of a professional expatriate.

So far my life has exceeded my wildest dreams. It has ushered me twice around the world and into places and situations that I could only have read about had I remained back home in Missouri. I spent three years diving for sunken treasures in Vigo, Spain. I was nearly lynched by a mob of angry Muslims near Casablanca, Morocco. I became the first American to sail and dive with Captain Jacques Yves Cousteau aboard his famous ship, the *Calypso*. I authored three books on SCUBA Diving, explored four of the world's seven seas, and had enough fun to fill several lifetimes.

All this happened more by chance than by choosing. It was more a matter of being in the right place at the right time, and a firm conviction that happiness comes with the freedom to work at what you most love to do and want what you already have.

Of course, everything has its price, even freedom. I had to forsake all vestiges of my Midwestern past. I will never know the intimate joys and comforts of a close-knit family and traditional home. They were simply not compatible with my nomadic way of life.

Life and death came knocking at my door more often than I care to remember. Such risks seemed part of the package. Ironically, however, it was not a dangerous adventure that brought me closest to death's door. It was a steamy but illicit love affair in the tropical jungles of Mexico.

Many friends warned me that such an affair was destined to fail. "It's not only illegal, it's downright perverted You don't know what you're getting into!"

I confess that history proved them correct. My "perverted love affair" has taken me over some rocky roads. I have been squeezed, bilked, terrified, jailed twice, shot at three times, taken on a "one-way ride," and expelled from my adopted country.

Granted, it would have been much easier to fall in love with a beautiful Mexican *señorita*, but that would have been too easy. I had to fall in love with a piece of Mexican real estate. For *gringos*, that was forbidden fruit.

Our relationship was typical of intercultural marriages. For me, it was love at first sight. From the moment I first laid eyes on her, I was smitten with desire. Her lush tropical beauty left me spellbound. I never dreamed that I could actually have her, make her my own. After all, she was a stunning beauty and totally Mexican. I was a horny hippy and very much a *gringo*. Nevertheless, we have been together almost forty years now and we are still in love.

In spite of our many differences, I still feel that we were simply made for each other. I think time has borne me out. We have ramined true to each other through good times and bad, and we are a synonymous and symbiotic part of each other. She is my passionate obsession.

Yet, I often wonder, even in the heat of enduring passion, what am I missing? How may I have been had I not followed my wanderlust and stayed back home in Missouri? What is the real price that I have paid for my illicit pleasures? What delights may my unborn children and grandchildren have given me? How may I be different had I stayed home and nursed my aging parents instead of gallivanting off to the four corners of the Earth? Am I crazy to have abandoned the "good life" of my family and friends to pursue the wild dreams of a love-struck romantic?

You be the judge!

Photo 1: Boulevard Raspail, Paris 1950

It all started in June of 1950 when I headed for Europe. Ever since I first read the stories of Ernest Hemingway, Elliot Paul, F. Scott Fitzgerald and Robert Service, the bohemian life of an American expatriate in Paris had always intrigued me. The mere mention of Paris conjured up sex-charged fantasies of wine, women and song that fired my imagination. As such, the academic aspects of my visit were only secondary. What mattered most was having a good time.

The adventure of escaping the familiar drudgery of the Midwest for my glamorous fantasies of post-war Europe compelled me to follow my professor's advice. Consequently, when my semester ended at Missouri University, I changed my major from journalism to French, crossed the Atlantic on a student ship to Les Havre and enrolled in the *Course de Civilization Françoise* at *La Sorbonne* in Paris.

When I arrived, Paris was basking in the heady ambiance of its post-war Renaissance. The streets and cafes of the Latin Quarter teemed with student life and activity. People from all over the world filled them with lively talk and laughter and among them were many Americans. Most of the Americans there were serious students, but some of us were there primarily to have fun and to bask in the *Gai Paris* that we had all come to know through our favorite authors. Most of the Americans were veterans of World War II or the post-war occupations, taking advantage of our G.I. Bill. Many were creative people who would later gain a certain measure of fame—writers such as Jimmy Baldwin, James Jones and Norman Mailer; artists such as Jackson Pollock, Larry Rivers, Mati Klareien and Jimmy Metcalf. Jacqueline Bouvier, President Kennedy's future first lady, was my classmate at Le Sorbonne. Ernest Hemingway and Henry Miller frequented the Café des Deuxs Magots. Across the street, at the Café des Flore, Jean Paul Sartre spent almost every afternoon at his own private table.

On my arrival in Paris, my first chore was to rent a cheap room with a bath, and that was not easy. The competition for rooms was especially stiff around the Latin Quarter, near the University. It was not unusual for up to a dozen students to share a single bath and water closet (WC). The WCs did not resemble modern toilets. They consisted of a porcelain bowl, about a yard square, with two raised stepping stones for your feet and a hole between them. The British called them "Turkish Delights."

I quickly discovered that a room with a private bath on the Left Bank of the Seine River cost much more than I could possibly afford. Therefore, I scanned the daily want ads in *Le Figaro* and found a room with a bath on the Right Bank at a price that I could afford. But even on the Right Bank the bath was not totally private. I had to share it with the son of my land lady. His name was Jean Jacques Flori, but everyone called him JiJi.

JiJi was a husky guy with a quick smile and a friendly manner. He had short curly hair and the ruddy complexion of an outdoorsman. JiJi spoke enough English to assure me that we that we would not have compete for the WC very often, because he was rarely there.

"I work aboard a ship, and most of the time I am at sea," he explained.

Curious, I asked "Are you a professional sailor?"

"Well, not exactly. I do a lot of sailing, but actually I am an underwater cinematographer."

"Underwater cinematographer? *Que s' que c'est ca*? What's that?"

"I take underwater movies," he explained. Then, he added, "In fact we are going to the preview of a film that I worked on this evening. Would you like to come along?"

"*Avec* pleasure!" I responded.

On our way to the screening, JiJi filled me in on the man who produced the film. By now, Jacques Cousteau's creative vision had already become a legend. As young French naval officers in occupied France, Cousteau and his friend, Phillippe Taillez, had a lot of idle time on their hands and an inquisitive curiosity about the hidden secrets of the seas.

Together, they created the first diving masks by simply attaching a flat pane of glass to an old automobile inner tube. Until then, everything underwater appeared as a mysterious blur. This was due to the optical distortion created by the water as it wrapped around the curvature of the human eyeball. By separating the curved eye from the water with a flat pane of glass, they brought the hidden wonders of the deep into sharp focus for the entire world to see.

A few years later, Cousteau and Emile Gagnon, a French engineer, adapted a standard hospital breathing regulator to work underwater simply by placing a one-way outlet valve over the exhaust port. This became the world's first self-contained underwater breathing apparatus, now known simply as SCUBA. They called it the Aqua-Lung.™

The invention of the Aqua-Lung broke the chains that kept people bound to the surface by their need to breath air. For the first time, man could swim through the water in three dimensions, as weightless and free as a fish, by taking his air supply with him in a tank.

Cousteau himself was astounded by the wild diversity of life, color and movement that he saw underwater and vowed to capture it on film. Shortly thereafter, he adapted an old World War II combat camera to fit inside an aluminum tube with a flat glass port. This enabled him to photograph the hidden splendors under the ocean and produce his first films for the French Navy. His early film clips won the attention of Louise Malle, a famous French film director. M. Malle suggested that they collaborate on a feature length motion picture which became the film that we were about to see—Cousteau's Academy Award-winning film called *The Silent World.*

Captain Cousteau introduced the film. He praised the work of JiJi Flori, Louis Malle, Albert Falco and the rest of his crew. *The Silent World* revealed the hidden wonders of the depths as they had never been seen before. Until now, every photograph of a man underwater showed him encased in a bulky canvas suit, wearing ten-pound shoes of lead and a huge copper helmet. A rubber hose fed air into the helmet and kept him tethered to an air compressor on the surface. Thanks to Cousteau's invention of the Aqua-Lung, divers swam gracefully through the water with rubber fins on their feet and breathing from a tank of compressed air strapped on their backs. Thus liberated, they explored underwater cities of coral populated by myriad forms of colorful marine life. In a wild kaleidoscope of living, changing form and color, they toyed with a friendly giant grouper named Jojo, rode the backs of mammoth-sized whale sharks and fearful "man-eating" sharks. I had never seen anything like it, and neither had anyone else.

The Silent World transformed my concept of Nature. It revealed that far from being a house of hidden horrors as commonly believed, the undersea world was a realm of ethereal beauty and enchantment. For me, the film was much more than mere entertainment. It changed the course of my entire life.

After the screening, JiJi introduced me to Captain Cousteau. The Captain received me with a gracious smile and a hearty handshake. He was tall and thin, almost gaunt. He had the beaked nose and chiseled features of an American Indian. His prematurely grey hair made him appear much older than he actually was, but his cheerful demeanor smacked of eternal youth.

When I met him, I was tongue-tied with awe and admiration. I marveled at what he had done and asked him if there were someplace where I could learn how to dive. He answered in the heavily accented English that was soon to become the signature voice of his popular television programs.

"A French colleague of mine has started a diving school in Palma de Mallorca in Spain," he said. "He is a protégé of my friend, André Dumas, but I don't know his name. Ask JiJi to investigate for you."

Throughout the following school year, I fantasized about the underwater world. As soon as the school ended in June, I left Paris for the Mediterranean island of Mallorca, intent on finding the diving school that Captain Cousteau had mentioned. Just before leaving, however, I became friendly with an elderly grey-haired lady who operated a Turkish Café stall in the central market known as Les Halles. When I told her of my travel plans, she offered to read my future. All I had to do was buy a cup of Turkish coffee and drink it. She would do the rest.

I accepted her kind offer, and when my cup was empty she placed it upside down in its saucer and let it set. After a couple of minutes, she returned the cup upright and studied the patterns that the coffee grounds had left inside the cup.

"Hmmm," she muttered pensively. "*Tu vas voyager beaucoup*. You are going to travel a great deal."

"Yes. I'm leaving for Spain in the next few days," I told her.

"Yes, but that will just be the first of many, many trips. I see you traveling all over the world for many years."

"That's good. I like to travel. But am I never going to settle down in one place?"

"Yes, yes." She studied the cup intensely and then went on. "You will live in that country south of your country. What's its name?"

"You mean Mexico?"

"Yes, that's it. You will live most of your life in Mexico. You will marry a Mexican woman and become a Mexican citizen."

"Why that's preposterous!" I exclaimed. "I don't know

anything about Mexico. I only vaguely know where it is."

She smiled and shrugged her shoulders. "I am just telling you what I see in your coffee grounds."

"You think there's any truth to it?"

"The coffee grounds never lie to me," she said with motherly assurance.

I accepted her predictions with bemused indulgence. I had never put much faith in such things as astrology, Ouija Boards and fortune tellers. They were like looking outside for what only lives inside. I must confess, however, that all her predictions came true, to the letter. And they lost no time in coming.

Palma de Mallorca

In June of 1951, I rode the overnight train from Paris to Barcelona. Then I took an overnight ferry to Palma de Mallorca. At that time, Spain was in the throes of a national transition. Under the dictatorship of Francisco Franco, Spain had been closed to all foreigners. When I arrived, however, Spain had just recently opened its frontiers to international tourism. The Balleric Islands had always been a popular vacation destination among Spaniards, so they were better prepared than the Spanish mainland to receive international tourism, and the tourists arrived there in droves.

As a result of its previous isolation, the ancient city of Palma turned out to be both cheap and charming. Around dusk, the tree-lined *rambla* teemed with people strolling up and down in the traditional evening promenade. *La Rambla* was the scene of much social banter and innocent flirtation. Antique trolleys rumbled along side of *La Rambla*, providing the island's only mode of public transportation. Signs fastened to each end of the trolley cars reflected the Mallorquin sense of humor. One end said, "By British

Airways to London." The sign on the other end said, "By Tram to Palma."

The few automobiles still running on the island were at least fifteen years old, and some were as old as thirty. Yet they were still in daily service. Antique car collectors soon bought them up, often paying for them with a brand new car.

Palma's pre-dinner social life was especially lively, and very cheap. In the many open sidewalk cafes, a glass of good wine cost the equivalent of ten cents. A three-course meal with impeccable service cost less than two dollars.

In Palma I enrolled in the Berlitz School of Languages to study Spanish. This qualified me to continue my studies under the G.I. Bill. My seventy-five dollar-per-month allotment went twice as far as it had in Paris. By exchanging my check at a bank in Tangier, Morocco, I doubled its value in Spanish pesetas. This enabled me to save about half of my allotment for diving lessons and travel.

I rented a small two-room apartment just off Plaza Gomilla for twenty-five dollars per month. It provided a million-dollar view of the entire bay and was only thirty meters from the water. The price included a part-time maid named Josephina who became a kind of surrogate mother. It gave me my first taste of true independence. I named it *Haute Hope Chateau*, or High Hope Castle.

Emilia

Mallorca attracted people from all parts of the world and among them were three people who greatly influenced my life. They were Emilia Laracuente, Robert Graves and Florent Ramager.

I met Emilia Laracuente in a crowded restaurant when she invited me to her table. She was a vivacious young Mexican-American.

Photo 2: With Emilia in Palma de Mallorca, 1951

Emilia had curly black hair, fiery brown eyes and a creamy complexion that turned honey-gold in the Mediterranean sun.

She was a vacationing student from the Chicago Art Institute. Emilia's Hispanic beauty and sometimes outrageous behavior quickly won my attention, then my heart.

Though Emilia preceded the Woman's Liberation movement of the sixties by a decade, she was among the most liberated women I have ever met. Whatever she did, she did with wild abandon, both in and out of bed.

I had been searching for a compatible traveling companion with whom I could tour mainland Spain and Morocco. Emilia volunteered to join me and even pay her own way. So off we went on a wild adventure that soon led to marriage and a close shave with death in Casablanca.

Inspired by the writings of "Papa" Earnest Hemingway, we first went to Pamplona for the Fiesta of San Fermi. There, we learned to drink from wine skins and I ran before the bulls. We then headed south for the Fiesta de Seville. There we drank dry *Manzanillo* from wineskins and learned to dance *las Seguidilla*s. After Cordoba, we toured the Alhambra and Palace of the Moors. Then we crossed the Straights of Gibraltar and entered the exotic world of Morocco and the Muslim culture.

In contrast to Spain, Tangier, Morocco seemed shrouded in mystery and intrigue. Within the walls of the Casbah, row upon row of white-washed houses climbed up a hill like bleacher seats in a giant amphitheatre. They gazed out upon the round harbor and a sheltered boat marina. In the narrow, twisting streets and alleyways, men sat in tiny sidewalk cafes, sipping mint tea and smoking kief through long-stemmed Hooka pipes. Most wore long, full-length kaftans with a bright red, black-tasseled Fez on their heads. Women peered out from behind the traditional veils imposed by their Muslim beliefs. The guttural chatter of the Berber language echoed through narrow passageways and mingled with the pungent odors of couscous and lamb. To me, it was as romantic as *A Thousand and One Nights*, and I could not wait to photograph these exotic people. That was when I got my first lesson in inter-cultural relations, especially those involving the Christians and the Moors. When I began shooting their pictures, the locals threw stones at my camera. I learned later that by taking their picture I was "robbing their spirit" and offending their religion.

In Tangier, we encountered an Australian couple whom we had met in Palma. They were headed to Casablanca to work with the Atlas Construction Company, an American conglomerate. It had contracted to build three B-52 air bases in French Morocco for the U.S. Government and was recruiting workers. Considering that my G.I. Bill was about to expire, getting a lucrative job seemed like an idea whose time had come. Emilia and I figured that we could afford to spend another summer in Mallorca before returning to the States if we both got jobs. We decided to join them on their trip to Casablanca.

In the course of celebrating our reunion, we entered into a place called the Parade Bar. It was a New York-style bar run by a gay couple from America who were both friendly and funny. There, even while submerging ourselves in the Islamic ambiance of Tangier, we embarked on a drinking party that lasted most of the week.

Towards the end of that week, we awakened under a drizzling rain. Since there was nothing else to do, we went to the Parade Bar and started early on Bloody Marys followed by Brandy Alexanders. Around two o'clock, Paul Bowles, an American writer, entered with a group of friends. They joined us at the bar, and we soon cranked up another party. The conversation turned to our sexual relationships. Paul and his friends urged me to "make an honest woman" of Emilia. They dared us to get married that very afternoon and Paul volunteered to make all the arrangements.

I said, "I'll do it if Emilia will do it." I don't know if I was just drunk or crazy as well.

"I know a protestant missionary in Tetouan who will marry you in a minute," Paul assured us. "I'll give him a call."

I really did not believe that Paul could arrange a wedding so quickly, but he did. In my drunken state, it seemed like a fair challenge, so I said, "Why not?" I admit that it was a poor reason for getting married, but what can I say? We did it any way.

We piled into two cars and drove fifty kilometers to the village of Tetouan, in Spanish Morocco. The Baptist mission was located in the beautiful foot hills of the Atlas Mountains. After some hasty paperwork, a personable protestant missionary performed a brief ceremony. Everybody cheered as we sealed our nuptials with the traditional kiss. It was over so quickly, it seemed like just another party prank. But alas, it turned out to be very real.

After the ceremony, Paul and his friends returned to Tangier while we four from Mallorca continued by taxi to an exotic village high up in the Atlas Mountains named *Cheuf Xauen*. Here, we spent an impromptu honeymoon with our Australian friends in a Moorish splendor of a Spanish *parador* hotel, replete with tropical gardens and numerous fresh water springs where monkeys gathered at dawn to drink and chatter. After three days in this exotic Berber community, we returned to Tangier and boarded the overnight night train to Casablanca.

Casablanca

Compared to the bucolic tranquility of Cheuf Xauen, Casablanca was a mad house of urban activity. The Atlas Construction Company had attracted an influx of foreign workers, engineers and technicians. Most were Americans, but many British and French were also there. Modern high-rise office buildings contrasted sharply with the ancient walled city called the *Medina*. Its handsome streets swarmed with antiquated traffic — cars, taxis, buses and numerous horse-drawn carriages. There were no rooms available, so we spent our first night sleeping in the chairs of some hotel lobby with our feet propped up on our luggage. The next day, we managed to rent a small apartment on the outskirts of the city. And before the week's end, we all had well-paying jobs.

Our two traveling companions from Australia had no trouble landing clerical jobs in an office building. Thanks to her drawing skills, Emilia got a job as an illustrator for the company newspaper. Because I spoke a fair amount of French by now, I landed a job as a labor foreman in a huge freight depot near the shipping docks. The jobs paid exceptionally well while they lasted. Compared to the paltry student stipends we both had been living on, we were suddenly rolling in money. Unfortunately, our jobs did not last very long.

The problem arose out of my ignorance about Islamic customs and beliefs. I knew no more about Islam than, say, President Bush did when he ordered the "liberation" of Afghanistan and Iraq. Therefore, we both paid dearly for our cultural naivety. For President Bush, it led to his political downfall. And for me, it almost led to my grave.

My boss was a burly Texan known as "Big Red Norris." He was the personnel manager for the three hundred Moroccan laborers who I was supposed to supervise. Ostensibly, the laborers were hired to do the maintenance work around the freight yard. But actually they did little more than just show up for work in the morning.

I divided my workers, military style, into three platoons of about 100 each. Each platoon had a French speaking leader who served as my translator and liaison with the others. Every morning at eight, we assembled in front of my little eight-by-eight-foot office for roll call. I then translated Big Red's work order into French for the three bilingual platoon leaders. They in turn translated the work order into Moroccan Arabic for their respective platoons. When dismissed, the three platoons then went off to fulfill their respective duties. In reality, however, all but a few simply vanished into a gigantic pile of scrap lumber for the remainder of the day.

The lumber had been salvaged from the various shipping crates that were emptied in the yard. The pile measured about forty feet high and over one hundred feet in diameter. Inside, it was honeycombed with dark passage ways wherein my workers gathered to chat and smoke Kef (hashish) until it was time to go home. No Frenchmen or foreigner would dare enter into this Muslim sanctuary for fear that they might never come out. Morocco was then in the midst of its rebellion against the French that would soon lead to its complete independence.

Big Red Norris hailed from Bartlesville, Oklahoma. Outwardly, he was as rough and tough as a bull, but once you got to know him he was as gentle as a pussy cat. Because I spoke a little French, he insisted of calling me "Frenchy" or "French Fry."

He didn't seem to mind the daily disappearing act of my workers. He explained that they had been hired more for public relations reasons than for their need or abilities. "By handing out jobs to the locals, the company wins the sympathy and support of the local politicians," Big Red explained. "So, no need to fuss or scold them," he advised. "Just let them do their thing."

Well, that was okay with me. But apparently it was not

okay with the Inspector General, who was the company comptroller. One day, Big Red came to me in a panic. "Frenchy, y'all gotta help me! The Inspector General is on his way here, and all your workers are hiding in the lumber pile and smoking pot! From all the smoke coming out, ya' might think that the lumber pile's on fire! You got to get them all out of there and put them to work before he arrives, or my ass is mud!"

With that, Red swaggered up to one of the many openings in the smoking lumber pile and started blowing on a police whistle. Then he started shouted inside, "All right ya'll, we know you're in there, so come on out *now*! Everybody out! Time to get to work!"

I joined his exhortations in French and, one by one, about three dozen men emerged from the lumber pile, squinting in the sunlight and rubbing the sleep from their eyes. Finally one of my French-speaking platoon leaders emerged. I explained the situation in French and asked for his help. I knew we could never mobilize all the workers who were still inside the lumber pile, so I told them to first gather up all the unmanned yard tools — the picks, shovels and rakes that lay about — and hide the evidence inside my little wooden office. Then I rallied all I could and led them to a nearby drainage ditch that needed clearing. I begged them to pretend that they were working on the ditch, at least until the Inspector General had passed. Most of them fell-to with admirable acting skill. But wouldn't you know it, one of them non-chalantly walked off in the opposite direction.

Now, normally I would not have given a damn. They all did what ever they wanted regardless. But this time, I wanted to make a good impression on the Inspector General for the sake of Big Red. So I shouted to the offender, "*Arête toi! Ou est-ce que tu vas?* Stop! Where are you going? The work is here inside the ditch!"

To my dismay, not only did the lone offender stop and confront me, all the others stopped as well and turned their attention back to me. Now I felt the need to assert my authority or they might walk all over me. "*Ou est-ce que tu vas?*" I repeated. "Where are you going? Come back here and work like the others."

The Moroccan looked askance at me and jabbed the air with his middle finger. Then, he turned and casually continued on his way. A disapproving murmur arose from the crowd of onlookers.

"Don't take that kind of shit from this guy!" commanded Big Red from behind me. "Go get his badge and tell him to get lost!"

"*Arête!* Stop!" I cried. "*Revien, tout suite!* Come back here!"

"Just take his badge from him and let him go."

"Give me your badge," I demanded. With that, the Moroccan put his thumb to his nose and wiggled his fingers.

"Can you beat that?" Big Red demanded. "Go get his badge and tell him he's fired."

My heart sank and I wished that I had never opened my mouth. Whoever this man was, I wished him no harm. However Big Red did not tolerate any insubordination. Not from me nor from anyone else. I figured that he probably had a wife and a bunch of kids to feed, and I really felt sorry for him. Now I felt obliged to confront him, take his identification badge and deprive him of his job.

I heaved a weary sign of resignation and ran after the offender. "*Ecoute! Donne moi ton badge.* Give me your badge," I pointed to the I.D. badge pinned to his tattered jacket. "Give me your badge and go home," I commanded.

He repeated his obscene gesture and turn once more to leave.

"Don't let him go until you get his badge," insisted Big

Red. “Don’t take any shit from him.”

I caught up with the offender once more and, taking him by the shoulder, spun him around. As he came around, he plowed his fist dead into my nose and caused it to bleed. Now furious, I countered with a flurry of punches of my own. Being smaller than me, he soon fell to the ground. As he lay on the ground, I bent over him to remove the badge from his jacket. As I did so, he kicked with his booted foot and caught me in the groin. With that, I furiously countered with another barrage of punches and left him on the ground.

As I returned to my workers, they murmured their disapproval. Then I saw the look of approval on Big Red’s face turn to alarm. But it was too late to avoid what was coming. I felt a heavy blow to my head and saw bright flashes of light as I fell to the ground. When I recovered my senses, I discovered that the rebellious Moroccan had run up behind me with a heavy clump of dried mud and stones and slammed it down on top of my head.

Now I was really pissed. Picking myself up from the ground, I laid into him with every thing I had. Once more, he fell to the ground, bleeding from his mouth. I was about to go after him again when two French security police jumped from their pickup truck, grabbed me by an arm and led me towards their vehicle. This time I read the alarm on Big Red’s face in time to save my life.

Glancing behind me, I saw the angry Muslim charge me wielding a huge sledge hammer. I knew that if that hammer ever made contact it would go right through me, so I dove between the tracks of a heavy caterpillar crane and scrambled out the other side. For the following ten minutes, the battered Moroccan and I played cat and mouse, circling each other around the crane. When he came around one corner of the crane, I ducked behind the next and thus kept him at bay.

Instead of helping, the two Frenchmen returned to their trucks to radio for help. Meanwhile, it was clear that the Moroccan intended to kill me, so I called out to Big Red for help. "Hey Red, this guy wants to kill me! Please help me!"

"Well, are you French or American?" Big Red demanded. "I can't get involved if you're French."

"I'm an American!" I screamed. "For crissake, do something!"

With that, Big Red started blowing his whistle again. "Alright, y'all leave him alone 'cause he's an American. Y'all hear?"

The effect was nil. In fact, the distraction had let my adversary get dangerously close. He was winding up to throw the hammer at me, but I managed to duck behind the crane again.

"That's useless," I scolded him. "Go get the security, quick! He's after my blood." Big red turned and ran for the security trucks, leaving me alone to cope with my adversary as we played our lethal game of hide and seek around the crane.

By now, all three hundred of my workers, and some of the crane crews as well, had abandoned the smoking mountain of scrap lumber and come to witness the unfolding drama. They surrounded the crane in a giant circle, and it was disconcertingly clear who they were rooting for.

Somehow, I had to get that hammer out of his possession before he killed me with it. I decided to entice him to throw the hammer at me by making myself a more tempting target. I danced before him until he looked like he was about to throw. Then I ducked back behind the crane. This went on for an unnerving number of false starts. Finally, the Moroccan, wound up and let the hammer fly. The hammer cart wheeled horizontally toward me and its massive head just missed me, but the wooden handle struck me at the waist, just above my belt. The blow knocked the breath out of me, but the worst was yet to come.

In the instant it took to recuperate, the Moroccan had picked up a steel lever bar that was even heavier than the hammer. The crane crews use such levers to lift heavy cargos high enough to pass a lifting cable underneath it. Holding the bar before him like a pole vaulter, he started towards me. Frantically, I looked for some way to defend myself. My eyes fell upon a piece of four-inch-thick timber about six feet long. It lay on the ground between us. As the Moroccan charged me with his heavy steel lever bar, I scooped up the timber and threw it broadside with both hands as he approached. The timber hit him across his chest. The blow knocked the steel bar from his grip and left him writhing on the ground. I lunged for the lever bar, but before I could disarm him one of his compatriots stood on top of it and held it to the ground until my attacker resumed his grip. By now, the crowd of spectators was pummeling me with small stones and clumps of dried mud. The fallen man staggered to his feet with the lever bar still in his grip.

I searched beyond the angry crowd for signs of Big Red or anyone else who might help, but there was nobody in sight. A few more flying stones and clumps of dry mud from the anonymous crowd of Moroccans made me realize that there was a good chance I might be killed.

In my benign world, the prospect of death had always been hidden out of sight and out of mind. If reason prevails, people do not confront life or death challenges unless they are trained and equipped professionals or an aficionado of some extreme participation sport. As far as we know, death is something that always happens to somebody else. Yet, it follows us around like a shadow, playing hide and seek with our animal consciousness. When the possibility of death does show up, it is usually where and when we least expect it — choking on a tough piece of meat from the butcher shop, in the wrath of a jealous lover, in the lethal overdose of a favorite drug.

Death is never ever very far away. It stalks us every day of our lives. Our abiding faith in our own immortality simply hides it from view. It is part of the grand illusion that we humans are somehow impervious to the immutable laws of nature. The threat of an impending disaster such as mine however, compels us to face the prospect of our own mortality. I suddenly realized that if I did not take some action to change my situation, I might very well be killed. I ran for my life.

But run where? The security post and the administration offices were out of my range. I knew I could out race them, for I was in pretty fair shape. However, I had to run somewhere that offered sanctuary, or at least far enough away to buy me some time or hide me from view.

About one hundred and fifty yards to my left was a veritable forest of crated Quonset Huts, those semi-circular metal buildings that were popular during World War II. The wood crates measured about ten feet squared by three feet deep. The crates were stacked four to six high in long rows, perhaps eighty yards long. They were my only hope. I spotted a hole in the circle of Moroccans that surrounded the crane and ran straight through it like a football halfback. The startled spectators parted ranks just enough to allow me passage, and I took off running as fast as I could for the rows of *Quonset* huts.

As I approached the first row of huts, I glanced behind me to appraise my progress. To my dismay, I saw my battered adversary running after me with the steel lever bar still in his hands. At least a hundred of his compatriots followed close behind him.

Now breathless and panicked, I dashed between the stacks

of huts and out of sight, then turned right and ran lengthwise between the rows, then left again. When I could run no further, I scrambled up one of the stacks, rolled over the edge and lay flat on my back, gasping for breath. By the time my pursuers arrived, my gasping had subsided, but I was still almost morbid with fear.

I tried in vain to dissolve into the wood surface of the top crate. Below me, I could hear their Arabic chatter as they milled around the stacks. They were getting closer and closer. To my dread, I then saw the head and shoulders of one of them emerge above a stack, just one row away. Our eyes met, and I knew I had been discovered. The spotter shouted to his comrades and pointed. As they crowded around me on the ground, I detected a note of triumph in their guttural jabber. Hearing a noise behind me, I looked back and saw the end of the dreadful steel lever bar rising in stops and starts as its bearer climbed up the crates to take his vengeance. I decided it was time to confront him so, reluctantly, I got to my feet.

As I stood up the Arabic jabber rose in pitch and a shower of stones and dried mud fell all around me. I clasped my hands before me and bowed in supplication for calm, but it had no effect. The mad man was now approaching with morbid determination and his lethal steel bar.

As his head appeared above the surface, I could see that he was just as exhausted as I was. We were both gasping for air and it occurred to me how ridiculous and futile it all was. *How ironic that I should meet my end like this,* I thought.

Nevertheless, when he began to raise himself up on to the surface, I scurried over and stomped on his hands. He quickly let go and fell back to the ground, the heavy steel rod landing on top of him. The instant that happened the crowd roared in dissent, and a hail of stones and dried mud rained down on top of me. I covered my head with my arms to protect myself. In the interim, my crazed suitor was already climbing back to the top and one of his friends was standing by to pass the steel bar up to him.

This time, instead of confronting him again, I took three running steps and managed to leap to the neighboring stack of crates. To my utter amazement, my obsessed pursuer managed to match my feat. However, the momentum of his heavy steel rod carried him further across the wooden surface until he was teetering on its far edge. A little push was all that I needed to send him the rest of the way over, and the poor man again fell to the ground.

His fall prompted another storm of rocks and mud. My old sport jacket offered a measure of protection, but I sustained some hits on my bare head that left me woozy and bleeding. When the storm of rocks finally subsided, there he was again, wearily receiving the same steel bar from another friend. I quickly bounded a few steps more and jumped to the following stack. Looking back in disbelief, I saw that he was preparing to follow suit. Therefore, as he ran to jump, I did the same thing, and I jumped to the following stack. That left one empty stack on each side of me. If he made it across the gap, I had only one more stack left to jump to. That was the end of the row. Also, I feared, the end of me!

From atop my stack of crates, I could see the entire expanse of the freight yard. In the distance I saw, with intense relief, the flashing red lights atop the company security truck as it came barreling in my direction. I knew then that help was on the way. However, it was still a good distance off and I was not certain they could arrive in time to save me. Even then, my dauntless opponent was hitching up his pants in preparation for yet another attack. Meanwhile, the shower of rocks and dried mud did not slacken, and I only had one stack of Quonset Huts left to jump to. My pursuer crouched down, and then sprang forward to jump.

This time, thank heaven, he did not make it. The tip of the steel rod hit the side of my crate and impaled itself in the wood. My opponent's momentum carried him down the rod and into the wall of crates from whence he bounced and once more fell to the ground. Thus, he diverted the attention of all his companions away from the approaching security truck.

As the truck came closer, I could see that Big Red was one of the three men inside the cab. I ran and jumped to the last stack of crates and frantically waved my arms. Red acknowledged me and waved back. Though the truck approached, it did not dare stop. Instead, it swerved around into a circle. As it passed just beneath me, Big Red leaned out the window of the cab, pointing frantically to the empty truck bed behind him.

I could not hear his words over the din, but I could read his lips. "Jump in the back!" he was shouting. "Jump in the back!" The truck continued in its circle and when it came around again, I knew just what to do. As it passed underneath me, I leaped into the empty truck bed and hung on for dear life.

By this time, the angry crowd of Moroccans had caught on. They surrounded the truck and tried to grab me. One of them actually got a hold on my left wrist, but I managed to shake him off. As the truck accelerated, a hail of stones and dry mud followed for a few seconds, but then we got away.

The two French security men drove me straight to their headquarters and put me in a barred jail cell. "Not to punish you," they assured me, "but to protect you. Because you speak French, they think you are French. And remember, we are at war!"

"As soon as we finish our report, I will drive you home," said one of the security officers.

"Take a couple of days off while we fix this," said Big Red. "I'll do the company report tomorrow. I will make sure that they know you are American and not French."

"Wait a minute, Red. Are you expecting me to go back to work with those guys?"

"I certainly am," Red replied. "You can't let 'em think that we are afraid of 'em. Can he, fellas?"

The two French security officers grunted and nodded in agreement. "Best you continue working just as if nothing happened," one said.

"My life wouldn't be worth two cents," I protested. "They'll kill me."

"No they won't."

"What about the one I beat up? If I were him, I would want to kill me, and I don't blame him."

"We will pay off the one you beat up. All you have to do is identify him for us. You don't have to worry about the others."

"Besides, I'll see that you get a gun to protect yourself," Red offered.

"I wouldn't even know how to use it."

"You don't have to. Just the fact that you have one is all the protection you'll ever need. A gun gives you authority."

"He's right," said the officers. Besides, we will keep our eyes on you. You can trust us."

Later that day, they brought in my bedraggled opponent for identification. He was a mess. "If this is the guy just sign this affidavit, and we'll take care of the rest," they said. "Incidentally, we found out that he did not work for you and Big Red. He was part of the crane crew."

"He had just done his prayers," added the other.

"How was I to know?" I moaned. "I'm really sorry."

"Just sign the paper," they said.

I signed the document. Then I took the opportunity to personally apologize to him. I clasped my hands before me in supplication. I said, "Please forgive me."

Then I offered my hand in friendship. Instead of taking it, he worked up a bloody quid and spit it out, right in my eye. I can't say that I blamed him.

It was not my intention to return to work the next day. Frankly, I had never felt comfortable in the presence of Islam's religious intolerances. Now, I was genuinely afraid that my former adversary, or one of his Muslim friends, would seek vengeance by killing me. Emilia agreed. "Maybe it's time to return to Mallorca," she suggested.

After a few days at home, Big Red came to visit me. "We have got nobody to take your place," he complained. "So if you come back just until we find a replacement for you, I will double your salary."

His offer was tempting. For every week we continued working there, we could remain another month or two in Mallorca. However, I confessed that I did not understand the Muslim mindset and was afraid of what might happen.

"What about the guy from crane crew?"

"We fired him and gave him a handsome severance check, so he won't bother you." he assured me.

"I wish I could believe that," I said.

"Besides, I will post a security guard in your office. I will also give you a gun to protect yourself," he promised. "In fact I insist on it."

The next day, I reluctantly returned to work at the depot, and my workers seemed genuinely pleased to see me. A French guard moved into my office that afternoon, and though I never discussed what happened that day, I made certain that they all saw the.38 caliber revolver that I now wore on my belt.

Three weeks passed and nothing out of the ordinary happened. Neither did Big Red manage to find a replacement for me. Meanwhile, we reveled in the idea that we had already accumulated enough of a nest egg to float us through the coming summer in Mallorca without worries. Then, because of my own carelessness, things suddenly changed.

I had become so comfortable in my work that I no longer wore the revolver on my belt. It was heavy and cumbersome, so I kept in locked in my desk with all the paperwork. However, I would sometimes not bother to lock my desk. One day, the resident guard and I returned from lunch at the company cantina to find the revolver missing. This threw me into a state of panic and paranoia. I left a note on my desk for Big Red and went directly home. That night Emilia and I hastily packed our bags and bid farewell to our friends from Australia. By the next night, we were back on the welcoming shores of Palma de Mallorca.

Robert Graves

With the legitimacy of a marriage license behind us, Emilia seemed to change rapidly. After returning to Mallorca, the incessant parties began to affect her personality. She became insanely jealous and possessive. I could not so much as look at another woman without incurring violent attacks and reprisals. It seemed that I was always defending myself for some offense, whether real or imagined. Most were completely unfounded, but the effect was the same. Her jealousy placed a tremendous strain on our relationship and eventually sent me to the hospital with a stab wound in the belly. However, for the first couple of months we were still getting along.

Posing as a freelance writer and photographer, I took Emilia to the small village of Deia where I hoped to interview a British writer named Robert Graves and perhaps write an article about him.

Robert's first book, *Goodbye to All That*, had already won him a measure of literary fame. Now, with the recent publication of *I Claudius*, Robert's literary genius was beginning to dawn on the world. Other books, such as *King Jesus* and *The White Goddess*, among others, would soon catalyze his stature as a poet and author of fiction. He won numerous prizes including a nomination for the Nobel Prize.

Meanwhile, however, Robert Graves was broke. In the course of our conversation, Robert complained that he did not have enough money at that moment to feed his copious family. By chance, I had just received an unexpected windfall and I volunteered to loan him a hundred dollars. Robert gratefully accepted and, thereafter, never stopped repaying me with various favors.

For reasons I can only imagine, Robert fell madly in love with Emilia. He christened her as his "Dark Goddess" and, after she and I had separated, he urged her to stay and live in Deia. Perhaps the biggest favor Robert did for me was to take Emilia off my hands. She was his mistress for several years, and he even bought her a house in Puerto Vallarta, Mexico.

Robert and I remained good friends. Three years later, Robert loaned me his little "Fisherman's Cottage" where I wrote most of my first two books on SCUBA diving, *The Complete Illustrated Guide to Snorkel & Deep Diving* and *The Skin Diver's Bible.*

Florent Ramager

Florent Ramager was the third major Mallorcan influence on my life. He was the French SCUBA diving instructor whom Captain Cousteau had referred to when I first met him in Paris. Florent was a descendant of French nobility and he looked and acted every bit the part. Handsome, suave and debonair, he was always elegantly dressed and impeccably mannered. He was a typical lover of the sea, but far from being a typical seaman. He had inherited a small seven-bedroom chateau on Mallorca. He lived there with his grossly overweight wife, whom he always referred to as "*Ma Petite Marielle*."

Andre Dumas, one of Cousteau's early diving companions, taught Florent everything he knew about diving. After which, on the deck of his forty-foot power boat, Florent opened the first and, at that time, the only

SCUBA diving school in the Mediterranean Sea. I felt privileged to be counted among his first paying students.

Florent made sure that my first dive fulfilled my expectations. With mask, fins, twelve pounds of lead weights on my belt and a steel tank of compressed air strapped to my back, I felt awkward and clumsy until I entered the water. Once in the water, however, I felt eerily weightless and free, despite my heavy weight belt. Until you have actually tried it, breathing underwater is a sensation that is hard to imagine. Suffice it to say, it blew my mind!

With a double-hose regulator feeding me air through a rubber mouthpiece, Florent escorted me below, following a weighted decent line that dangled from his boat. As we submerged into the depths, Florent looked over me like a mother hen. From time to time, he paused to equalize the pressure in his ears, then he motioned for me to do the same. About thirty feet below the surface, we arrived at the sandy bottom. Dancing fingers of sunlight radiated down from the restless surface and frolicked among the shadows of the submarine terrain. Some eighty feet away, the sandy bottom merged with the cobalt blue of the Mediterranean sea, and the two became one.

Only a few fish were evident and, at that depth, they all looked gray. Where were all the wild colors I had seen in *The Silent World*? I soon learned that water gradually filters out all colors of daylight except for blue and green. That is why the surface of the sea always appears to be blue or green.

Tapping my shoulder, Florent signaled that it was okay for me to release the decent line and follow him. Then we took off, swimming weightless and free. I followed him deeper into the blue We paused to observe a school of graceful angelfish gliding over the rocks. For me, it was like a visit to another planet, an unearthly realm of ethereal beauty and charm that I had never before suspected. As Florent turned to begin our ascent, I knew that I was hopelessly hooked on SCUBA. I have remained so ever since.

Photo 4: Robert Stenuit, John Nathan, Myself, Florent Ramager, and John Potter

My three classmates at Florent's diving school and I became fast friends. We were so compatible that we all became major influences on each others lives. They were Robert Stenuit, a marine archeologist from Brussels, Belgium; John Potter, who hailed from Martha's Vineyard, Massachusetts; and John Nathan who came from San

Francisco, California.

True to his academic calling, Stenuit took up diving to expand his academic horizons as a marine archeologist. Like me, Nathan wanted to learn to dive just because he had always wanted to and now, at last, he could. However, John Potter had other motives. With only one lung, John Potter was rather frail to be taking up SCUBA diving, but he was highly motivated. He had been an avid coin collector throughout his entire life. His specialty was collecting coins from sunken treasure ships. He had spent years in the musty naval archives of Spain, France, England, and Holland researching the various maritime disasters and recording their sunken cargos of treasure. He had already compiled a list of over three hundred possible treasure wrecks and was now compiling a book about them (see *The Treasure Diver's Guide,* ©1957 John S. Potter, Doubleday & Company).

Now that the new Aqua-Lung enabled people to swim unrestricted by air hoses over the seafloor, Potter saw the timely opportunity to use SCUBA to find these sunken treasures before somebody else did. Over post-dive drinks at Joe's Café in *La Plaza Gomilla*, I learned the common thread that had brought us all together.

"The invention of the Aqua-Lung has brought ninety percent of all sunken treasure within human reach," Potter boasted, "and I intend to be the first to reach them!"

When he said that we all responded in unison, "Can we come with you?"

Potter's impish grin spread from ear to ear. "There are several possible wrecks that can make us all rich," he assured us, "and I will tell you all about them, tonight at nine at Joe's Bar." His eyes shined with mischievous anticipation, and we knew he was not fooling.

That evening, as usual, we all met at Joe's Bar. Also as usual, Potter arrived late, but he was carrying a large manila envelope. Fixing his gaze on each one of us, he did not return our greetings. Instead, he silently withdrew four sheets of paper from the large envelope, very purposefully placing one sheet in front of each one of us.

"Alright boys," Potter said. "These are your tickets to fame and good fortune. I've gone over my list of the fifty best sunken treasure wrecks of the world and these are the four best, the best candidates to make us all rich. Read each page and then pass it to the guy on your left. After you've read all about them, we will vote on which one we want to go after first."

"Did anybody ever tell you that treasure hunts cost a lot of money?" I inquired.

"Who cares what it costs?" cried Robert gamely. "Let's just do it!" Johnny Nathan echoed his sentiments. Then so did I.

Potter waved an accusing finger at us. "Don't you worry your little heads about money," he scolded. "I've got that all taken care of, almost. I'll tell you about that later. But for now, to work! Read each paper, then we have to vote. After we choose, I'll tell you my secret."

Eagerly, we each read the paper before us, then passed it on for the next to read. Each sheet contained the description of a different wreck with sunken treasure, its approximate location and the value of the treasure it was logged to have carried.

Of the four wrecks Potter described, by far the richest one was a paddle-wheel steamship named the *S.S. Central America*. She was a side-wheel steamer carrying over four hundred passengers and twenty-one tons of gold from the famous California 49ers near San Francisco, bound for Boston. In September of 1857 she sank in a hurricane off the coast of North Carolina with a loss of all life. However, the water off the coast of North Carolina tends to be very deep, probably up to ten thousand feet deep. That is well beyond the limits of air-breathing breathing divers (see *Ship of Gold in the Deep Blue Sea*, ©1999 Gary Kinder, Vantage Books).

The next of the four richest wrecks was a Spanish galleon named the *Atochca*. She sank in the seventeenth century somewhere south of the Florida Keys. The *Atocha* carried over fifty million dollars worth of Mexican silver and gold that was destined for the King of Spain.

The third candidate for salvage was the wreck of a British merchant vessel named the *S.S. Teel*. She was carrying another rich cargo of gold bullion from the vaults of San Francisco to New York. She had run aground in a hurricane somewhere on Scorpion Reef, some eighty miles off the eastern coast of the Yucatan Peninsula.

The fourth and final candidate was the one we all voted for. It consisted of a flotilla of Spanish treasure galleons that was sunk in a mighty naval battle on the third day of October 1702, just fifteen miles north of the Portuguese border in the Bay of Vigo, Spain. Stuffed into their bulging holds was a three-year hoard of New World gold and silver worth over $140 million.

Its story began with the death of King Carlos V of Spain near the end of the 16th century. Charles II was a descendant of the Habsburgs of Austria, but France and Spain conspired to put Bourbon into the empty throne of Spain. The British and the Dutch were afraid that such a powerful alliance as France and Spain would dominate the world's seven seas. Therefore, they allied themselves with Austria and declared war. It was known as The War of Spanish Succession, which lasted from 1700 to 1714.

As an act of war, Britain and the Netherlands blockaded Spain's major port of Cadiz, the home of Spain's annual treasure fleet from Mexico. The blockade deprived Spain of the "King's Fifth," a twenty percent tax on all foreign imports that entered the country. Spain badly needed that money to help finance their war, but could not take the risk of an encounter with the enemy in Cadiz. The stakes were too high.

The Spanish galleons waited out the blockade, riding at anchor in Havana, Cuba. After three years of languishing in the warm, tropical waters of Havana, wood-eating worms took their toll on the galleons, and they badly needed overhaul and repairs.

They could wait no longer. Their French allies sent twenty-three warships to Havana to escort Spain's seventeen treasure galleons back to Spain. The combined flotillas did not attempt to run the blockade of Cadiz. Instead, they turned north and on September 23, 1702 they sailed into the Bay of Vigo, Spain.

Once safely inside Vigo Bay, the fleet of cargo galleons anchored in defensive positions deep inside the Bay. Their armed escort of twenty-three French warships anchored in a defensive circle to protect them. French and Spanish marines barricaded the narrow entrance to the Bay with a floating chain of tree trunks. They fortified the narrows and the beaches with ships, cannons and garrisons of infantry.

Nevertheless, a British spy soon discovered their whereabouts and notified his superiors in Cadiz. On October 23, 1702, exactly one month after they had entered Vigo Bay, the combined British and Dutch fleets from Cadiz sailed into the Bay to attack.

The battle raged for three full days and nights. On the third day, the British Flagship the *H.M.S. Torby*, managed to break through the floating barrier of tree trunks that blocked the narrow entrance to the inner bay of Rande where the treasure fleet waited behind their protective shield of French war ships. What followed was one of the greatest naval massacres in history. All twenty three of the French warships and the seventeen Spanish cargo galleons were either sunk, captured or scuttled. Over three thousand French and Spanish were killed or captured and many more were wounded or maimed. The invading British and Dutch lost over eight hundred men.

Photo 5: Partial engraving of the Battle of Rande in Vigo Bay, October 23, 1702

No sooner had the smoke cleared from Vigo Bay then a stream of treasure seekers plunged into its muddy depths in search of wealth. If you read Jules Vern's masterpiece, *20,000 Leagues under the Sea*, you would discover that the sunken treasures of Vigo Bay were the principal source of financing for Captain Nemo's immortalized voyage aboard his fabled submarine, *The Nautilus*.

Many diving expeditions followed, but none of them enjoyed the flexibility and freedom of movement that we did. Being tethered to the surface by their need to breathe air, they were limited in both depth and range. As John Potter pointed out, we alone would have the means of moving independently in three dimensions while breathing air underwater.

"No matter how efficient our predecessors might have been, pockets of treasure are bound to still be there," Potter insisted.

Of course, we all agreed with him. We all pursued the same boyhood dreams of finding treasure as he did. Nevertheless, there were practical matters to consider.

"At risk of being a party-pooper," I said, "How do you plan to finance this operation?"

"Ah ha!" admonished Potter. "I knew that was coming." He waved accusing finger at us. "I told you I had a plan. And here it comes." Then he cleared his throat and raised his glass. "I propose a toast to my little baby sister," he proclaimed, "for she is the little angel who may soon answer our prayers."

"Your sister is rich, then?" Nathan questioned.

"No. Not exactly rich. Just charming and cute. Maybe even sexy. I wouldn't know. I'm not that kind!"

"Then what does your sister have to do with us?" Florent inquired in his heavily accented English.

"Well, I have never mentioned this to any of you, because

it was none of your damned business. But now, I guess it *is* your business, so I might as well tell you. My little sister recently got married."

"About time!" Nathan chuckled.

"I'll drink to that," I offered.

"I still don't get it," Florent said.

"The point is that my little sister did not marry just any old slob like you or me. She has better taste than that. She married Hank Luce Junior, the son of Mister *Time*, *Life* and *Fortune*, all of which need a good adventure story about successful treasure hunters like us!"

"I'll drink a double to that one!" I exclaimed

"Hank Junior is a really nice guy, very open and friendly. When I talked to him after the wedding, I told him that I was learning to SCUBA dive in order to find sunken treasures. When I mentioned the treasure of Vigo Bay, he was really excited. 'It sounds like there might be a story there,' he said. 'If you sell us exclusive rights to the story, maybe we can help finance.'"

"*Et voila!"* Stenuit exclaimed.

"That's what he said to me, I swear to God. And why not? For *Life* magazine a treasure story is a natural."

"*Life* magazine? Who is ziss?" Florent asked, scratching his head.

"It's not a person. It's a magazine," Nathan explained to Florent, "something like *Paris Match."*

Florent threw his head back and cried, "*S'ailler*! Now, I got it! Zay want to print the story. *Magnifique!* Do you zink zay will pay?"

"Yes, it's practically a done deal." Potter proclaimed. "But it won't happen over night. I will probably have to return to New York to nail down the deal, but I think they'll go for it. It's just a matter of time."

"Bravo!" Florent put in.

"Double Bravo!" Robert echoed.

"Ah-ha, me too!" Nathan called.

"I propose a toast," said Potter, raising his glass again. We all raised our glasses of Fundador. "To the Treasure Divers of Vigo Bay!" Potter exclaimed. We all clinked our glasses and echoed his words, "To the Treasure Divers of Vigo Bay!" We laughed and drank, far into the night. Somehow, we all sensed that our treasure hunt would come true.

Potter was right on both accounts. Our adventure story was a natural for Life magazine, and it took some time to iron out the details, over eighteen months to be exact.

Meanwhile, I could not wait. When my semester ended at the Berlitz School, so did my G.I. Bill and its student stipend. That meant no more of my care-free life on the Isle of Mallorca. I had to find a job, and do it quickly.

TV Wasteland

In the mid 1950s, the American economy was still basking in the glow of its post-war boom. New York City was on a roll and so was the entire country. It was a good time to find a job, but you had to be choosy. Otherwise you risked selling out your precious lifetime on Earth for mere survival. Personally, I had always felt that if you would not willingly pay to do the job you are paid to do, it is a job not worth doing. In other words, you had to love it or leave it.

Not everybody had equal access to a good job. Most people settled for less than the best they could do for themselves merely for the sake of expediency, usually to feed their children, then wound up stuck in the job for the rest of their lives. As that old saying went, "Finding the right job is not so much what you know, as it is who you know." It had been my experience that in order to get a job that you really wanted, you had to get to know the right people first, and then volunteer to work for just for the love of doing it.

In New York City, I had the good fortune to know enough of the "right people" to land a job as an advertising copywriter in a schlock mail order advertising agency. The agency was located on East 46th Street, near Madison Avenue. I rented a tiny fourth-floor walkup apartment on West 45th Street, so I could walk to work in a matter of minutes.

For a small-town boy from Missouri, Midtown Manhattan was an exciting place to live. The daily scene was charged with energy. However, the physical ambiance was very cold and impersonal. After three months there, it occurred to me that I had not seen a plant nor blade of green grass since I had arrived. I yearned for some vestige of nature that was not so contrived.

One day, I visited Washington Square Park in Greenwich Village. At that time, Washington Square was still a green meadow of grass. Three well-worn footpaths trisected the meadow like a pie, piercing the heart of Little Italy and China Town. I felt more at home in Greenwich Village than I did in Midtown Manhattan. Consequently, I ran want ads in a new local newspaper called *The Village Voice*. The ad read, "Seek rent-controlled apartment in Greenwich Village for under $50."

I never really expected to get a reply, but after a few weeks, to my great surprise, an elderly Italian lady offered me an apartment on the third floor of 548 West Broadway (now LaGuardia Place) near the corner of West 4th Street. It was right in the heart of Greenwich Village, and the rent was only thirty dollars per month.

When I went to see it, I realized why the price was so low. The place was revolting. Plaster slabs peeled off the walls like dried fish scales. A full inch of old newspapers covered the rotten wood floors. The bottom layers of newspapers dated back to the early 1930s. To make matters worse, countless animal droppings were sandwiched between the old newspapers, imparting an odor that could stop a freight train. Furthermore, the dappled surface of the crumbling plaster was inhabited by millions of New York's famous tiny cockroaches. The walls were covered with them! It was enough to turn your stomach.

But what a location! I tried to not look at the disgusting filth and instead see it as a unique opportunity. To find a comfortable yet cheap apartment right in the heart of Greenwich Village was a major accomplishment.

I rented the apartment and had it fumigated. Then, while continuing to sleep in my mid-town digs, I started its total renovation. Working at night and on weekends, I stripped the interior down to its bare brick walls and broad-planked floors. Then I gradually rebuilt it to my own taste. In retrospect, I think that renting that apartment was the wisest move I ever made. By releasing me from the burden of having to pay the high rents common to midtown Manhattan, it liberated me and greatly expanded my horizons. While providing me with a great place to live and work, it also became my ticket to freedom, to live my life just as I pleased.

The advertising agency that I worked for was very active in the brand-new medium of black and white television. For me, black and white television was even more exciting than SCUBA diving. television was, and still is, the most powerful means of disseminating knowledge and wisdom ever conceived. Its power to inform and persuade, for better or worse, boggled my mind just as the underwater films of Captain Cousteau once did. I dove into the medium with the same enthusiasm I dove into the sea.

However, there were not many schools qualified to teach the new medium. It was still too new. People had to learn it by doing it, and I offered to do it, gratis, until I became of value to the team. I often worked twelve-hour days. As soon as it was offered, I studied TV writing and production. I even studied the maintenance and repair of Arriflex cameras. Soon, I was not only writing, but also producing and directing my own TV commercials. It was beginning to look like I could have a successful career in television if I wanted it. As I got to know the medium better, however, I became disillusioned with its conveyance of "knowledge" and "wisdom."

If the world's powers had used the persuasive abilities of the television medium for all it was worth, I think we would be living in a much different world than the one we know today. It would have been a world in which the electronic dissemination of knowledge and wisdom could have transformed our relationships to be in harmony and balance with the eternal truths of Nature rather than with the egocentric fantasies of mankind. We might even have avoided the consequences of Nature's rebellion—the growing ozone hole, acid rain, global climate changes, murderous storms, draught, floods, world hunger, global warming, earth quakes, and tidal waves.

I believe that the wise use of the electronic media can and could have saved mankind from many so-called "natural" disasters that are actually induced by human activity. TV is, after all, the ultimate tool of education and reform. At the same time, I feel that we humans are failing to live in sustainable balance and harmony with Nature, simply because we have not been taught how to do it.

The electronic media is capable of teaching the entire world how to live in balance and harmony relatively cheaply and quickly. Unfortunately, however, the people who run the media are obviously not inclined to use it for all its humanly worth. Instead of exploiting its uncanny powers of persuasion to establish global balance and harmony with the universe, they use it to promote the ever-growing demands of an ever-expanding consumer population. Of course, such growth is doomed to ultimately fail, for it defies mathematical logic. Yet we continue on this self-destructive course even in the knowledge that our children and their children will eventually have to pay the bill.

Instead of disseminating knowledge and wisdom, the medium appeals to the lowest common denominator of popular taste. I read that most TV story scripts must meet a prescribed computer profile to even qualify for production. Violence, smut, mayhem and conflict are required elements in every successful TV story. A respected research company claims that by the time a child turns fifteen, he or she has already witnessed over fifteen thousand murders on the family telly.

Because of all this, the idea of pursuing a life-long career in television began losing its appeal. I now had to ask myself, *Is this what I really want?*

As much as I loved the medium, I determined that it was not what I really wanted. It seemed to me to miss the point of living, just as TV had missed the point of being a great medium of communication. The world did not revolve around the TV mail-order sales of Charles Antel's Lanolin Hair Spray. *There has to be something fulfilling than this*, I thought. And sure enough, there was.

I was wrapping up the last half hour of a daytime beauty show, when I got a fateful phone call from John Potter. He was calling from Vigo, Spain.

"Heya' old buddy, good news! I closed the deal with *Life* magazine. They will finance us for up to three years in return for exclusive rights to the story. That means that the treasure hunt is definitely on. And we need you here to help us find the treasure, and maybe make a film. Are ya' interested?"

"Hey! Well yes, of course I'm interested. It's just that… is Johnny Nathan there?"

"Yes. Robert and Florent are on their way. All we lack is you."

"How much does it pay?" I asked.

"The divers get $100 a month base pay plus forty percent of whatever treasure is found," Potter answered. "But first, the Spanish Government gets fifty percent off the top, so that's only forty percent of the $50 million estimate, divided between the five of us, that comes to about $10 million each. Hey, not bad eh?"

"And if we don't find the treasure?" I asked.

"Not much, a hundred dollars a month plus expenses."

"Jeez," I whined. "I make that much every day."

"Yeah, but ya' know, this is not about money," Potter admonished. "This is about love, passion, freedom. It's about doing just what you always wanted to do instead of doing what somebody else wants you to do. It's about adventure, romance! Think of all the fun we'll have. How many guys can even think about going on a real treasure hunt like this? And if we find treasure, well, there should be plenty for everybody."

"Can I have the rights to shoot a film about the expedition?"

"I don't see why not." Potter answered. "Of course *Life* might want first crack at it."

Had I been able to see something more rewarding in my future than making television commercials, like making fiction films or even good documentaries, I would not have given Vigo a second thought. I would have remained in New York City where all the action is. However, my chances of ever breaking out of commercial TV seemed hopelessly remote. What I saw in my future was a bird in a gilded cage — perhaps another marriage to another jealous wife, a home in the suburbs with a forty-year mortgage, the daily grind of commuting to work and the usual crop of renegade kids, their cars, their teenage rebellions, their university tuitions, insurance policies and hospital bills. I could read the hopeless resignation on the faces my colleagues. I could see it in the jealous tirades of my ex-wife. To me, it was a trap. My own dull feelings of creeping resignation were reason enough to flee while I still had a choice.

Meanwhile, I missed diving. Every dive was a new adventure, a new exercise in freedom. Moreover, I loved the idea of living and diving in Spain. Even if we did not find the treasure, what better way to spend one's youth? If worse came to worse, I figured I could always find another job. But how often could dive for sunken treasures in Spain? To share the adventure with my old diving buddies and party pals would be a dream come true. Now, if I could use my new talents to do a film on the expedition, I would have the best of both worlds.

The next day, I phoned Jean Jacques Flori in Paris with my proposition. "How would you like to come to Vigo Spain and shoot a film about diving for sunken treasure?" I asked.

"I can't," he answered. "I'm about to go to Nepal to shoot a feature-length documentary."

"I don't mean to do it right now. The treasure hunt may last for years."

"Do you mean would I like to do it some time in the future? *Bien sure*? Why not?"

JiJi's response put my mind at ease. It somehow legitimized my leaving a good-paying job in New York City to go hunt for sunken treasures in Spain. It gave my move a legitimate purpose.

I phoned Potter and informed him of my intentions to participate and film the expedition. Then I gave notice to my clients, friends and employers. Through them, I had no trouble renting my apartment for five times what I had paid for. it. Once again, I commended myself for having spent the time and money to remodel it. The rent was my ticket to freedom to do as I pleased. Within two weeks I was on my way to Vigo, Spain.

Treasure Divers of Vigo Bay

Photo 6: Florent's Dive School

John Nathan picked me up at the airport and drove me to meet with Potter who was now living in Vigo. Within the following week, first Florent, then Robert Stenuit showed up.

As Potter handled all the permissions and paper work, we divers focused on the logistics and supplies. First, we leased an old diesel-powered sand barge named *Dios Te Guarde.* God guards you, proclaimed the name of our vessel, but the uncertain chug-chug of one-cylinder diesel made us dubious of its durability. Nevertheless, we fitted it out with a steel A-frame crane and winch, water pumps, hoses, lines and heavy tackle. Two high-volume air compressors were installed in the bilge to feed the Air Lift Pump, a device needed to vacuum away the thick overlay of mud and muck using air.

Finally, we began scouting out the locations of the sunken galleons. The local fishermen revealed where they snagged their fishing lines or nets or encountered concentrations of fish. Both might indicate the presence of a shipwreck. We then used underwater metal detectors and probes to verify that metal lay buried beneath the mud. Thus we located at least a dozen wrecks.

Next, we used the air pumps like underwater vacuum sweepers to excavate the mud and debris from first one, and then two more galleons. Within a month, their bilge timbers lay exposed to human eyes for the first time since 1702.

Using our hands like a fan, we swept away the silt to examine between the planks and ribs for signs of treasure. And what did we find? Canons, over a dozen of them, and some weighing as much as two thousand five hundred pounds. We also found hoards of cannon balls melded together with piles of heavy ballast stones. They were probably carried in the ship's bilge to serve as ballast.

But what of the $140 million worth of Spanish gold and silver? After almost two years of searching almost every day, we had found only six silver pieces of eight, all of them embedded into the orange oxidation that coated one of the cannons.

Meanwhile, new research revealed that most of the treasure had been successfully removed immediately preceding the battle and sent to Madrid on the backs of burros. This did not bode well for our treasure hunt. However, one possibility still remained viable.

Photo 7: Treasure Divers at work

Photo 8: Cleaning encrustation from cannon

Photo 9: Treasure Divers of Vigo Bay

Britain's share of the captured treasures had been stowed aboard a captured galleon that was taken away by a British warship named the *H.M.S. Monmouth.* A professional researcher had found the *Monmouth's* log in the British Naval Achieves in London. The log revealed that, "on leaving Vigo Bay to return to England, the galleon *Monmouth* struck a shallow rock whereupon it bulged and sang immediately." After much debate, we deduced that the rock in question must have been the one called Carumeros.

Among the local fishermen, Carumeros Rock was well known as a shallow fishing shoal. It lay in just three meters of water off the southern tip of the Cies Islands, twelve miles offshore. On our first dive there, John Nathan and I discovered several ships' cannons, hundreds of cannon balls and an old cutlass handle. There was still no trace of the galleon, or of its three hundred-ton cargo of silver ingots, however. That meant that after striking Carumeros Rock, the galleon must have floated free and drifted off with the southerly currents before it finally sank. Consequently, while Florent and Robert continued searching the galleons within Vigo Bay, John Nathan and I rented a small motor launch and moved to a little house near the outlying village of Bayona to focus our search on the *Monmouth's* galleon.

On a nautical chart of the area, Nathan and I divided the area down current from Carumeros Rock into sections like the slices of a gigantic pie. We defined each slice by laying two weighted lines on the bottom. We visually searched in between the two lines, diving twice each day. When one slice was searched, we moved the outside line over to make a new slice and began again. Thus, over the following two years, we visually searched every square yard within a mile radius down current from Carumeros Rock. Nevertheless, the treasures of the *Monmouth's* galleon continued to elude us. We could only surmise that the Spanish themselves, or perhaps some previous treasure expedition, had found the treasure before us.

Our failure was embarrassing. We feared that if we did not find treasure soon, the editors at *Life* magazine might cancel our contract. However, Robert Stenuit saved the day. He discovered six encrusted silver pieces of eight that were stuck to a cannon. That revived their interest. A couple of weeks later, the editors of the magazine renewed our contract for another year.

During the warm summer months, the magazine sent two reporters, Anne Chamberlin and Ken McLeish, to keep tabs on their investment. Every morning, they earnestly asked us the same question, "You think you guys will find the treasure today?" We could easily read the picture in their minds — the classical treasure chest on the seafloor, its lid open, its coffers overflowing with gold doubloons and silver pieces of eight, with a few strands of pearls spilling over its sides. We had all entertained the same naïve fantasy.

Consequently, we always responded with the same earnest sincerity, “Well, ya’ never know. This could be our lucky day!” Beneath our cheerful veneer of optimism, however, we all sensed that unless we hit pay dirt soon, our days as paid treasure divers would soon end.

Shooting the Film

Photo 10: Owen with Underwater Camera

About that time, JiJi Flori finally made contact by phone. He declared himself ready to shoot the movie of the expedition. By now, however, the expedition was on its last leg. Our dive suits were patched and tattered. Our steel air tanks were pocked with rust. Our boats leaked and needed repairs. Worse yet, our spirits were crushed. We were not in top show form. Nevertheless, I asked JiJi to come, and within a week he showed up with his assistant, Yves Piard, a 16mm Éclair camera and about five thousand feet of 16mm commercial Ecktachrome film.

In anticipation of JiJi's eventual arrival, I had prepared a half-hour shooting script of what had transpired, so it would be relatively easy to re-enact the scenes for the camera. However, we would need the collaboration of every one in the crew, so I called them together to get their vote.

"Since we never actually found much gold or silver, the hunt itself is our only treasure," I explained. "The chances are that John Potter's book and this film will be the only treasures we will ever take home with us. So do I have your pledge to collaborate?"

We all voted "yes" and for the following two weeks we all became actors playing ourselves.

I could not imagine how I would manage to scrape together the necessary funds to actually develop and copy the film and finally edit it into a viable program, but with the kind help of a New York producer named Dale Reardon, it somehow got done. Two years later, my film *The Treasure Divers of Vigo Bay* won an award at the third annual Underwater Film Festival in Los Angeles, California. It also won the attention of Ruth and Jimmy Dugan, who were Captain Cousteau's main collaborators in the U.S. This eventually led to my joining the staff of Captain Cousteau aboard the *Calypso*. But more about that later.

Fond Farewells

No sooner had we finished shooting the film than the editors of *Life* notified us that our contract would not be renewed, just as we anticipated. This imposed some drastic changes on all of us. For JiJi, Robert and Florent, it was no big problem. Being Europeans, they simply packed up their belongings and went back home from where they had come. For us Americans, it was not so simple.

By now, Potter owed so much money that he could not leave Vigo, even if he had wanted to. Before leaving, Potter had to finish the book he was writing for Doubleday & Company, collect the second half of his advance on royalties and pay off his debts.

As for me and John Nathan, we didn't know what else to do so we just keep doing the same. We stayed where we were and hired ourselves out as commercial divers. For a few months, we survived by scavenging the bottom of Vigo bay for scrap metal, lost anchors, fish traps and sunken mussel beds. This bought us a little time, but we barely earned enough to live. Furthermore, we had lost the glamorous aura of being real Treasure Divers. Now we were simply two more of the local maritime workers. We were different people.

My eventual salvation came in the form of a letter I received from Ken McCormick, Potter's editor at Doubleday & Company. In my spare time, I had written a short novel based on my experiences in commercial television in New York City. At John Potter's suggestion, I had submitted the novel to Ken McCormick. The letter asked me to contact him regarding my novel, so I phoned him with hopeful anticipation.

When Ken answered the phone, he said, "Well, I read your novel, Owen, but I'm afraid we can't use it."

"Dare I ask why not?"

"Frankly, we don't think it has a ready market."

"Do you think it's badly written?"

"No, to the contrary. The novel shows me that you can write quite well, but it simply has no marketing prospects. Books are like any other product. Right now, books about television are a glut on the market."

I could not conceal my disappointment and I was about to hang up when Ken threw me a pleasant surprise. "However, I have a proposition that may interest you," he added. "You guys are pioneers in SCUBA diving. I think that SCUBA diving has an enormous market potential, because nobody has yet done a book about it. Do you see the difference?"

"Well, yes, I see the difference all right."

"If you would be willing to write the book about SCUBA diving, I can arrange to pay you a ten thousand dollar advance on your royalties."

I literally shouted with glee. "Wow!" I cried. "That is music to my ears!"

With my own salvation assured, it was now John Nathan's turn. One rainy day in the fall of 1958, John and I were having a snack on the open veranda of our house when a beautiful eighty-five-foot motor sailor slid gracefully into the Bay. We watched with admiration as she came about, hove-to and set her anchor less than eighty yards offshore. We watched curiously as three men on board lowered an inflatable dinghy over the side and started heading in our direction. On such gloomy days, company was always welcomed.

"They must be coming to see us!" exclaimed John. And indeed, they were.

John grabbed the umbrella that we kept behind the door and trudged off through the rain toward the beach. I watched as he exchanged greetings and helped to drag their dinghy up onto the sand. Then he escorted them towards the house. As they approached, I recognized that one of the men was Paz Covera, a friend we had met at the Fontana Cabaret.

Photo 11: Owen & Johnny at a Halloween party

Paz was a short, jovial little man who shared our lust for the girls at *La Fontana*. His round ruddy face always wore a quirky little smile, and he was quick to laugh for the slightest reason. He had the thick neck and broad shoulders of a body builder. We exchanged *abrazos*, that hearty, back-slapping embrace that is the standard macho greeting in many Latin countries. I exchanged names and shook hands with his shipmates. John Nathan emerged from the house with a bottle of Fundador and some glasses. We all gathered around our big round table as he poured the brandy.

"Paz, I really like the way you travel," John said as he poured the drinks. "Most people arrive here by car or by tram."

"Well, as a matter of fact, we came here especially to see you," Paz said.

"How so?" John inquired.

Paz nodded towards his two companions. "I had the good fortune to meet these two gentlemen at the *La Fontana Cabaret.* They informed me that they are delivering that beautiful yacht to Miami via the Canary Islands and the Caribbean."

"Hey, that sounds fabulous!" John cried.

"They also informed me that they just lost one of their crew to an attack of appendicitis and are now looking for someone to replace him."

"Fantastic!" I cried.

"The last time we talked, you mentioned that you were looking for a way to sail back to the States. Well, if you want to go, here it is." He turned to his two British friends, "Isn't that right, fellas?"

"That's right," they nodded. "We could definitely use a couple more hands on the crossing. Our auto pilot is out, and it's just too much steering for the two of us."

"That sounds great," I said.

"The only catch is that we can't wait," explained one of the Brits. "We're on a tight schedule, so if you can go right away, we can even pay you."

"You can count on me," John assured them. "I've been ready to go for some time."

Paz turned to me. "How about you, Owen? Do you want to go along?"

"It sounds mighty tempting," I answered. "But I just got a contract to write a book, and Robert Graves has offered me a little cottage in Mallorca where I can hang out and start writing. If I go with you guys, I know that I'll never get any writing done. So, I think that I had better stay and get some work done."

"Well OK," Paz said, "have it your way." Then he turned to the two sailors. "How much time does John have to get his things together?"

"As soon as you can move aboard," answered one of them. "There's no urgent hurry but…"

"The sooner the better," interjected the other. "We want to reach Miami before the hurricane season."

"How about two days?" the first inquired.

"Two days is plenty," said John.

We helped the two Brits launch their dinghy to return to their boat, but Paz stayed ashore for a couple more drinks. "I'm really gonna miss you guys," said Paz. "I don't have anybody else to drink with." Both his words and his sight were beginning to blur. We accompanied Paz to the trolley stop and he rode the next tram back to Vigo. His departure saddened us. It symbolized what was going on inside our heads and our hearts. It made us realize that after almost three years of fun and games on the beach, the party was really over.

I helped John dig out his luggage and start packing his belongings. We worked silently, each lost in our own reverie. For me, it was a nostalgic review of all the adventures we had shared. For the past three years, we had been closer than brothers. Our lives had literally depended on each other. We had been the closest of buddies, not only underwater, but above it as well. We shared not only the same job, but the same house, the same meals, even a few of the same girls from *La Fontana Cabaret*. In the process, we logged more than fifteen hundred dives together.

Finally, I broke the silence. "Well, we never found the mother lode," I admitted, "but it's been a fabulous three years, old buddy. I'm really going to miss you."

John stopped packing and turned to me. "Yeah, I was just thinking the same thing," he said.

"You will always be my number one buddy, no matter where you are," I said.

"The same goes for me," Nathan said, "both under the water and on top of it."

We exchanged *abrazos* and slapped each other's backs. "I wish you the best luck in the world, old buddy," I croaked.

"Yeah, yeah, I wish the best for you too."

That night we went to *La Fontana Cabaret* for one last fling. In those days, Spain was still ultra conservative. "Decent girls" could not go out with us without dragging along a Madonna or chaperon. Consequently, they were off limits and not worth cultivating. For that reason, the showgirls of the *La Fontana Cabaret* became our principal source for fun and games. They all knew us by name and showered us with kisses. When *La Fontana* closed at three o'clock in the morning, we often invited our two favorites, Juanita and Carmencita, to come home with us. This time, when we invited them, we partied until dawn.

The two girls were still asleep at noon when the two yachtsmen came knocking at our door. "Are you about ready to go?" they asked. Of course we were not. Nobody could just walk out on the life we had shared for so long without some reluctance. However, the two sailors indicated that they were anxious to leave, so we all obliged. The girls and I helped to carry John's luggage down to the dinghy that waited on the beach. We stowed the luggage in the bow, then helped to drag the dinghy to the water's edge.

"Let's keep in touch, old buddy," I croaked. We embraced each other with a final *abrazo*. "I'll let you know as soon as I arrive," John said.

"Arrive where?" I queried. "Where are you going?"

He shrugged his shoulders. "Wherever the ship takes me," he answered, smiling.

The two girls and I gazed after them until they had transferred John's luggage onto the yacht and climbed up the boarding ladder. When they hoisted the rubber dinghy aboard, we started waving goodbye, but it was way too soon. There was a lot more deck activity as they prepared for their departure. At last, they started the engine, and we watched as they winched up the anchor and lashed it to its chocks. Finally, with a loud blast form her air horns, the yacht motored up into the wind and set sail.

The yacht had the buxom beauty of a typical motor sailer. Her mainmast soared forty feet through the roof of her spacious deckhouse, while aft of the cockpit a smaller mizzen mast stood by at the ready. The unfurling of the jib and mainsail from their roller reefing canisters was a joy to behold. The mainsail seemed to climb up the mainmast of its own volition, luffing and snapping in a light ocean breezes. Finally up went the mizzen sail, like an infant mimicking a bigger brother.

Under full sail, the yacht glided out of the Bay, as graceful as a swan. Although, we always phoned each other on the twentieth of January, our common birthday, that was the last I ever saw of my old diving buddy. John Nathan died of emphysema on the Island of Barbados in May of 2005.

As for me, the melancholy loneliness of Vigo's rainy winter soon got to me. The following month, I reluctantly bid John Potter farewell and returned to Mallorca, where it all began. Robert Graves had kindly offered me the use of one of his guest houses which he called the "Fisherman's Cottage."

On arriving in Deia, I was surprised to encounter my ex-wife, Emilia Laracuente. She had been living in Deia for the past couple of years, part time as a bachelorette in the heart of Deia and part time as Robert Graves' mistress in another one of his buildings. When Robert learned of my presence, I feared that he might be jealous. I assured him I harbored no designs or grudges. He kindly reiterated his offer to loan me his Fisherman's Cottage without my even asking.

Robert's Fisherman's Cottage was simply an oblong shed made of white-washed stone and stucco. Inside, it measured perhaps ten by twenty feet long. It offered neither electricity nor running water. Its furniture consisted of a double bed with a mattress, a table and chair made of raw wood and a ceramic wash bowl on a wooden stand. It had only one door and one small window above the table. It was here where I wrote the major portion of my first book on diving. It was here, also, where I met Marshall Allen, an eccentric millionaire from New York City. Marshall was destined to become a major influence on my life in the near future.

Homesick

Around mid summer, I finished the first draft of my book on diving. About the same time, I got word that the tenant who had sublet my apartment in New York City would soon be leaving. Furthermore, I had not seen my parents is almost nine years and I was feeling guilty about neglecting them. After all, they had given me a great set of genes and a wonderful childhood. They raised me as best they could. The least that I could do for them was to pay an occasional visit.

About that same time, my parents inquired about the possibility of coming to visit me in Europe. Since they had never been to Europe, I thought that was a great idea. The only problem was that I was now on a schedule. I had recently promised a yacht captain that I would go back home on his sailboat that was departing from Palma on the 5th of November. Sailing the Atlantic was something I had always wanted to do, and this seemed to be an ideal time to do it. I phoned my parents and urged them to meet me in Paris as soon as possible so I could set sail in November.

"If you come soon, I can drive you around and translate for you," I promised.

On the 25th of August, I flew to Paris and met my parents in Le Bourget Airport. I was shocked to see how much they had aged. Nevertheless, it was joyful reunion. After dinner that evening at the Tour D'Argent, my dad spread out a map of Europe on a cocktail table to review his plans for our grand tour. They had just six weeks of vacation and they wanted to see as much of Europe as they could before returning.

"Don't try to squeeze too much into one trip," I warned them. "Better to do less and enjoy it more." But they were determined.

The next day, my Dad purchased a small Renault car and we took off for Bordeaux. Within the following six weeks, we did our best to visit every country in continental Europe. Heading East from Bordeaux, we stopped first in Carcassonne to stroll its famous ramparts. In Provence, we scaled the roman ruins in Arles, danced on the famous Pont D'Avignon, ate *bouillabaisse* on the quay de Marseilles. Then, we pressed onward to the Cote D'Azure, Nice, Cannes, St. Tropez and Monaco.

In Italy, we ate pasta on the *quais* of Positano, supped in the green hills of Tuscany and marveled at the beauty of Miguelangelo's David. In Rome, we explored the Coliseum, got blessed in the Vatican and gazed at the ceiling of the Sistine Chapel. We walked the rutted streets of ancient Pompeii, rode gondolas through the canals in Venice, then drove onwards to Greece.

In Athens, we explored the ruins of the Greek Acropolis and drank our share of tart Ouzo, then headed north to the

Swiss Alps, the elegant shores of placid Lake Como. In Germany, we drank beer with students in Heidelberg, ate Sauerkraut and rode a boat up the Rhine River. We safely navigated the St. Barnard Pass into France, and then headed cross-country for the tree-lined *ramblas* of Barcelona. The idea was to get me back to Mallorca in time to return to the United States under the sails of an old gaff rig schooner called *The Don Quijote del Mar*.

Leaving the car in Barcelona, we flew to Palma. There, my parents accompanied me to Deia to gather up my meager belongings, then saw me off on my crossing of the Atlantic under sail, and later returned to St. Louis via Paris and London.

The European tour had left me and my parents totally exhausted. Like most tourists, we had tried to squeeze too much into too little time. Furthermore, we were totally saturated with each other's company. Therefore, there were no tears or regrets over our parting. We no longer felt guilty about living far apart from each other. It had been a wonderful trip and a touching reunion, but enough was enough We departed with much love and a much better understanding of our differences. Now, we were all perfectly willing to go our separate ways.

While living in Mallorca, I had become acquainted with several yacht captains and determined that they comprised a special breed. A good yacht captain must not only be a good sailor and navigator, he must also be a jack-of-all-trades, a person who can repair almost anything even while at sea under the most brutal weather.

Professional yacht captains are a nomadic breed of nautical know-it-alls who roam the seas at the behest of their boat's owners. Usually, they live with a wife or a girl friend of similar inclination who also serves as a deck hand and cook. I grew to admire them as a lot, because most of them were living by doing what they loved to do most, which is my definition of a wise person.

One such couple was Arthur and Esther Watkin, the paid crew of *The Don Quixote del Mar*. Arthur hailed from Southampton, England and Esther from Hampton, Rhode Island. They lived aboard *The Don Quixote* in the Marina of Puerto Pi. After several social encounters, I had become quite friendly with Arthur and Esther and often admired their nomadic lifestyle. One day, over drinks, they informed me that the owner of their boat had asked them to sail it across the Atlantic to Miami, Florida. Remembering John Nathan's departure from Vigo, I volunteered to go along as crew, just for the experience. After all, it had been my dream since boyhood. They gratefully accepted, and on the 3rd of November 1959, we set sail for Miami and home.

Sailing the Atlantic

Every extended sailing voyage becomes a major rite of passage, like it or not. As the last sight of land slips below the horizon, so do all your earthly problems. Granted, your earthly problems do not really vanish. They are simply overwhelmed by a brand new set of problems relating to the sea. The few earthly problems that survive an extended sea voyage are those that stow away in the labyrinth of your subconscious mind. For that reason, an extended sea voyage provides the perfect opportunity to review who you are and decide where you are going.

Among other things, a long voyage at sea reveals just how unimportant all your earthly problems really were. When alone at the wheel of a sailboat, with nothing but an endless canopy of stars sparkling amidst the endless tracks of sea and sky, you are likely to discover an astounding number of hidden thoughts and emotions underlying that social veneer that you present to others. You become an integral part in your immediate environment and intimately connected to the entire universe. It is a divine reunion with the cosmic reality that everything is intimately connected to everything else. I suppose that's part of the allure of sailing. It is very likely to change your life.

Photo 12: The Don Quijote del Mar at sea

The Don Quixote del Mar was a three-masted schooner-yawl. She measured fifty feet long with a twelve-foot beam. Below decks, she accommodated our five-person crew with comfort and ease. In addition to Arthur, Esther and myself, there was Alaister Reid and his wife Mary.

Alaister was a friend of Robert Graves and a staff writer on *The New Yorker Magazine*. He was also a brilliant conversationalist. His witty comments and urbane stories helped to relieve the inevitable periods of boredom that come with long crossings.

We were like five peas inside a tiny can. With one of us standing wheel watch at all times, the two couples took turns sleeping in the double-sized bed up forward of the main mast where there was a modicum of privacy. I had to share my single bunk space in the galley and salon with all of them, however, so I took to sleeping on deck above the foc'le under an ebony canopy bearing a billion stars.

By the time the *Don Quixote* reached the Canary Islands, she had lost one of the three cylinders in her diesel engine. Without power, we had to backwind our main sail in order to heave to a stop and drop anchor in the port of Lanzarote. Captain Arthur phoned the owner and asked him to send a new cylinder sleeve and piston assembly via air freight. But apparently, the parts got lost in transit. After two weeks, Arthur phoned again. Once more, the parts never arrived. Finally, Arthur phoned the owner and threatened to abandon the boat as is, where is, and that seemed to do the trick. After two months of waiting, the parts finally arrived.

We jury-rigged a block and tackle to lift the engine from its mounts. With our boat still rocking and rolling at anchor, Arthur managed to replace the faulty cylinder sleeve and piston assembly. It was then I realized that professional yacht captains must be jacks-of-all-trades while at sea.

Three months after our arrival in the Canary Islands, we finally weighed anchor to continue our crossing.

Throughout our voyage down the eastern coast of Spain and also from Gibraltar to the Canary Islands, brisk breezes from abeam moved us along at six to nine knots on a broad reach. With such a breeze, the mizzen sail could be trimmed so that the vessel virtually sailed herself. But from the Canary Islands, west to the Caribbean, the prevailing trade winds blew directly from astern. With the trade winds billowing first one, then the other of our twin headsails, our little craft yawed and wallowed like an overstuffed pig. It was a constant struggle for the helmsman to keep her on course. We each took our turn at trying to repair the automatic pilot system, but nothing worked except the person on watch.

After thirty-two uneventful days at the helm, we made our landfall on the island of Antigua and treated ourselves to a fresh food dinner ashore. A few days later, we sailed northward, working our way up the Leeward Islands. The Caribbean Islands are conveniently close to each other, permitting sailors to sail by day and to sleep in a different port almost every night. If we especially liked where we were, we simply stayed a few days.

After two glorious months of sailing through the Caribbean and the Bahaman Islands, we finally arrived in Miami, Florida. It was exactly one year from the day we had departed from Mallorca.

With the last quarter in my pocket, I phoned my parents collect and asked them to buy me a ticket home. A week before Christmas, I was back in my boyhood home in Brentwood, Missouri, almost ten years after I had left it for summer school.

My visit home was sweet and nostalgic. I delighted in visiting my parents and my old school chums. But as somebody said, "Home is where the heart is," and after a few weeks the novelty waned. With the excessively familiar tranquility of Brentwood, Missouri, I started wondering, *What's new? What next? What am I missing?*

As always, my parents urged me to stay home, settle down, get a J-O-B, get married, and produce some grand children to amuse them in their old age. But family life was not my calling. I sincerely felt then, as I do now, that there were already too many kids in this world. I worried about their future, even though they were not even mine. Furthermore, my rent controlled apartment in New York City was soon to be vacated by my sublet tenant. I returned to the Big Apple to finish writing my SCUBA book and edit my film about treasure diving.

The Big Apple

By previous agreement, I moved back into my New York City apartment while my rental tenant was still in it. My tenant was an actor named Gregory Workman. In order to survive, however, he worked as waiter in an Italian Restaurant on McDougal Street. After a couple of frustrating years of auditioning in New York City, he had decided to pursue his acting career in Hollywood and was due to leave in just three days.

Greg had many contacts in show business. After hearing about our treasure hunt in Spain, he arranged for me to appear on a daytime television quiz show that was appropriately titled *Treasure Hunt*. A comedian named Jan Murry was the host of the show.

In order to qualify as a quiz show contestant, I had to fill out volumes of questionnaires and forms. Therefore, the producers and writers already knew what the contestant knows and does not know, before he or she goes on the stage.

In that way, I figured, the writers and producers controlled the contents of each show. As long as they wanted to keep a contestant on the show, they would simply ask questions that they already knew he would know. When they wanted a contestant off the show, they simply asked those questions that they knew he did not know. Before they asked me a question they knew I did not know, I had the good fortune to win $18,000 in cash plus prizes.

That was enough to kick-start my new life in the Big Apple. With money in hand, I phoned JiJi Flori in Paris and asked him to air freight the unedited film footage that we had shot of the treasure hunt in Vigo, Spain. When it arrived, I sent it straight to the lab to be copied and edge numbered.

Fire Island

Meanwhile, throughout the summer months, I spent every weekend that I could on Fire Island, a long sand bar that lies just offshore of the southern coast of Long Island. My millionaire friend, Marshall Allen, maintained an elaborate complex there where he entertained his friends and I was privileged to have a standing invitation. The complex included a huge octagonal guesthouse that could sleep up to twenty people and a large swimming pool. Marshall himself lived in a private little cottage at the opposite end of the pool. He would emerge only occasionally to participate in the endless party, then retreat to the privacy of his cottage when he had enough. However, he saw to it that nobody in the guesthouse need ever lack anything. His bar was always stocked with plenty of beer, booze and refreshments. His refrigerator was equally well-stocked with cheeses, meats and snacks. And if that weren't enough, there was always an open bowl full of pot sitting in the middle of a big round cocktail table.

When the summer ended, Marshall did not let the party die. He simply moved it to his luxurious three-story townhouse on West Thirteenth Street. From Saturday night until Monday morning, his friends could count on the same perks and amenities that he offered them on Fire Island. If you wanted something different for a change, a *Village Voice* reporter named John Wilcox offered a free list of alternative parties every weekend via his telephone answering machine.

It was in this ambience that I first met Dale Reardon. In the course of casual beach-party conversation, I found him to be bright and personable with a good sense of humor. When I learned that he produced films for such rich clients as IBM and the U.S. State Department, I told him about my film, *The Treasure Divers of Vigo Bay,* and asked him to recommend someone to do the editing and post-production work.

"Let me see the footage," he said. "If I like what I see, I will do it cheaply. If I don't like it, I won't do it."

I grumbled about being poor, and then asked, "How much would you charge?"

"How can I tell you until I've seen the raw footage?" he demanded impatiently. "I've got to see it first. And if I really like what I see, I might even do part on speculation."

After I showed him the film, Dale volunteered his editing talents and the use of his post-production studio on fifty percent speculation. He also guided me through the post production process and taught me everything I know about editing. Even if a bit temperamental at times, Dale was always ready, willing and extremely able to help me. As a result, we produced a neat little half-hour documentary on *The Treasure Divers of Vigo Bay* in just a few weeks.

When I first met Dale on Fire Island, he had told me about his impending divorce and complained that it was driving him crazy. In revolting against his mundane role as a responsible middle-class father of two, Dale had abandoned his comfortable midtown apartment to his wife and kids and proclaimed himself to be a "free man" but, in fact, he was not free. He dragged the burden of his guilt with him to his third-floor film studio in the West Fifties together with a queen-sized bed and an electric hot plate. In his effort to drown out his marital anguish, Dale jumped into the New York party scene with both feet. Haunted by his failed marriage, he tried every possible alternative to it, including all the varieties of "sex, drugs and rock and roll."

Dale cultivated an impressive coterie of beautiful, liberated women, They came to share their newly acquired independence with him, and I was invited to join the fun. Consequently, our editing sessions at the Movieola became shorter and shorter while our parties lasted much longer. We did not break any post production speed records, but we had a ball and we did finish the documentary.

In the process, Dale and I became more than fast friends. We were adult playmates. Soon, we were ready to give up work entirely and devote full time to our diversions. However, we both got involved with other commitments. Dale was involved in editing a feature film, and I still had still had my film to promote.

I screened my *Treasure* film at the first annual Underwater Film Festival in Los Angeles, California. The film won the attention of Ruth and Jimmy Dugan. As a correspondent for *Stars and Stripes* during World War II, Jim Dugan wrote an article about some young French naval officers in the port of Toulon who had developed a new way of deep sea diving. One of them was Lt. Jacques Cousteau.

Jimmy Dugan and Cousteau were so taken with each other's talents that Cousteau asked Jimmy to help him write a book about their diving experiments. Cousteau's first book, *The Silent World*, was the startling result. It became an instant bestseller and revolutionized man's concept of the oceans. It soon evolved into the Academy Award-winning film of the same name that I had first seen in Paris with JiJi. Ever since, Ruth and Jim Dugan had worked as Cousteau's official media representatives in the United States.

After seeing my film, Jimmy and Ruth came to congratulate me. Then they added an intriguing postscript. "Commandant Cousteau is looking for a French-speaking American film maker to join his team aboard the *Calypso*," Jim informed me. "If you would be interested in the job, please send me a copy of your film, and I will make sure that the Commandant sees it."

I happily gave him the film I had just shown, but I regretted it almost immediately. Having spent the last of the prize money on the post production, it was the only copy I could afford to print. Therefore, I anxiously phoned Ruth and Jimmy for possible results far too often. Each time, Jimmy assured me that he had sent the film to Cousteau and urged me to be patient. More time passed, and after several months of silence, I virtually forgot about it.

Meanwhile, survival in the Big Apple came to dominate my existence. The money I had won on the television show was now gone. Furthermore, I was a failure at keeping books because I was not accustomed to paying my own expenses. Throughout my year aboard the *Don Quixote del Mar*, I had practically no expenses. Before that, in Vigo Bay, *Life* magazine paid our expenses and gave us divers a monthly stipend. Before that, I had lived on the G.I. Bill. Somehow, I was always taken care of.

But the Big Apple knew no such largess. New York had always been a cold, cash-and-carry city. It was clear that there was little hope of returning to the commercial TV business any time soon. By now there was a long line of recent graduates from the NYU Film School standing ahead of me. Seeing no alternative, I simply continued diving.

Commercial Diver

I christened myself, "Tech Divers, Unlimited" and placed a two-line ad in the yellow pages of the New York City telephone directory. By so doing, I managed to attract enough business to survive, barely.

However, commercial diving proved to be very different from treasure diving. After a few months, I began to suspect that I got only those jobs that none of my competitors were willing to accept. For example, The New York City Water Commission hired me to burrow eighty yards into a five-foot diameter black water outflow in the East River to repair a broken section with quick-drying cement.

Later, International Underwater Contractors (IUC) hired me to pour the underwater cement footings for the locks of the St. Lawrence Seaway throughout the winter. Topside, the wind chill often dipped to twenty below zero. Underwater, it was warmer, but we had to keep jiggling our air hoses to prevent the entry hole from freezing solid. Off Andros Island, I was hired to protect a photographer's backside from aggressive sharks and only narrowly escaped being bitten myself. However, my most dangerous work was for the U.S. Navy.

Photo 13: Commercial Diver, 1959

The U.S. Navy hired me to film stereophonic motion pictures of air-charged water as it flowed along hulls of its warships while moving at various speeds. This produced audio-visual recordings of what the Navy calls a "ship's signature." To get the shots, we divers had to be within ten or fifteen feet of the hull as the ships passed by. Stabilizers, antennas and sonar transponders protruded through the hulls of such vessels, so we never knew what was coming, and several times they only narrowly missed us.

I soon learned that if I wanted to survive the risky business of commercial diving, I should get some professional training. Therefore, I enrolled in the Commercial Diver Training program offered by IUC of City Island, New York. For three months, I learned the fast-evolving techniques of underwater construction, demolition, cutting, welding, drilling, well capping, saturation and mixed gas diving. Needless to say, the school taught me a lot. But what I really learned, at the end of the day, was that I did not want to be a commercial diver. Rather than run the risks and discomforts of commercial diving, I began to think along the lines of the burgeoning new world of sport diving. Teaching bikini-clad beauties to dive in the clear, warm waters of some tropical seaside paradise was much more appealing than risking my ass just for the money. However, fate had something even better in store.

Occasionally, I wrote press releases for Andre Galerne, the president of IUC. One day, he invited me to an extraordinary meeting of his Board of Directors. The purpose of the meeting was to welcome the Honorary Chairman of the Board who was paying a surprise visit. To my astonishment, the Honorary Chairman turned out to be Captain Jacques Yves Cousteau.

Over pre-dinner cocktails, I reminded Captain Cousteau of our first meeting in Paris, but he did not remember it. Disappointed, I was about to withdraw, when he asked me an important question, "Perhaps you can help me find someone. Andre tells me that there is an American film maker in the company named Owens something. Do you happen to know him?"

My heart skipped a beat. "Owens? No, nobody by that name. But my name is Owen. So maybe he was referring to me!"

"Are you the one who made a film called *The Treasure Divers of Vigo Bay*?"

"Yes, yes! That's me, Owen Lee!"

Photo 14: Owen Lee meets Captain Cousteau

"Then you are the one I am looking for." He took my elbow and guided me to an empty corner of the room. Then he spoke confidentially. "Jimmy Dugan recommended your film, and before coming here I finally got to see it. It is nice work."

"Thank you," I said.

"I especially like your narration."

I thanked him again, and he continued. "Jimmy and Ruth Dugan recommended that I should talk to you about the possibility of joining our staff. We have many requests for lectures in America, but I have no time to do them. So we are looking for a French-speaking American who can help us part-time as an underwater cameraman aboard the *Calypso* and part-time as a lecturer on the American lecture circuit. Might you be interested? I have already talked to Andre Galerne, and he is willing to lend me your services."

I could not believe what I was hearing. "Are you serious?"

"Yes, indeed."

"It would be a privilege, sir, a dream come true!"

"Then you should talk with Jimmy Dugan. He is expecting your call. He will make all the arrangements regarding your contract with W. Colston Leigh, our lecture agent. He will also book your passage to join us in France."

I returned home that night ecstatically happy. I could not quite believe my good fortune, so I phoned Ruth and Jim Dugan in Philadelphia to confirm. They assured me that I was not dreaming, that Cousteau's offer was real. From then on, I simply followed their instructions.

Jimmy came to New York by train, and we went together to sign a contract with W. Colston Leigh Inc., the lecture agency. The deal was that I could keep whatever lecture fees I garnered, but I would not be paid for my work aboard the *Calypso*. That seemed super OK to me, and within two weeks I was flying over the Atlantic to join the *Calypso* in the port of Marseilles.

I found the *Calypso* tied to the municipal pier in the heart of the city. Having appeared in a National Geographic television series, the *Calypso* had already become an icon of travel and adventure that was known to millions. Amidst the creaking flotilla of rusty trawlers, the distinctive lines of the *Calypso* were easy to spot. The bulbous observation chamber protruding from her bow, her unique flying bridge, all made her distinctive and different.

Photo 15: The Calypso visits the Dios Te Guarde

As I approached the ship, a uniformed *gendarme* stopped me at the gang plank. When I showed him Jimmy's letter of introduction, he took it aboard and soon reappeared with Albert Falco in tow. Falco, better known aboard as Bebert, was Cousteau's first mate and chief diver. Short, stocky, and built like a tank, Bebert Falco was an imposing but very sympathetic person. His dark eyes shined with a twinkle beneath a crown of tasseled black hair.

He greeted me with friendly smile. "You must be Owen Lee." He leaned over the deck railing to shake hands.

"And you must be Albert Falco," I said. "Jimmy Dugan sends you greetings from Philadelphia."

"Ah, good ol' Jimmy Dugan. Welcome aboard!" He motioned me to come aboard, and we went forward into the forecastle.

The forecastle was a space in the bow of the ship. It was filled with steel lockers and about thirty pipe-rack bunks.

"This is where you will be sleeping," Bebert said. "Find yourself an empty bunk and a locker. The head and showers are up forward. When you're ready, come aft to the galley. We will be eating soon."

Photo 16: Captain Cousteau with Owen Lee

When I found my way to the galley, the crew was already seated around a spacious table made of varnished wood. There were about nine men of assorted shapes and sizes. They were drinking red wine. I learned that the wine, being that it was a French ship, was stored in a two hundred-gallon water tank and came from a spigot like water.

As I entered, Falco stood to greet me and introduced me to the others. I shook hands with everyone around the table. It was a ritual that would repeat itself every morning, noon and night.

After a few minutes of lively conversation, Captain Cousteau appeared with his wife Simone and his sixteen-year-old son Phillippe. The crew stood respectfully, and Captain Cousteau gave me a warm welcome, introducing me to his wife and son.

When they sat down, the crew resumed their seats and Daniel, the cook, served dinner. As one would expect aboard a French vessel, the dinner was delicious, as was the conversation. The crew was full of jokes and good humor. They were all patiently indulgent and helpful as I tried to improve my French. It was a cozy, familial scene which I soon grew to love.

Dive into History

My first dive from the decks of the *Calypso* was a thrill that I will always remember. For some weeks before my arrival, the *Calypso* divers had been excavating the remains of a Roman Galley. It lay in one hundred-fifteen feet of water about thirty miles off the coast of Marseilles. The crew referred to the Roman galley simply as *Le Grand Congluee,* the name of the island near which it had sunk perhaps two thousand years before.

With double-hose Aqua-Lungs on our backs, we sank through the turquoise blue waters of the Mediterranean leaving trails of silver bubbles in our wake. At a depth of a hundred feet, we leveled off, suspended in limbo above the ghostly outline of a large boat, perhaps twenty feet below us.

The wooden hull had long ago vanished, consumed by torero worms, marine bacteria and the ravages of time. Now, only the remains of the ancient cargo defined the galley's shape. Its hold had been stuffed with hundreds of *amphora*, elegant clay jars with conical bottoms. When embedded in sand that also served as ballast, the conical bottom held the earthen jars upright.

Photo 17: Diving into history

In Roman times, the *amphora* served as containers for wine, grain and produce. They were the Roman equivalents of our cardboard boxes. The *amphora* had been stacked in neat, military rows, thus delineating the shape the wooden hull which had been eaten away. The purpose of our mission was to salvage some *amphora* for the Musée Oceanographique of Monaco, which Captain Cousteau was soon to inherit from Monaco's Prince Raniér.

By fanning the sand away with our open palms, we

loosened a dozen *amphora* from their ancient bed. Then, one by one, we turned them upside down and injected air from the mouthpiece of our SCUBA regulators. The instant an *amphora* became buoyant, we released it to rocket towards the surface. As the air inside expanded, it expelled the water out the bottom, until it burst through the surface like a Poseidon rocket. Once on the surface, crewmen in an inflatable dinghy rushed to wrestle the *amphora* aboard before it could turn turtle and fall back to the bottom.

When the dinghy was full, the crew struck a partially submerged metal rod with a stone. The sound, clearly audible to the divers below, signaled them to wait while the dinghy transferred the *amphora* to the *Calypso*.

As we divers waited on the bottom, a shimmering cloud of tiny silversides appeared overhead, in hungry pursuit of invisible plankton. They moved slowly over the remains of the wreck, like a blimp hovering over a football stadium. The fish were so numerous and tightly clustered that they seemed to move and act as one.

Around the shimmering mass, a couple of snapper and a large grumpy-looking grouper stalked their movement like hungry vultures. From out of the blue, a marauding pair of yellowtail jacks darted through the cloud, shattering it like shards of broken glass. This triggered the other predators into frenzied action. As they emerged through the cloud, hundreds of wiggling silversides spilled from their mouths and gills. No sooner had the marauders passed, then the survivors hastily regrouped into a single shimmering mass as before.

Within seconds, the marauding pair of jacks returned for another pass. This time, however, one was left flailing on a hook. The ship's cook had dropped a line over the side of our vessel and he hauled the jack, struggling, up to the surface. Later that day, we ate it for dinner.

As Bebert served himself a second helping, he chuckled at the memory. "This is a very noble Jacques Crevelle," Bebert observed to Madame Cousteau. "He put up a valiant struggle, but the poor fish fell victim to his appetites."

"Just as we all do," added Madame Cousteau.

"They must have been feeding on plankton," I said. "You could not see them, but you knew they were there."

"Then you guys got to see the whole life drama unfold right before your eyes," observed Madame Cousteau. "From the invisible schools of tiny plankton, to the massive school of little silversides, to the mouth of this Jack Carville, to our mouths sitting here at this table. It's the whole pyramid of life incarnate!" she cried gleefully.

"That is the beauty of diving," Falco said. "We can actually see how everything fits into the big picture."

"We need schools where people can go to have experiences like that," Madame Cousteau observed. "People need to see how we all fit into the big picture on a personal level." I did not know it at the time, but Madame Cousteau had just defined my chosen mission in life.

The Captain's Wife

The *Calypso* served throughout World War II as a U.S. Navy mine sweeper. Therefore, the hull was entire made of wood so as to avoid setting off a magnetic mine. Only one hundred-forty feet long with a thirty-foot beam, the *Calypso* was not big enough to accommodate any more than a few persons in private cabins. Besides Captain Cousteau and Madame Simone, Bebert, Captain George Allinate, the navigation officer, and Henri Leban, the chief engineer were the only ones lucky enough to have a cabin of their own. The rest of us slept on the pip-rack bunks in the forecastle.

Photo 18: Onboard the *Calypso*

The number of persons aboard the *Calypso* varied from eight up to forty, depending on the type and duration of the mission. We all shared a communal bath, ate at a communal table in a communal galley and relaxed in a communal lounge. Needless to say, there was never much privacy.

Madame Simone presided over this communal enterprise like a mother hen presides over her chicks. Silent, watchful and always in good humor, she spent much more time aboard the *Calypso* than the Captain did. However, she forbade any mention or photos of her to the media. Her personal privacy was the price of her presence. Whereas, Captain Cousteau came and went according to the dictates of his multi-faceted career, Madame Simone was ever-present, mothering, supervising, cajoling, negotiating, and entertaining *mes mic*, "my guys." She was the catalyst that bonded our motley crew of sailors, divers, engineers, producers, cameramen, scientists, and technicians into an efficient, smooth-working team.

Beneath a wind-blown mop of yellow hair, her brown eyes sparkled and her smile could light up a room like the rising sun. Her high spirits and easy manner were contagious, reflected in the faces and behavior of our crew. Under her motherly influence, we functioned like one big happy family. As a result, the *Calypso* was the happiest and healthiest ship on which I had ever sailed.

The enthusiasm of the *Calypso's* crew was inspiring. Our life at sea was the epitome of comradeship and team spirit, even through the longest passages. The entire crew was aware that we were sharing in one of the greatest adventures of our day, and we worked and lived accordingly.

Although each us had our special job, there were no specialists. We all pitched in whenever and wherever we could, be it in the diving locker, on the bridge, in the galley, or even in the engine room. As such, we all became well acquainted with the *Calypso* from stem to stern.

Money was of little importance to us. It was that kind of job. Through we never discussed it, we reveled in our shared dream, proud to be among the pioneers of Earth's last and largest frontier, proud of our role in revealing its hidden secrets to the world. Proud to be a member of *L'equipe Cousteau.*

Photo 19: The Calypso lifts the Deep Diving Saucer

Photo 20: The Diving Saucer underwater

Albert Falco

Albert Falco was in charge of all operations aboard the *Calypso*. Robust, friendly and very professional, he was the perfect male counterpart for Madame Cousteau's motherly care. "Bebert" as we called him, had a knack for handling people and getting things done. He was more than his title of Master Diver and Boatswain implied. In many ways, he was Cousteau's alter ego.

When "The Pasha" was not aboard, Bebert took charge, making decisions, setting the style, analyzing and solving a myriad of problems that came his way, then showing the way by his own example. He never asked anything of us crew that he would not willingly do himself. He could get diverse groups of people working together like a well-oiled machine without ever raising his voice. Everyone aboard loved and respected him, even under the most trying conditions. When filming in shallow depths, as Bebert liked to do, we often spent the entire day underwater. Yet, he never demanded more than he would willingly give of himself. He was always right there with us, and the crew happily repaid him in kind.

Captain Cousteau

Whether Captain Cousteau was physically aboard ship or not, he was always the dominant presence. After all, everybody aboard the *Calypso* was hired to advance Cousteau's mission however and whenever one could.

In the late fifties and early sixties, life aboard the *Calypso* was relatively casual and relaxed. When not shooting a film project, Captain Cousteau occasionally chartered the *Calypso* out to worthy scientific or engineering projects to help pay the ship's expenses. On such occasions, he was especially friendly. Since they were not his personal projects, he assumed the role of host and took a more active role in shipboard social life. After dinner, he and Madame Simone would often hang around the table and shoot the breeze. Our after-dinner conversations ran the full gamut, from dirty jokes to serious debates over global issues.

I loved these talk sessions. They gave us an intimate glimpse into the minds of some of the world's brilliant people in a casual and non-judgmental ambiance. There was no room for any kind of snobbery. We were all one big family, floating in limbo on the endless expanses of the open sea.

Later, as Cousteau's name became a household word throughout the world, that kind of intimacy gradually vanish, and life aboard the *Calypso* changed radically. Whenever Captain Cousteau came aboard the *Calypso*, he was likely to arrive with a large entourage of writers, directors, producers and technicians, all of whom competed for his time and attention. The urgent business of film production took precedence over all else. This usually entailed the re-enactment of vital scenes of shipboard activity involving close-ups of Captain Cousteau aboard ship or narrating the lip-synchronized bridges and transitions that would later hold the voice-over sequences in a coherent format.

Most production days began with an early morning meeting around the galley table after breakfast. Captain Cousteau, Bebert Faclo, Captain Allinant, Henri Leban, and the various writers, producers or directors would determine the agenda for the day. By eight o'clock the work was usually well under way.

Throughout the work day, Captain Cousteau displayed amazing stamina. He willingly repeated the same lines over and over again until everyone was satisfied. Nevertheless, by the end of the day, the stress was clearly visible. His tall, lean frame appeared slightly stooped with fatigue. The normally ruddy face beneath his prematurely gray hair appeared gaunt and gray. His engaging smile was not so evident, and he appeared much older than he actually was.

When *The Pasha* began to show signs of fatigue, Madame Simone would gently entice him into their cabin, and we would not see them for the rest of the evening. After a good night's rest, however, they always reappeared, looking refreshed, happy and ten years younger.

Cousteau and his film collaborators managed to capture Nature's magic with eloquence and style. To millions of television viewers throughout the world, Cousteau became Mother Nature's most articulate spokesman. With three award-winning motion pictures, more than forty books and over one hundred-fifteen television programs, Cousteau took the world on a vicarious exploration of Earth's hidden secrets. For the first time in history, people could actually witness and participate in the wonders and workings of the global ecosystem on both land and sea. *The Adventure's of Captain Cousteau* on TV created a global awareness of Nature's wonderful ways as they had never before been seen. It also revealed how intimately each living species is related to all others.

Nature's Spokesman

Cousteau's fame catapulted him into the political arena as one of the world's foremost authorities on Global Ecology. Twice he addressed joint sessions of the U.S. Congress. He warned of the accelerating degradation of our global ecosystem and worried openly about the welfare of our children. He proposed a Bill of Rights for Future Generations that was quickly sanctioned by the General Assembly of the United Nations.

"Future generations have a right to inherit a pristine and undamaged planet," he told them. But his words apparently fell on deaf ears.

Discouraged by the lack of political response, Cousteau joined forces with other ecological visionaries in a Coalition of Concerned Scientists. Among them were Dr. Barry Commoner of Washington University, Dr. Paul Ehrlich of Stanford University, Dr. James Lovelock of the University of London, and Dr. E.O. Wilson of Harvard University. All had written best-selling books forewarning us of the emerging ecological crisis that is now in full bloom and calling for appropriate action. Even Al Gore, the Vice President of the United States, pitched in with a book titled *Earth in the Balance* (©1992 Al Gore, Houghton Mifflin Company).

Cousteau lamented the fact that the world well knew what the ecological problems were and even knew how to resolve them, yet neglected to take appropriate corrective action. Ever since Cousteau's death in 1998, there has been a lot of talk about the ecological crises but relatively little action. In some cases, the United States. and a few other countries have backed out of the few international agreements that were ratified. Such moral blindness weighed heavily on Cousteau's conscience. To him, it was a form of species-wide insanity.

In his post-humously published autobiography, *Man, Octopus and Orchid*[6], Cousteau summed up his feelings as follows, "Man's road into the future leads us smack into a wall. We simply ricochet off the alternatives that destiny offers; a demographic explosion that triggers social chaos and spreads conflict, death, disease, nuclear delirium and the quasi annihilation of our species."

Later he added, "If we are to bequeath future generations a life of dignity instead of despair, we need to reintegrate humanity into harmony and balance with the global ecosystem before it is too late to try."

Scientists generally acknowledge that ninety percent of

world's ecological problems are the direct result of human activity. Therefore, we can no longer hide behind our claim of ignorance or impotence. We have proved that we can change Nature for worse. Now we must prove that we can change it for better. Otherwise, we will only prove that we have failed as a species.

As I see it, the time has come for us humans to stop fighting amongst ourselves and start fighting together for our lives. It is painfully clear that we can no longer leave the responsibility for the health of our planet up to our social, religious and governmental institutions. They are no less intimidated by the global character of our ecological problems than we are as individuals. Institutions have their own survival agenda that always take precedence. Consequently, our planet, the common property of everybody, has become the responsibility of nobody. Rather than confront the reality, our government and religious institutions have chosen to ignore it, deny it or leave it up to future generations. Therefore, our institutions are not the solution, they are part of the problem. This leaves the chore of finding solutions up to each individual.

We were discussing this dilemma on board the *Calypso* one evening when Captain Cousteau claimed that the ecological crisis was basically a problem of definition. "A problem well-defined is a problem half-solved," he observed. "We humans have been educated to believe that we are the masters of Nature and therefore impervious to Nature's laws. What we need now is a global shift in the context of our thinking, but that requires awareness, which in turn requires education, and such educational programs do not yet exist. So there you have the Big Challenge. Come up with a program to re-educate the world to live in harmony and balance with Nature, and you might just save the world for future generations. It is that simple."

On the Road

When not aboard the *Calypso*, I represented the Captain and crew on the winter lecture circuits, and I thought a lot about Cousteau's challenge. Throughout my career with him, I narrated Cousteau's 16mm films in three hundred-five cities and towns, schools and clubs, churches and universities. Life on the lecture circuit contrasted sharply with life aboard the *Calypso*. There was no privacy aboard the *Calypso*. Except for the long hours of wheel watches at night, there was neither time nor place to be with alone. Somebody was always sharing your space, whether you liked it or not.

By contrast, the four-month lecture circuit was the loneliest period I had ever experienced. Except for one year, when Paulette Brioude, a charming French expatriate, accompanied me around the country, I was always alone. Driving up to three hundred miles through endless tracks of corn or wheat, I was alone. I was even lonely in crowded airports. Regardless of how I traveled, it seemed like my destination was always the same—loneliness in some anonymous motel room.

My booking agent, W. Colston Leigh Inc., insisted that I memorize my entire ninety-minute spiel and repeat it word-for-word in every show. Delivering the same old commentary to the same old film only intensified my loneliness. After my lectures ended, I was usually left alone to fend for myself. In the worst case scenario, my hosts would sometimes stage a post-lecture reception for me. During such ordeals, I was more alone than ever. We all stood around with silly grins painted on our faces, while I tried to answer the same old questions with the same old answers without falling asleep.

At the end of most lectures, however, I would emerge from the lecture hall, wide awake and raring to go places and do things. But the only night life in most of my lecture cities, was usually some homeless animals asleep in the street. If lucky enough to have a quarter, the best I could hope for was fifteen minutes of mechanical massage from *The Magic Fingers* machine in my motel room. By the end of my lecture season, I was more than eager to exchange my solitary lifestyle on the road for the public life of a *Calypso* diver.

My second season aboard the Calypso was the most memorable summer I ever spent. With a full crew aboard, the Calypso motored east along the Cote D'Azure. Each night, we anchored in a different port, and some of us would go ashore. Rounding the boot of southern Italy, we explored the enchanted islands of the Aegean Sea, emerging from the sea like gems set in blue velvet. Alone the way, we filmed the work of Dr. George Bass, an underwater archeologist from the University of Pennsylvania. He had the enviable job of excavating ancient historical wrecks for the Greek and Turkish governments. After a brief visit to the Egypt, we turned into the warm clear waters of the Red Sea. Here we encountered coral reefs of spectacular beauty and variety. Each one comprised a wild kaleidoscope of living, changing forms and colors.

Coral reefs are true underwater cities. Amidst the graceful forms of hard and soft corals, myriad schools of colorful fish — pork fish, wrasses, grunts and angels — floated in limbo. Nearby graceful lionfish lolled fearlessly within easy reach, as if tempting one to touch their poisonous quills. Timid octopus, so perfectly camouflaged that they were virtually invisible, hid amidst the corals. Around the parameters of the reefs swam rays, jacks, sharks, and other predators.

When we were filming straight natural life, four cameramen sometimes worked under the boat at the same time. Since water selectively filters the color spectrum of natural light, we relied on powerful 24-volt underwater lights to reveal all the true colors. These lights were powered by thick, wire cables attached to the *Calypso*'s big generators. Each of us worked with an assistant who handled the lights and electrical cables. The results were well worth the effort. The Red Sea provided Captain Cousteau with some of the best natural-life footage in his entire film library. Of course, only a tiny fraction of it ever made it to the TV screen. For every foot of film that one might see on *The Undersea Adventures of Captain Cousteau*, hundreds, perhaps thousands of feet of film went unused.

From his unique perspective, Cousteau revealed the mind-boggling complexity of the global ecosystem as few others could. In the process of revealing the hidden secrets of life under the sea, Cousteau discovered how intimately the marine ecosystem related to and depended on the terrestrial ecosystem on land. By the end of his first two television series, one made for the French Government and the other made for National Geographic Society, Cousteau's vision embraced much more than just the oceans. As his fascination with the interdependence of life matured into theory, so did the subject matter of his books and films. He began to reveal the inner workings of the global ecosystem with the same elegance and style that he had displayed when revealing the hidden secrets of the sea. Thus, his vision now embraced the past, present and future of life itself.

Cousteau ultimately agreed with Dr. John Lovelock, creator of the GAIA theory. "There is only one world and only one life," he maintained, "And like it or not, we are all an integral part of it. Every living species is a vital part of and dependent on all other living species."

When Captain Cousteau died, I think he died a disillusioned man. Cousteau envisioned humanity reunited with Nature as an integral part and participant in the whole life process. Instead, many of Cousteau's most dire predictions are now coming true and little is done to stop it. The hole in the ozone continues to expand, global temperatures continue to rise, so-called natural disasters continue to increase, and population stretches towards the seven-billion mark. The work of Cousteau and his colleagues seems to have been in vain. We have come to a turning point in the story of life on Earth. It is time to stop complaining about the weather and actually do something about it. The reintegration of mankind into balance and harmony with Nature's ecosystem is a global problem that requires global education, global awareness and a global program of positive action.

The Sexy Sixties

In 1967 a freak boating accident shattered the meniscus in my left knee. The pain forced me to leave the *Calypso* and return to America for surgery and a long convalescence. I could meet my lecture commitments, but my usefulness as a working diver was severely hampered. I tried to justify my disappointment by convincing myself it had been destined. It was a God-given opportunity to enjoy my New York apartment and perhaps to plan a Nature Study Center to meet Captain Cousteau's Big Challenge about the need to live in balance and harmony with Nature.

Although I had acquired my New York pad in the early1950s, I had never really taken the time to enjoy it. My nomadic lifestyle had kept me on the move ever since graduating from Brentwood (Missouri) High School in 1945. The *Calypso* was a beautiful adventure. But it could not compare with the Big Apple in the "Sexy Sixties." New York City was the epicenter of the biggest and most peaceful revolution in history. And it was happening all around me, in the very heart of Greenwich Village.

My parent's generation raved about the fast life in the "Roaring Twenties," but I can't imagine that their "fast life" moved half as fast as life in New York City did during the 1960s. In New York City, and throughout American, the sixties came alive with revolutionary changes in race, religion, social welfare, minority rights, sex, and many other aspects of contemporary life. It began with the timely demise of the presidencies of Richard Nixon and Gerald Ford welcoming the ultra-liberal administration of Jack Kennedy.

President Kennedy's heady combination of compassionate wisdom and enlightened youth, mobilized a whole generation to action. His power and spirit breathed new life into an otherwise stodgy world and wrought many changes. With his gorgeous wife Jacqueline by his side, the vivacious Kennedy Clan encouraged innovation, creativity and reform in both government and society. They opened the doors to a new age of truth, exploration and experimentation. President Jack Kennedy kicked off this wave of enlightenment by launching the exploration of Earth's last two remaining frontiers, that of Outer Space, the moon and our solar system, and that of Inner Space, the sea.

Kennedy promised a "brave new world" full of high hopes and expectations and delivered it. The revision of archaic customs, mores and attitudes led to progressive legislation that produced revolutionary changes. Discrimination based on race, gender, creed, or sexual orientation was now illegal. No longer were women, blacks and gays treated as second-class citizens. For the first time in U.S. history, they could now enjoy the same social, professional, moral, and political rights as their white male counterparts.

Spurred by a lively post-war economy and plenty of easy money, the Roaring Sixties became the decade of excess as well as success. With the legalization of abortion and the availability of voluntary birth control, sexual mores and practices changed over night. Gays, lesbians and swingers came out of their closets in droves. Open marriages became *au currant. Ménages* of three, four and more were not uncommon. In the rural countryside hippies set up open communities, while urban gays created the new bath house society.

"Sex, drugs and rock and roll!" became the war cry. Timothy Leary and Richard Alpert, two rebellious professors of psychology at Harvard University, captured a following by offering youth two new alternatives to the ultra conservative norms of the day. After serious studies in India, Richard Alpert changed his name to Ram Dass and returned to his homeland as a spiritual guru. Dr. Timothy Leary, his former colleague, discovered lysergic acid, otherwise known as LSD Dr. Leary urged his followers to "turn on" with LSD, "tune in" to the universe, and "drop out" of conventional society. And they did so by the thousands.

Around midnight each night, an entire subculture of nocturnal party goers seemed to materialize. One block from my apartment, the top three floors of a legitimate bank building were devoted to bacchanal orgies of sex, drugs and rock and roll that often did not end until the bank was already open for business. In the anonymity of virtual darkness, hundreds, perhaps thousands, danced the nights away in a haze of marijuana smoke and amyl nitrate "poppers."

When not dancing, many hung out in the midnight bath houses, wherein nothing was taboo. Out of curiosity, I joined in an orgy involving over a hundred people. It was the kind of open, unlimited, care-free excess that made communicable diseases, like gonorrhea and HIV Aids, almost inevitable. It was these diseases that eventually brought the Roaring Sixties to a whimpering end. It also precipitated a backlash of ultra conservatives and born-again Christians who were collectively labeled as "yuppies."

Rebecca's Gift

Photo 21: Becky and her puppets in New York City

I first met Rebecca Slaton while attending a photography seminar in Miami, Florida. She was a beautiful blonde flight attendant who hailed from Mississippi. Her face was lightly peppered with freckles, and she spoke with a soft southern drawl. In fact everything about her was soft. And also very sweet.

Becky worked for Eastern Airlines. She also had a graduate degree in education and was writing her thesis on the use of puppetry as a teaching tool. The airline granted her a two-year leave of absence to test her theories while doing volunteer work in a Tibetan orphanage near Katmandu, Nepal. She had just recently returned and Louis Marden, a *National Geographic* photographer, invited Becky to come see his film of her work in Nepal.

Becky's story fascinated me, so I invited her to lunch during the break. Becky and I discovered that we had a lot in common. For instance, we were both adventurous freelancers who were facing a major turning point. Having just returned from her sabbatical in Nepal, Becky was offered an internship with the New York Puppet Theatre in Central Park and she wanted to change her base from Miami to New York City before resuming her flight career.

I told her about my work with Captain Cousteau and my plans to scout out the right location for a Nature Study Center, somewhere the tropics. "Captain Cousteau told me that such places were needed to clarify our personal stake in the health of the global ecosystem," I explained.

We enjoyed each other's company so much that we agreed to meet later for dinner. Before the end of the evening, it occurred to us that we might be able to help each other in more ways than one. In order to move her flight base to New York City and further her career in puppetry, Becky needed a place to live. Meanwhile, I had a great place to live there, but needed a cheap and easy way to scout the right location for my Nature Study Center. It seemed like a symbiotic combination. So why not get together?

The next day, we drove to Fort Lauderdale for lunch. We went to a nice restaurant that faced the beach. As I seated Becky at the table, she smiled coyly and said, "I've got something to show you."

"I can't wait." I sat facing her across the table and sent her a questioning glance.

There was a mischievous sparkle in her pretty blue eyes as she slowly unbuttoned her blouse. Then she opened it wide, revealing a pale blue T-shirt. The shirt molded itself around the delicious curves of her shapely breasts. Printed in bold red letters across the shirt it said, "MARRY ME & FLY FOR FREE!"

I laughed heartily. "Is this is a proposal?" I chortled.

"It is, if you want it to be!"

I smiled broadly and took her hand in mine. "With great

pleasure," I cooed. "I was about to ask you the very same question."

We sealed our deal with smiles and a kiss. Later that night we went to bed and it was wonderful. "Well, there goes the straight business deal!" I laughed.

The following day I had to return to New York City. Becky promised to follow as soon as she could, but frankly, I was skeptical whether or not I would ever see her again. However, in just eight days, her sweet southern drawl came in over the telephone, and suddenly there she was standing at my door, bag and baggage. I was amused at my own excitement. I swept her into my arms as if we had been lovers for years and kissed her.

Over the next few weeks, Becky, always sweet, bright, beautiful and open, melded into my life as if she had always been there. We were surprisingly comfortable and happy with each other, accepting each other as is. All my New York friends loved her, and she loved living in New York. It was almost too good to be true.

Once settled in, Becky lost no time getting into her own routine. Not only did she continue working as a flight attendant, she also worked part-time at the New York Puppet Theatre and did volunteer work at an uptown Buddhist Center. At least once a week Becky spent two or three days out of town with the airline, and that gave us just enough time apart to keep our love fresh and new. I always missed her when she was away and we were always happy to see each other when she returned. Even though our relationship was supposed to be a straight-forward business deal, I found myself falling hopelessly in love with her.

Meanwhile, Becky was becoming more independent with each passing week. She had developed her own coterie of uptown friends and her agenda was full of outside interests. When she began seeing other men, I confessed to a tinge of jealousy and finally yielded to my own emotions.

"When are we getting married?" I inquired sardonically.

"Whenever y'all are ready," she replied sweetly.

The Acapulco Wedding

The idea of getting married in Acapulco was not ours. It came from Marshall Allen, my millionaire friend from Fire Island. When I told him about our wedding plans, he latched on to the idea as if they were his own. "Perfect!" he cried. "You can get married aboard my boat in Acapulco. And I've got the ideal place for you to spend your honeymoon. It's a funky little Mexican fishing village called *Zihuatanejo*."

Marshall went on to inform me that he had recently bought half interest in an eighty-five-foot sailboat which was waiting at anchor in Acapulco. Marshall's partner, a bilingual American named Freddy Mohr, was already living aboard and would be happy to take care of us, Marshall assured me. Marshall had met him in Benidorm, Spain and together they had found the boat in the port of Alicante, and had had her shipped by freighter to Acapulco. There, Freddy Mohr had refitted her from stem to stern and hired a local crew. They planned to sail the boat from Acapulco one hundred-thirty miles northwest to Zihuatanejo. But Freddy, himself, was not a sailor. He had never been to sea. Although he had hired a crew of three, none of them could read a chart. That is where I came into the picture. Because of my nautical background with Captain Cousteau, Marshall reasoned that I could help Freddy safely deliver the boat to its final destination, then spend our honeymoon aboard.

"What did you say was the name of the port was?" I asked Marshall.

"It's called *Zihuatanejo*," he said, "pronounced Zee-what–tan–nay-ho. It's just a tiny little fishing village north of

Acapulco. Freddy showed it to me, and I think you'll like it."

"It sounds like a great place for a honeymoon!" exclaimed Becky. And that convinced me.

"What is your partner going to say when Becky and I show up for our Honeymoon?" I asked.

"No problem," Marshall assured us. "You and Freddy will love each other."

"Can I ask him a few questions about the boat?"

"Yes, sure. We can phone him right now."

Marshall led us downstairs to his office, gave me a wireless telephone and phoned Freddy Mohr in Acapulco. To my surprise, I recognized Freddy's distinctive voice. We had met once before on Fire Island. I remembered the occasion and recalled that we laughed a lot. When Marshall told him our wedding plan, Freddy was just as enthusiastic as Marshall had been. He volunteered to make all the legal arrangements and handle all the logistical details. Had he not done that, I think that I would have gone no further. However, their kind offer convinced Becky and me to actually pack our bags and get on an airplane bound for Acapulco.

Both Freddy Mohr and Acapulco were delightful. Freddy was one of the funniest men I had ever met. He was one of those rare people who could inject joy and laughter into almost everything he said and did. Almost from the moment he greeted us at the airport, he had us convulsing with laughter.

On our way to the marina, we stopped off for a drink at the hilltop bar of the hotel *Las Brisas*. From our perch on the hill, we marveled at the panoramic beauty of Acapulco Bay. On the verdant foothills surrounding the Bay, rows of luxurious villas gazed out upon the sparkling green water of the Bay like opulent spectators in a gigantic amphitheatre. Broad crescents of golden palm-lined beaches rimmed the water, playing host to tourists from around the world. Behind the beaches, the busy *Costera Miguel Alemán* bustled with chaotic automobile traffic, most of which was bent on pleasure, for pleasure was Acapulco's only business.

Acapulco touted itself as the "jet set capital of the world." It offered something for everyone. With enough money in your pocket, there was nothing one could not buy or do there. The many fine restaurants were packed with happy diners. Revelers could dance until dawn in over a dozen crowded discothèques. An air of naughty decadence permeated its busy streets. Whether rich or poor, man or woman, white or black, straight or gay, Acapulco promised fulfillment.

When we arrived at Acapulco's yacht club, the boat itself was a shocking surprise. Named *El Viejo*, "The Old Man," the boat had none of the graceful lines of a classical sailing yacht. She looked more like, well, like exactly what she was — a floating boxcar and a moveable feast. Eighty feet long by fifteen feet wide, *El Viejo* had started life in 1928 as a Thames River sailing barge. Built in Southampton, England, her original job was to carry bulk cargos of sand, coal, cement, and gravel back and fourth across the English Channel. A collapsible mast and a pair of giant leeboards vaguely qualified her as a sailing vessel, but without the help of her one-lung diesel engine, she barely made headway against a three-knot current. Her collapsible mast enabled her to squeeze under low bridges and motor through the elaborate canal systems of continental Europe.

What distinguished *El Viejo* now were the luxurious trim and furnishings that Freddy and Marshall had added. Below deck, the spacious cargo hold was now a luxurious three-bedroom apartment with two baths, a working fireplace and an opulent round dining area for twelve. In the salon, thick carpeting covered the decks from gunwale to gunwale. Up forward, a plus leather sofa spanned the entire width of her beam. Two modern Eams chairs stood on either side of a round rosewood cocktail table, and cool jazz filled every corner of the vessel.

Topside, the spacious roof of the raised cargo hatch was covered with thick foam rubber encased in cream-colored artificial leather. Here guests could lounge in the shade of an enormous blue deck awning suspended between the two side stays and the fore stay. Two large hammocks swung rhythmically between the forestay and two side stays. In short, Freddy had converted *El Viejo* into a luxurious floating Greenwich Village party pad, not very different from Marshall's luxurious digs in New York City and Fire Island. As such, it was easy to forgive *El Viejo's* innate homeliness. She was like a winsome fat lady with a great sense of humor. Even though she was fat and ugly, we all loved her just the same.

Freddy escorted us to a cabin, then invited up topside for a drink under the deck awning. There, he demonstrated that not only was he one of the funniest people alive, he was also one of the most accommodating. He had researched everything that we would need to know and do in order to get married in Acapulco. Furthermore, he volunteered to personally escort us through the entire process.

The following day, Freddy drove us to a medical lab to get our blood tests, then to the department of Foreign Relations for the permits, then on to the Registo Civil where we waited in line for the Justice of the Peace, signed as a witness and literally became my Best Man. He even shed mock tears during the brief ceremony.

When we returned to the boat, iced champagne awaited us along with a small wedding cake. Soon, three other couples joined us for a delicious seafood dinner, which he and the crew had already prepared. Thus, Freddy single-handedly transformed our wedding day into a regal celebration that Becky and I would never forget. He contributed far more than we had ever expected, and we oozed with gratitude as well as good cheer.

Freddy did not even pretend to be a sailor. He had graduated from Cornell University's school of gastronomy and hospitality. Therefore, he left all nautical considerations to me and his paid three-man crew and, instead, focused on the shipboard amenities.

Photo 22: Freddy Mohr (right) with friend at my Acapulco wedding

As I saw her, *El Viejo* was no sail boat but she was any match for the slightest bit of bad weather. Nevertheless, Freddy insisted that she had just been recaulked and was perfectly seaworthy and the crew perfectly capable of taking her to Zihuatanejo.

"After all, it's only one hundred-thirty miles away," he insisted. "We could almost swim it!"

For the next three days, we helped Freddy provision *El Viejo* with food, fuel and water. Around four o'clock on the fourth day, we weighed anchor and headed north. Once out of the Bay, we simply followed the coast about a mile off shore. Around sunset, the wind dropped and the surface of the water became as smooth as glass. The wash of our bow wake and the throaty chug-chug of our engine seemed to syncopate with the mellow sounds of Stan Getts and Astrid Gilberto. About two hours out, we had the rare privilege of watching a fiery sun set off our port side while the full moon rose like a big yellow balloon out of the darkening foothills of Sierra Madres off our starboard side.

As the near-invisible crew steered the boat from the wheel house full aft, Freddy, Becky and I lolled on the soft foam mattresses that covered cargo hatch. We sipped white wine and marveled at the sparkling causeway of silver that led to the moon and danced on the water's surface. The slow chug-chug-chug of our old one-lung diesel left us little choice but to surrender to the magic spell. "Forget about wherever you have been or think that you are going," the engine seemed to say. "For the moment, at least, I am in command. I am the captain of this ship."

As the night wore on, a chilly dewfall prompted Freddy to go below and then return with a blanket and three pillows. He gave us the pillows then we all cuddled up beneath the blanket with Becky in between Freddy and me. That's how we slept throughout the night. It was as if we were sailing on a magic carpet.

We could see Point Gorrobo Lighthouse blinking from the distant entrance of Zihuatanejo Bay long before dawn. However, we did not actually arrive at the Point until well after sun up. As we rounded Point Gorrobo the pristine bay of Zihuatanejo opened up before us like a boyhood dream. *Vogue* magazine had once described Zihuatanejo Bay as "one of the ten most beautiful natural harbors in the world," and indeed it was, and still is.

The narrow entrance blossomed into a mile-wide basin of warm protected waters that was surrounded by five beautiful palm-lined beaches. Each beach beckoned us to come play and swim. The village itself sidled up to the main beach, where a dozen fishermen were preparing dugout canoes for a day of fishing on the open water. In the early light of the morning, the village of Zihuatanejo was just awakening.

El Viejo coasted slowly up to the middle of the main beach and dropped her anchor in about twelve feet of water. We were perhaps forty meters from the village beach. Behind the beach, a deserted basketball court gave way to a small plaza of cement and a network of streets made of rust-colored dust. The streets were still empty except for one immobile burro and a variety of pigs, cats, dogs and chickens busily scavenging for food. Behind them was a motley assortment of adobe houses whose tenants were just coming awake. As we watched from our sheltered anchorage, several women emerged with pails of water. Each splashed the water onto the thick dust in front of their doors, momentarily converting the dust into a gooey mud that would soon dry and return to dust.

Nestled beneath a stand of giant coconut trees on the beach, a palm-thatched roof sheltered several men drinking beer at a make-shift bar. A sun-bleached sign proclaimed it to be "The Bongo Bar y Cantina." Freddy examined it through the ship's binoculars. "I bet we can get some breakfast there," he remarked. The crew launched the inflatable dinghy off our stern and we soon set off to join the party.

The Bongo Bar could have served as a set for some

romantic south sea island movie. Beneath its shaggy roof of palm fronds, a half wall of woven twigs supported wide sun-bleached planks that served as the bar. Rustic awnings of woven coconut mats swung open from the overhead beams and were propped up with bamboo poles. Atop the thatched roof lay mounds of dead coconut fronds that had fallen from the trees overhead. A stalk of green bananas hung from one beam in a shady corner and a small mountain of green coconuts lay heaped on the sand floor.

We sat on stools that were once part of the trunk of a coconut tree and gleefully exchanged our first impressions. After checking us out, a bearded attendant came to take our order. We ordered beers and *huevos Mexicanos,* which he fried over a wood fire on a stove made of mud. Freddy asked the now-curious locals how many people lived in Zihuatanejo. They debated amongst themselves whether the number was closer to two thousand or three thousand. Nobody seemed to know for sure, nor did they particularly care. Whatever it was, it was okay by them.

Zihuatanejo

After breakfast, we set off to explore the rest of the village. Only four blocks wide and six blocks deep, the village itself was a relic of the past in both mind and matter. Until the completion of the coastal highway from Acapulco in 1967, the rugged terrain of the Sierra Madre Mountains kept the area in psychological and geographical isolation from the rest of Mexico. Throughout the summer rainy season, its only access was by boat or light aircraft. The unpaved streets became sodden canals of gooey mud. The same mud also covered the uneven walls of the simple, one-story dwellings that lined the streets. The adobe walls were re-enforced with woven sticks and dried coconut husks. The roofs were covered with baked tiles, round *palapa* leaves or tarred roofing shingles. Few people owned a watch or a pair of shoes. They were not needed. The people did things in their own way and in their own time.

Photo 23: Zihuatanejo, 1967

Although the flat coastal areas produced an abundance of coconuts, papayas and bananas, the local agriculture was primitive. To produce a single crop of corn for tortillas, farmers often slashed and burned a small fortune in lumber. Farming was hard work, so there was not much agriculture, even at that. After all, there was always plenty of fish in the sea and fresh fruit on the trees, so who needed anything more? Life in primitive Zihuatanejo was relatively sweet and simple.

The isolated care-free subsistence of Zihuatanejo produced a local population that was uniquely self-sufficient and fiercely independent. Few paid taxes or wished for capital improvements. They were smugly content and did not want to change. Therefore, when the Federal government moved in with a $500 million loan from the World Bank to develop local tourism, many of the locals felt threatened by the change. They resented having to pay taxes and having to prove ownership of the land where they were born. They were part of the land and the land was part of them. Worse yet, they resented having to show up on time or do as they were told. They had always done just as they pleased, whenever they pleased, so why should they change?

As a result of their resistance to change, an invasion of outsiders moved in and took over the well-paying jobs. This relegated the locals to the more menial service jobs like waiters, bellboys and doormen. This created a social and economic cleavage within the local population that persists to this day.

Whatever Zihuatanejo lacked in social amenities, it more than made up for in its copious gifts from Nature. Of the five beautiful beaches that surrounded the Bay, the closest to town was the *Playa Municipal*, the home of the local fishing fleet of dugout canoes. Two hundred meters further inland was another beautiful beach called *Playa Madera*. *Playa Madera* means "wood beach." It was so named because of an old steam-driven sawmill whose rusty remains still stood in the middle. The mill had processed and exported the last stands of precious *Bugote*, *Parota* and *Granadillo* trees that once grew in the hills surrounding the Bay. Because of such high quality woods, the first of the so-called *Naos of China* were built right there on Madera Beach in the latter part of the 16th century. The *Naos of China* were the Spanish galleons that first opened the trade routes to China, the Philippines and the Far East.

The *Naos of China* soon left Zihuatanejo for their home port of Acapulco. Because Spain was at war over who would ascend to occupy its empty throne, paid pirates and privateers from England and the Netherlands took up residence in Zihuatanejo simply because it was the closest protected anchorage to Acapulco. Their duty was to prey on those same galleons as they returned from the orient laden with treasures from the Far East. Local legend says that one of the *Naos* once blundered into Zihuatanejo Bay by mistake, thinking that it was Acapulco. Legend says that the pirates sank the *Nao* without even having to lift their anchors. The *Nao's* cargo of oriental fabrics washed up on the shore and thus endowed La Ropa Beach with its name. In English *La Ropa Beach* means "fabric beach."

The single dirt road that led out of town ended at the Hotel Catalina, at the beginning of La Ropa Beach. Excepting a few hippie chicks that lived there with their Mexican lovers, La Ropa Beach was the exclusive domain of stray burros, dogs and cows. The only other lodging in the Bay was the Casa Elvira on the Municipal Beach and the Hotel Avila in the heart of the village.

The Hotel Catalina had just been sold to Don Carlos Broyer, a German expatriate. Like many others that followed, he had first come as a tourist, fallen in love with the tropical setting and stayed. Until Don Carlos had brought it, the Catalina Hotel had sat virtually empty. People complained that it was too remote, too lonely or too dangerous. Some even saw ghosts of the ill-fated *Nao* that had sunk in the Bay. Don Carlos solved low-occupancy problems by renting the entire hotel to just one person, the one and only Dr. Timothy Leary, the renegade, acidhead shrink from Harvard University.

Harvard University had fired Dr. Leary for urging his students to "turn on, tune in, and drop out" of contemporary society. He maintained that the appropriate antidote to the prevailing decadence of our bourgeois capitalistic society was the mind-bending drug known as LSD. Dr. Leary sublet the rooms of the Hotel Catalina to his entourage of young disciples and, for a couple of years everybody had a high old time. Before long, however, a local authority had a bad trip and ran Dr. Leary out of town. In 1963, Dr. Leary abandoned La Rope Beach and moved his entourage of followers to Millbrook, New York.

Among other expatriates who came to Zihuatanejo on vacation and succumbed to its tropical allure were Isabel Fortune, Margot Chapman, Estella Buena Ventura, Tanya Scales, Linda Fox, and Elizabeth Williams, to name just a few. Even if they had come for the love of some person, they actually found fulfillment in their love for the place. The lush tropical beauty of Zihuatanejo Bay proved irresistible to them all.

And so it was for me, Marshall Allen, Freddy Mohr, and even sweet little Becky. It was a case of love at first sight. The pristine nature of Zihuatanejo's beautiful bay fired our imaginations. On the golden sands of its five virgin, palm-lined beaches, we saw the possibility of realizing our childhood dreams. We willingly surrendered to its hypnotic spell.

Then, as now, it was against the law for foreigners to own land within fifty kilometers of Mexico's frontiers or seashores. However, hundreds had gotten around that law, usually through the use of a friendly "name lender." We did the same. Using the name of their local partner, Freddy Mohr and Marshall Allen built a chic, seaside bungalow hotel called El Capricho del Rey. As for me, I envisioned my Nature Study Center as a place where people could experience their personal integration with nature, and Zihuatanejo was the ideal setting for such a place.

El Capricho Del Rey

For her square chines and lack of a keel, *El Viejo* tended to rock and roll whenever at anchor, even in the calmest weather. Therefore, Marshall ordered that we seek out the calmest corner of the Bay in which to anchor. That turned out to be as far as he could get from the busy pier in Zihuatanejo, just fifty yards offshore of the steep rocky hills that separated La Ropa Beach from Las Gatas Beach, a distance of about two hundred meters.

There were other considerations as well. At that time, 1967, La Ropa Beach was still deserted. It had no roads, no electricity, no water, and no restaurants. Meanwhile, Las Gatas Beach was already a popular daytime tourist destination. Thanks to its unique reef, its protected swimming lagoon and its four seaside restaurants, a fleet of over twenty taxi boats shuttled excursionists back and fourth between Las Gatas Beach and the Municipal Pier. This gave us easy access to the restaurants, the taxi boats and to town. Last but not least, it also gave us a convenient place to play. This was very important, because being stuck on a boat was no fun. It bred "island fever," that sick longing for other people that comes from living in imposed isolation. Unless there is some means of escape, boats can be as lonely as any jail cell, especially in the company of an eccentric drunk like Marshall.

In all fairness, Marshall spent most of his time quietly reading on the leatherette and foam hatch cover in the shade of the blue deck awning. In the process, he often consumed a full bottle of Gordon's gin a half-gallon of fresh orange juice. He also smoked up to a half-dozen joints and popped a couple of pills. By mid-afternoon he was usually stoned and looking for someone to engage him in a philosophical discussion about something that nobody else knew or cared. Usually, it was about some book that only Marshall had read. This was the cue for me and Becky to dive over the side and swim to Las Gatas Beach to have lunch.

Chez Arnoldo's was the third restaurant from the taxi boat landing on Las Gatas Beach. Unlike its name, the restaurant itself was nothing fancy. Like the other three restaurants on the beach, it consisted of a rustic palapa-roofed pavilion with half-dozen tables inside and a few chaise lounges out in the sun. The fancy name was simply a reflection of the owner's sardonic sense of humor.

Arnoldo Veerboonen was a direct descendant of the Dutch pirates and privateers who first came to Zihuatanejo during the war of Spanish succession in the 17th century. With a name like Veerboonen, his ancestors must have been part of a Dutch contingent that worked with Captain George Anson, a British privateer who eventually became the Commodore of Her Majesty's entire fleet. As a young naval officer, Anson spent seven years in Zihuatanejo. When at last he was ordered back home to England, his motley crew refused to go. Many had wives, children and houses scattered amidst Zihuatanejo's five beautiful beaches. They were not inclined to trade this care-free lifestyle in a tropical paradise to be indentured servants in frigid old England.

To solve their problem, they burned their ship, leaving young Captain Anson to return home as best he could. Two centuries later, Arnoldo Veerboonen and his neighbor, Oliverio Maciel, found and salvaged the ship's enormous anchor. They moved it to the shallow waters of the lagoon in front of Arnoldo's restaurant on Las Gatas Beach, where it has been a popular attraction for snorkelers ever since. However, the main attraction on Las Gatas Beach for us at that time was Arnoldo himself.

Arnoldo Veerboonen was a handsome, charming and relatively well-educated man. He had learned English as well as Spanish while going to school in Mexico City. When he returned home to Zihuatanejo, his urban education produced many social advantages. For example, it enabled him to marry Sarah Espino, the eldest daughter of Don Salvador Espino, who was Zihuatanejo's first elected mayor. Thus,

Arnoldo served as the city's Commissioner of Water.

We ate lunch at Chez Arnoldo's almost every day. Arnoldo shared Marshall's love for booze, books and jazz. This made him a favorite recipient for Marshall's drunken afternoon discussions, providing the rest of us with a certain measure of relief. Even though they only vaguely understood each other, they soon became fast friends, so it was only natural that they should also become business partners.

Arnoldo had garnered the *ejido* or homestead rights to the entire hillside near which *El Viejo* rode at anchor. When Arnoldo showed Marshall and Freddy the boundaries of his *ejido* land, they made him an offer that was most tempting. "If you will put up your land, we will put up the money to build a small hotel on it, and we will all be equal partners."

Arnoldo was ecstatic. We all were. We became happily involved in conceptualizing the perfect little boutique hotel in the perfect tropical setting. Although none of us had ever gone beyond mechanical drawing in high school, we were now architects with a *carte blanche* to do as we pleased. The only condition was that the buildings had to be individual free-standing bungalows. There would be no multiple dwelling units. Each living unit had to be made of materials and labor that were locally available. The winning design would exploit the natural gifts of the environment and set the theme and style of all succeeding structures.

The planning and creation of the hotel evoked profound changes in everybody involved, both as individuals and as participating members of the group. By giving each of us a personal goal to achieve for the group, it endowed us with a noble purpose for being there, besides pure pleasure. Marshall even cut down on his drinking in order to fully participate. Thus, the project bonded the five of us into an intimate and close-knit creative unit of mutual love and respect. Our reward was to see the incorporation of our personal ideas into the master plan. I had never felt so richly paid for anything I ever did. I had never been happier.

For the next few days, we followed a little routine. First, each of us went off to be alone, to think and work as an individual. Shortly before sunset, we all came together to judge, to vote, to compare notes and to brainstorm possibilities. All decisions were made by consensus. First, we all agreed on the basic design and infrastructure, the foundation, the plumbing, the drainage, and septic system. Then we selected all the amenities—spa bath, wooden bar, boat dock, etc. Next we studied other people's ideas. By agreement, we freely adapted whatever appealed to us. We each did our best to visualize what we wanted to see on paper. Our sketches varied according to the talents of the individual. Nevertheless, we all managed to convey our ideas quite effectively. It was a creative contest between the five us and, we were all winners. Getting the right result was the goal of the game. Eventually Marshall hired a pair of bright young architects to incorporate our ideas into their plans and put them to work.

I found the project so exciting that I could not tear myself away from it. Even when Becky returned to her work in New York, I chose to stay in Zihuatanejo and work just for the fun of it.

About ten days later, Becky showed up looking exhausted. She explained that she was on an overnight working trip to Acapulco and had ridden five hours on the bus in order to spend the night with us. She also reminded me that I had a lecture date the following week.

I returned with Becky to New York City. Although I had planned to return to Zihuatanejo immediately after my lecture, I became a willing slave to my sexual appetites. Being with Becky in New York City was so pleasant that I stayed six weeks. After all, it was the Big Apple and in the heat of the Sexy Sixties.

Just when I was on verge of returning to Mexico, Marshall showed up and invited us to his place on Fire Island. "Don't worry about going back to Zih for the project," he advised. "The two architects I hired have it well under way. The first of six bungalows is already half done."

"Did you ever come up with a name?" I asked.

"We are calling it '*El Capricho del Rey.*' That means 'the caprice of the King.' Do you like that name?" he asked rhetorically. "I think that it refers to the *Calzontzins*, the tribal Kings of the Tarascan or Purepuecha Indians that live in the area. Legend says that they were ones who built the barrier reef in front of Las Gatas Beach."

"I hope it remains his caprice and not yours," I joked.

Marshall laughed. "Yeah. Those building costs are getting out of hand."

"That's because everything has to come in by boat," I offered. "Boats always jack up the price."

By the time I returned from New York, the young architects, and a forty-man crew had already cleared Arnoldo's property and poured the cement footings and floors for three of the six bungalows planned. Since there were still no roads to La Ropa Beach, the forty workers all arrived and departed either by foot or by dugout canoes from the village pier. So did all the material, sand, cement, bricks, reinforcing rods, even the water. While half the men cleared the land and dug the footings, the other half laboriously carried the materials up the hillside. From the deck of *El Viejo*, anchored fifty yards offshore, they appeared like ants as they labored up the steep incline.

Now that the conceptual work was over, there was really not much more I could do since I could now fly for practically nothing, I spent roughly half of my time with Becky in New York City and half with Freddy and Marshall aboard *El Viejo*. I really had the best of both worlds. Whenever Becky had an overnight trip to Acapulco, I would accompany her so we could have some fun in the sun before returning to New York. It was during one such trip that I fell hopelessly in love.

Las Gatas Beach

One day, as was our habit, Becky and I swam to Las Gatas Beach to meet Freddy and Marshall for lunch at Chez Arnoldo's. We asked Arnoldo about the history of Las Gatas Beach. Arnoldo explained that *Las Gatas* literally means "the cats." In this case, however, it did not mean those furry felines that we keep as pets. *Las Gatas Beach* referred to the toothless nurse sharks that once lived in the reef-protected lagoon. Local legend said that the reef was built by the Calzontzins, the leaders of the Tarascan Indians, which are the predominate ethnic group in the area. The Tarascan Indians originated on some islands located in the middle of Lake Patzcuaro only three hours drive inland at an altitude of seven thousand feet where the winters were cold. At the first sign of winter's chill, the Calzontzins bundled their families into dugout canoes, and paddled down through the roaring rapids of the Rio Balsas and down the coast of the Sierra Mountains to take up residence on the "King's Point" at seaward end of Las Gatas Beach. That made the Calzontzins Zihuatanejo's first "snowbirds."

Legend said that the Calzontzins ordered the reef built to protect their children from the open waters of the Bay and Las Gatas, or the catfish which the beach is named. Judging from the size of the stones that comprise the reef, my guess is that Mother Nature did most of the work herself. Whatever its origin, Las Gatas Beach was blessed with the only reef-protected swimming lagoon on Mexico's entire Costa Brava.

But there is much more to the story.

Shortly after the conquest of Mexico, the King of Spain sent armed cadres throughout Mexico to levy taxes on the various tribes. The legend says that when one of them confronted King Calzontzin on Las Gatas Beach, the good King pleaded with them to spare his humble people. Instead, the King offered them anything from his personal possessions that they might desire.

"In that case," exclaimed the heartless tax collector, "I shall take your lovely daughter!" When Calzontzin protested, he literally lost his head. Thereafter, the King's entourage abandoned Las Gatas Beach never to return. People have been losing their heads over Las Gatas Beach ever since, and I was soon to become one of them.

Paradise Found

I asked Arnoldo exactly where the King Calzontzins had lived on the beach. Arnoldo pointed to the seaward end where a point of land jutted into the water. Curious to see if any signs of their presence remained, I excused myself and wandered down the beach to explore. At the seaward end, the beach vanished into a dense jungle of mangrove trees. The mangroves grew well into the water and obscured the entire point from view. The faint signs of a footpath led me through the leafy tangle until I emerged in another world on the other side.

Dozens of coconut palms towered above a canopy of dense green underbrush. Birdsongs accompanied the sound of waves as they washed upon the shore. I followed the path as it meandered through the underbrush until I came upon the rotted vine-covered remains of some old wooden *cabañas.* As I explored the ruins, a giant boa constrictor, perhaps twelve feet long, slid out of the rotting lumber and vanished into the underbrush. I could sense the ghostly presence of those who had first lived here.

The thick jungle growth obscured the entire bay from my view, but I could hear the ebb and flow of the waves on a nearby shore. It was a sensuous whisper that beckoned me. Breaking through the dense underbrush, I emerged into a sandy clearing near the rocky edge of the Bay. In the waning sunlight, the Bay unfurled itself before me like a sparkling carpet of blue-green diamonds edged with the white ribbons of its five palm-lined beaches.

To one side of the clearing, the charred remains of an abandoned campfire gave evidence of a visit. Vicariously, communing with ghosts, I shared in their pleasures. I lay back on the sand, savoring the feeling of its warm embrace. High-flying frigate birds circled lazily in a cobalt sky, floating on invisible cushions of air.

As the waves marched down the rocky shoreline, they rushed and hushed and played their eternal music on the rocks, then wrapped around the rocky point and rolled onto the sandy beach in the distance. The point break was a surfer's dream come true. The sound was hypnotic, as if Mother Nature were singing some sweet siren's song. The sensual combination of her physical beauty with her sounds and textures simply overwhelmed my senses. I was too dumbstruck with awe to even think straight, a gibbering fool who was smitten with desire. All right, let's face it, it was love at first sight.

But alas, I was not falling in love with some sexy mistress who would one day be the mother of my children. That would have been okay, normal, approved by my family and condoned by law. But no, that was would have been too easy. I had fallen in love with a piece of Mexican real estate.

For *gringos* like me Mexican beach property was forbidden fruit. By Mexican law, foreigners were not allowed to rent, buy or even covet Mexican coastal or frontier land. But I knew the way around the law, and by the time I returned to Arnoldo's restaurant I was burning with desire.

Freddy, Becky and Marshal complained about my absence. "Where have you been?" Becky demanded. "We thought we had lost you!" Freddy complained. Almost breathless with excitement, I tried to describe what had I had just discovered and invited them to accompany me and see for themselves.

When Arnoldo emerged from his kitchen with our bill, I told him of my experience and asked him who owned the property. "A man named Carlos Barnard owns it," he said, then casually added, "I heard that it's for sale."

My heart skipped a beat. "How much?" I demanded.

Arnoldo shrugged his shoulders. "I don't know. But why don't you ask him? He lives in the last house on the Municipal Beach, next to the canal."

The idea that such a beauty could actually be mine triggered a rush of adrenalin that threw me into a fit of stuttering. I could not speak. I simply motioned for my three companions to follow me.

Tingling with anticipation, I led them down the beach. When we penetrated the tangle of Mangroves and entered the jungle sanctuary, the scene had the same effect on them as it first had on me. "Wow!" they exclaimed. "It's another world!"

Retracing my steps, I showed them the overgrown ruins. Then I led them to the clearing by the water. I swept my hand over the horizon, then back to the land. "Wouldn't this be a great place for my Nature Study Center?" I asked, not needing an answer. For them, as for me, it was love and first sight.

"You have got to get it!" exclaimed Freddy Mohr. "It's

incredibly beautiful."

"Gorgeous!" Becky agreed.

"Yes," Marshall added, "I agree." He nodded his head approvingly. "You should get it if you can," he said. He must have been reading my mind, for he then added, "If it's not too much, I will loan you the down payment."

I couldn't believe my ears. "Wow!" I cried. But I could not say more. I gathered the three of them into my arms and gave them a communal hug. They responded in kind. Needless to say, I was ecstatically happy. Not even in my boyhood dreams did I ever imagine I could possibly acquire something so beautiful.

And, as it turned out, I ultimately could not.

The Ultimate Perversion

Falling in love is such a common form of madness that it would not be worth mentioning except for what it reveals about the human condition. When one falls in love with another person, one often suspends good judgment simply to prolong that giddy high. Love sweeps us off our feet and out of our minds. Logic vanishes. Imagination overpowers reality. Love makes us feel better, so it's not surprising that it is such a popular addiction.

Woe is he who has never exchanged love. Love can put us on an express highway to Nirvana. If we let our selfish egos enter into the relationship, however, it can also take us in the opposite direction.

Either way, love invariably leads to major life changes. That overwhelming feeling of desire often leads to sex, marriage, children, fulfillment and ethereal bliss. However, it can also lead to in-laws, responsibilities, insurance, tuitions, servitude, resentment, conflicts, and divorce. They all seem to come in a package with our species.

As I see it, the way that we love determines our relative measure of frustration or fulfillment in our lives. Love is a gift. So long as we offer it as a gift, it is the most precious gift that we can either give or receive.

Yet, too often, we let the selfish desires and expectations of our unbridled egos pollute our new-found Nirvana. Our ego will have us think that we and it are really one, but that is a bald-faced lie. The ego lives independently. It has its own life and its own survival agenda. Our bodies are only a convenience for it and, therefore, of secondary importance. Our ego does not function in our own best interest, but in its own. The ego interprets everything we experience only in so far as it pertains to its own survival, not ours.

Furthermore, the ego is a shameless time robber. Instead of allowing us to fully enjoy the magic of each moment, it keeps us busy rehashing our past mistakes or worrying about what mistakes we may make in the future. These are the techniques that have enabled the human ego to survive throughout history. It is small wonder, then, that the ego-mind relationship is such a disaster.

We can still rescue our species from total destruction by the ego if we use our intellect to away wrestle control of our destiny and give it back to the human intellect. Once familiar with our own ego, we can see and understand how it works, then simply acknowledge that it is doing its job without succumbing to its seductions.

Thereafter, we need never worry about the past nor the future, as neither exists. The present is precious. Nature intends us to live each moment as best we can. Living in love and harmony with Nature is the best way I have found to do it.

Such was my state of mind when I went to see Don Carlos Barnard about "buying" or renting his property on Las Gatas Beach. I had been hopelessly smitten with love and desire.

One way or another, I intended to make her mine. But even as I approached his door, I felt that I was kidding myself, that I was merely testing reality. I recalled Freddy Mohr's mocking satire on AM radio, "This is only a test. If this had been a real life, you would have been told where to go and what to do. This life is only a test."

I was told that Don Carlos was rich, but that he lived in a very modest house at the end of the Municipal Beach. Don Carlos revealed himself to be a short, pot-bellied gentleman with a bald pate, a mild manner and a pleasantly sincere smile. Don Carlos thought nothing of bending the law for his own convenience, and I, a *gringo*, thought nothing of doing the same.

When I revealed that I wanted to buy his property at the end of Las Gatas Beach, he seemed pleasantly surprised. He seemed especially pleased that I intended to build a Nature Study Center on his land to promote Captain Cousteau's ideas about living in harmony with the environment. He readily agreed to cooperate in any way he could, though he confessed he could not actually sell me the land. Until the law changed, he could only lease it to me for ninety-nine years. His only condition was that I fulfill his homestead requirements by building a house with an adequate septic system on each of his five lots.

When I asked him how much, I found his price to be very reasonable, only $30,000 for over three acres. I asked if he would accept $10,000 down and give me five years to pay off the balance. He agreed, so I hired Marshall Allen's lawyer to draw up the contract. Shortly thereafter, I gave him Marshall's check for $5,000 plus a check of my own to cover the down payment. This left me penniless but happy. I had no idea how or when I could ever pay off the balance of $20,000. I just knew I had to have it.

We were all aware of what we were doing, so this had to

be an agreement between friends. In this way, both Don Carlos and our lawyers bought into my fantasy by creating one of their own. We were playing an adult game of "Pretend." We all knew that the legal ramifications could render our agreement useless or possibly put us both in jail. Yet, we did it anyway.

The Law of the Land

A brief review of Mexico's turbulent history might clarify some of the confusion surrounding Mexican real estate laws. Mexico drags her history behind it like a ball and chain.

On February 18, 1519, a young Spaniard named Hernan Cortez set sail from Havana, Cuba with eleven ships, five hundred-eight soldiers, a hundred sailors, sixteen horses and eight cannons. On arriving near Veracruz, Cortez did what no other Spaniard had ever done. He trained his men until they had become a cohesive fighting force. Then, declaring himself and his men independent from Cuba, he burned all his bridges by burning his ships. Thus, in one bold move, he committed himself and his entire retinue to survival in a strange land, full of strange people.

The local Indians were awestruck by his mere appearance. Having little body hair themselves, they had never seen a heavily bearded red-head or a horse or a firearm. When they saw Cortez on his horse with a blunderbuss, they thought he was a god. This gave Cortez immediate access to Mexico's most powerful leaders, including Montezuma, King of the Aztec Empire.

Perhaps even more importantly, he bought an alluring young princess from a band of iterant merchants and made her his mistress. This was "*La Malinche,*" one of the most extraordinary women of all time. Having been born to a king of the Paynala Indians, Malinche was relatively sophisticated and well-educated. Nevertheless, when a brother and heir were born her parents, she was cast off and sold to a band of itinerant merchants. The merchants in turn traded her and thirty other maidens to Hernan Cortez in return for some mirrors and metal hand tools.

Having learned many languages during her travels with the merchants, La Malinche soon became Cortez's chief translator and advisor, as well as his mistress. Seeking vengeance against her own people, La Malinche recruited over two hundred thousand Indians to fight on the side of Cortez. Thus, with the help of La Malinche and his well-trained cadre of soldiers, Cortez managed to conquer the entire country in the name of God and the King of Spain.

After the Mexican conquest, the King of Spain divided the country into huge blocks of land, which he parceled out to his friends as gifts. The lucky recipients became known as the Viceroys of Spain. Few of the Spanish Viceroys had any idea of where or what Mexico was and could not have cared less. Most had scant interest in their remote windfalls, abandoning them without ever seeing them. The indigenous Mexicans, who actually lived on the land, took little interest in farming or developing land that was not their own. The property of no one became the responsibility of no one. Consequently, large parts of Mexico lay fallow for centuries. The entire country wallowed in the doldrums, personified by the icon of the Mexican peasant asleep by a cactus under his sombrero.

Finally, the Mexican people revolted. On September 15, 1810 Father Miguel Hidalgo proclaimed Mexico's independence from Spain with the famous cry, "*Viva Mexico!*

Agrarian Reform

In 1928, Mexico's Agrarian Land Reform ended the stranglehold that the Spanish Viceroys had on their land. The huge Spanish land grants were divided up and awarded to the indigenous residents who qualified as homesteaders, known in Spanish as *ejidos.* To qualify as a homesteader (*ejidatario)* under the Agrarian Reform, every candidate had to meet certain conditions — build a house, plant fruit trees or viable cash crop and pay a modest land tax called an *Impuesto Predial.*

Don Carlos had inherited his *ejido* land on Las Gatas Beach from his grandfather who had qualified as an *ejidatario* by planting eighty coconut, tamarindo and banana trees. The only thing still lacking from his claim, was a house on each lot. This was why Don Carlos insisted in our contract that I build a house on each lot. By building the houses, I would ratify his claim to the *ejid*o land.

An ironic twist of fate effectively postponed my early day of reckoning with reality. Without much warning, my beloved father took ill and died. His death was a brutal blow to me, for I loved him dearly. On the other hand, his demise automatically released to me a trust fund of some $250,000. It was a cruel irony that his death should provide the means for me to stay and survive in Zihuatanejo. My distraught mother pleaded with me to invest the money in money markets or local real estate.

But love is blind. I saw it as the means to realize my dream of creating a Nature Study Center on Las Gatas Beach. I did try to compromise, thought. I put half of the trust money in time deposits to please my mother and used the other half to pay off Don Carlos and start construction.

I would have gladly done without the money if it could have brought my father back to life, but so be it. Now it was up to me to prove myself worthy. With my sister looking after my mother and with money in my pocket, I could now focus my time, energy and money on the creation of my Nature Study Center.

My Beach House

My first step was to build a little house where Becky and I could live while we designed and built the structures needed for the school. For me, the design of our house was a delightful challenge. I wanted to take advantage of Zihuatanejo's benign climate by designing my house to invite the outside inside, yet still embody the comforts of my New York City apartment. Zihuatanejo's subtropical climate boasts an average of two hundred-eight days of sunshine every year, and the temperature rarely drops below seventy degrees Fahrenheit (twenty degrees Celsius). Therefore, no doors, windows or walls were actually needed. Mere bug screens and partitions were all that was required.

Anticipating how difficult it might be to verbally convey my ideas to Mexican workers, I wisely decided to first build a miniature model on a scale of one hundred to one. This would prevent misunderstandings. It would also allow us to make corrections on the model before actually starting construction.

At a model airplane store on West 33rd Street, I bought sheets of balsam wood, glue and miniature house fittings. Since I loved the size and floor plan of my Greenwich Village apartment, I simply adapted them to my new model home. The result was a charming model beach bungalow with a palm-thatched roof. By removing the roof, you could see every drawer, closet, door, fixture, and furnishing. To invite the outside inside, it had no solid doors or windows, only screened openings with shutters that could be raised or lowered in accord with the weather.

Once I completed the model in New York City, I put it into a cardboard box and carried it by plane to Zihuatanejo. There I discovered that, by chance, Marshall Allen's two architects had just finishing work on his Hotel El Capricho Del Rey and were looking for another job. I invited them to accompany me to the very spot where I wanted my house built.

Withdrawing the scale model from its box, I said, "Please, how much to build this house right here, just as you see it?" Over a year later, Becky and I moved into the real thing, and it far exceeded our expectations.

In order to fulfill my commitment to Don Carlos and also to provide lodging for at least thirty students, I gave the workers a month off, during which time I designed four additional lodgings and a central kitchen. When we resumed construction, I soon discovered how demanding island living can be.

Because fiberglass boats had not yet arrived in Zihuatanejo, every brick, every bag of cement, every grain of sand, even the water had to be brought in by motorized dugout canoes. With an *adze*, an ax and a giant pair of calibers to measure the thickness of the hull, a good boat carpenter could produce a twenty-foot canoe out of a single branch of the giant Parrota tree in just ten days. Meanwhile, I missed the convenience of automobiles as never before. Frankly, the need to rely on outboard motorboats for every day needs was a colossal pain in the ass.

Marshall's Mexican Wedding

While Becky and I were busy with our construction projects, Marshall was busy falling in love. Rosalin Kirkland was a familiar face around Greenwich Village and at Marshall's place on Fire Island. Although we often saw each other in

New York, I really did not get to know her until she showed up aboard the *El Viejo* the same day Freddy Mohr vanished.

Pretty, bright and very sharp, she was a perfect mate for Marshall's erratic demeanor. They were soon talking marriage. The only problem, as far as I was concerned, was that Rosalin's aversion to Freddy Mohr deprived me of his delightful company. Because he was openly gay, Rosalin couldn't stand him. She saw him as competition for Marshall's money and attention. She forbade his presence aboard *El Viejo*. To my dismay, Marshall indulged her. Marshall bought Freddy out and sent him back to his home in Florida. Thereafter, *El Viejo* literally became the proverbial *Ship of Fools*.

The wedding took place aboard the deck of *El Viejo* at about five in the afternoon. I was designated to be Marshall's best man. A colorful assortment of Ros' and Marshall's friends flew in from Greenwich Village and Fire Island to witness the ceremony. Meanwhile, Rosalin had invited Zihuatanejo's three-time mayor and all of his political cronies to participate in the ceremony. It was the first time they had ever been invited aboard and they were all there, dressed in their tropical best.

It was the only occasion that Marshall had ever invited local society aboard his boat, and he felt awkward and lost in their presence. Since the bride and groom spoke no Spanish and the attending officials spoke no English, the wedding ceremony was surreal and confusing. Intercultural differences popped up throughout the evening. After the wedding ceremony was over, he shook a few hands, and only a few hands, then insisted that I accompany him behind the wheelhouse to avoid the crowd and smoke pot.

Rosalin would appear from time to time to plead with him to come participate in his own reception, but he would have none of it. Soon her supplications turned to sour warnings, then vociferous threats. "Marshall, if you don't come out here right now, I am going to throw everything overboard! Do hear me?"

I stood to go placate her, but Marshall caught my arm and pulled me back down. Then we heard a pronounced splash, followed by Rosalin's screams. "Did you hear that, Marshall? That was the punch bowl! And now, here goes the bottle of Chevas whiskey." Splash! "And now your gawddam bottle of Gordon's gin." Splash!

And so it went. Rosalin's honored guests from the community panicked and scrambled for cover, or else frantically signaled for help to passing boats. However, all those present who had known them in New York and Fire Island simply took it in stride. They had all seen it before. With such shenanigans, it was not long before the ship was abandoned by all but the latter mentioned group of die-hards. With the "foreign element" removed, it turned out to be one hell of a party.

Nevertheless, Marshall's Mexican wedding did not bode well for their marital future. Nor did it bode well for Freddy and me. We both lost Marshall's support and participation. Rosalin tried to take over where Freddy left off, but the results were not nearly the same. Meanwhile, I was still trying to finish the construction of my student housing for the Nature Study Center.

Labor Laws of Mexico

When you hired workers in Mexico, it was almost like getting married. The courtship, the wedding, the romantic honeymoon, the familiarity, the boredom, the disillusionment, the contempt, the divorce, all the elements of a dysfunctional marriage entered your relationship. Furthermore, the divorce process could be just as traumatic, often with both parties in arbitration court, blatantly accusing each other of the most outrageous lies.

After just thirty-one days, an employer cannot discharge an employee unless he is paid a full-month's severance, a full month's vacation, a half year of costly social security fees, two weeks of sick leave, and a Christmas *alguinaldo*. If an uninsured employee got sick or injured on the job, he or she qualified to receive all of the above, plus all medical and hospital expenses, full pay throughout the convalescence, and all legal fees paid. Since the legal arbitrators get one-third of the employee's take, the laws were heavily stacked in favor of the employee. In other words, once an employee got you in the door for labor arbitration, you had already lost your case and chances were that it would break your business.

I suffered my first run-in with Mexico's labor laws when I contracted Odelon Lara to put a *palapa* roof on the big four-unit bungalow I called the "Hotel California." Odelon was tall, slim and as nimble as a cat, Odelon was a happy *palapero* — an expert in palm thatched roofing.

A *palapero* makes palm-thatched roofing by weaving the leaves of the round palm tree onto a latticework of wood called *barras*. Palm-thatched roofs are handsome to look at and delightful to live under. They provide perfect insulation against the tropical sun and they are almost always a work of artistic beauty. Unlike an ordinary roof, a *palapa* roof is a living, breathing organic entity. Its life span varies from four to eight years, depending on its inclination. The steeper the roof, the longer it lasts. It is like a favorite pair of old shoes, just when you really get comfortable with it, a hole wears through and they spring a leak. Once it springs a leak, there is no use in trying to patch it. Nothing to do but to tear it all off and start over again.

Odelon was the first of several *palaperos* I worked with.

He was the captain of a five-man *palapa* team. After buying and cutting some five thousand *palapa* leaves from a rancher, he had to truck the leaves to Zihuatanejo, then load them on a boat to carry them across the Bay to Las Gatas Beach. Once ashore, each leaf was spread out flat to dry in the sun. While the new leaves were drying, the crew removed and burned all the old *palapa* leaves. They also repaired or replaced all the wooden framing and bars that held the leaves in place. Then they painted the entire wooden framework with burnt motor oil, diesel oil or toxic poisons to ward off the termites.

To watch Odelon at work was an awesome experience. He could go tripping across the steep, oiled infrastructure with the agility of a cat. His crew lifted loads of fifteen *palapa* at a time up to Odelon by means of a barrel. The barrel was part of a block and tackle system that passed through a pulley attached to the ceiling. From his perch on the framework, Odelon would fish the barrel into his reach and then set to work, busily weaving each leaf into the wood. In this way, he created three beautiful *palapa* roofs for me on just as many buildings. But they were more than mere roofs, they were beautiful works of art.

When he built the first *palapa* roof on my house in 1968, *palapa* was the cheapest kind of roof you could buy. *Palapa* leaves were abundant, and the price of each leaf was only five cents. Today, however, *palapa* is in vogue. Every fancy hotel, bar, restaurant, park, or gazebo in neighboring Ixtapa now boasts a *palapa* roof. Thus, the demand for *palapa* leaves has grown exponentially and so has the price. As of January 2006, the price of *palapa* hovers around eighty cents per leaf. In less than the lifespan of a *palapa* roof, the price has jumped sixteen-fold, from being the cheapest kind of roof on the market to the most expensive.

As the price of *palapa* continued to soar. I decided that I could no longer afford another *palapa* roof. Therefore, the next time a roof began to leak, I vowed to replace the *palapa* with ceramic tile. When that time came, Odelon refused the job. After working with *palapa* for so long, he was unaccustomed to both the character and the weight of tile. It seemed to me that the tile would be much easier to place than *palapa*, so I convinced him to do the job anyway. That turned out to be a total disaster, which I deeply regretted.

Odelon was a great guy who would never intentionally harm anybody. He had a twinkle in eyes and wore a perpetual smile, preferring to see life through the proverbial rose-colored glasses. To know him was to love him, except when he had been drinking.

Odelon was a cheap but terrible drunk. Just two bottles of beer transformed him from mister nice guy into a manic-depressive monster you would rather not know. When booze went in, all reason went out. Under the influence, Odelon could run the whole gamut of emotions, loving, tearful, despotic, sentimental, subservient, suspicious, angry, morose, remorseful, rebellious, belligerent, and back to loving again, all in a matter of minutes. At such times, I simply tried to avoid him. I never knew if he would try to kill me or kiss me. Yet, after a night of sleep, he would return to his work without a trace of a hangover, nor any memory of what happened.

After finishing the tile roof behind the Hotel California, Odelon left several buckets of surplus tiles sitting high up in the *cupola* of the building. One fell off and almost landed on a guest. The next time I saw Odelon, I gave him hell for being so irresponsible. Odelon burst into tears and promised to fix it *ahora mismo*, right now. That is when I should have known that he had been drinking.

I reminded Odelon that it was Sunday, that there was no one around to help him. With that, he sniffed haughtily,

"Wazza matta you? You no zenk Odelon can do it alone?"

"Well, OK," I conceded. "If you want to try it alone, go ahead. But I think you are going to need help." I felt so uncomfortable, that I invented some excuse to go to town. I was not actually present when the following took place, however, those who were there later told me what happened.

Odelon stubbornly set out alone to remove the offending tiles from the *cupola*. Using the same block and tackle system he had used to lift tiles, he now hoisted the empty barrel to the top and tied the ropeer end to a post. That done, he climbed up to the *copula* and filled the empty barrel with tiles. Then he returned to the ground and untied the rope.

The barrel full of tiles now weighed much more than Odelon did. The instant he untied the rope, the barrel hurdled downward, pulling Odelon off his feet. In his attempt to stop it, Odelon hung on. Half way up to the ceiling, Odelon collided with the barrel. The impact fractured his collarbone, but he managed to continue his ascent. At the same instant Odelon's head struck the ceiling, the heavy barrel full of tiles struck the ground. Shards of broken tiles and barrel stays went flying everywhere. With nothing to counter-balance Odelon's weight, he came crashing down upon the shards of broken tiles.

Many feared that the fall had killed him, but Odelon was invincible. After three months in the hospital, he emerged fat and as good as new.

Unfortunately, I did not recover so easily. As his employer, I was responsible for his medical bills, his hospital stay, his obligatory year-end bonus, and his lost pay. It took two years for me to pay off the debt.

Guererro

Even though the United States and Mexico share the same two thousand-mile border, the vast differences between their cultural, political, social, religious, and economic pasts has made them very distant neighbors. Each geographical area leaves its distinctive stamp on the mental, as well as the physical character of the people who inhabit it.

Just as different as Mexico is from the United States, so the state of Guererro differs from all the other states in Mexico. This is especially true regarding the northern half of the state which is known as the *Costa Brava.*

Until Zihuatanejo's international airport opened in 1973, the Costa Brava was among the most primitive areas in the country. Isolated by the Sierra Madre Mountain range on one side and by the Pacific Ocean on the other, the Costa Brava wallowed in the antiquated past until 1967 when the World Bank decided to invest over $550 million to develop its budding tourism industry.

Geography isolated the local people, but despite their independence, or maybe because of it, the people of the Costa Brava tended to be kind and accommodating, almost to a fault. They could not bear to disappoint anyone and would go out of their way to please you. If you asked them for directions, for example, they would happily oblige you, whether they knew the way or not. Rather than disappoint you, they would create some directions for you right on the spot.

In Guererro, getting to the truth of a matter could become a surrealistic adventure. Direct questions only rarely begat direct replies. Rather, they were likely to lead you through the whole realm of possibilities. Therefore, it was often difficult to determine what to believe and what not to believe. Promises were especially suspect, probably due to a distorted concept of time. In Guerrero, *mañana*, tomorrow, only rarely lived up to its billing. *Mañana* could mean tomorrow, but it could also mean days, weeks or months into the future. Or it might never come at all.

On the Costa Brava of Guererro, corruption, lies and deliberate misrepresentation were as common as the cold. This produced serious consequences for the entire community. Half-way through the installation of Zihuatanejo's original drainage system, I noticed that the diameter of the piping suddenly diminished from about two feet to eight inches. Now when it rained, the systems did not drain the streets, it flooded them. I surmised that the difference went into the pockets of the local politicians and contractors. When the water treatment plant failed, they did not fix it for eleven years. They simply pumped the only partially-treated sludge into the Bay under cover of darkness. In 2004, a front page expose in *La Reforma* newspaper of Mexico City caused a steep drop in tourism. Only then was it finally fixed.

Professional aptitude was also a problem. Until recently, there were few trade schools where one could acquire professional skills. Consequently, there were many jacks-of-all-trades, but masters of none. Professional ineptitude made it extremely difficult to get things done well or on time. Trying to motivate *Guererreses* with perks and bonuses was costly and ultimately ineffective. In hot sultry Zihuatanejo, nothing ever seemed to get done well on the first try. "That's how they invented refried beans," Freddy Mohr always insisted. "They couldn't get it right the time!"

After almost forty years of trying to fathom the mind of the typical *Guererrese* still defied my comprehension. Contradictions abounded in number. Objective reasoning seemed useless. Impersonal considerations were taken very personally. Personal matters were often aired in public. Their typical reaction to honest criticism, however well intentioned, was to walk off the job, to break down in tears or to charge with a machete.

After working with such perfectionists as Captain Cousteau and the various film crews, I found it hard to cope with such work ethics with. Nothing I tried seemed to make any difference. Frustrated and impatient, I began to loose my temper, to rant and scream. This robbed much of the joy from my work. What should have been a creative party became a nightmare chore.

I began to doubt my own sanity. I concluded that the problem must be me, not them. I feared that if I did not get psychiatric help soon, I might provoke one of my workers into killing me or, worse yet, provoke myself into killing one of them. I retreated to the relative sanity of New York City to seek some professional help.

After sessions with two so-called psycho therapists, I concluded that they needed help more than I did. As an alternative, I signed up for a two-week, new-age self-help seminar called the "Erhard Seminar Training" or simply EST.

EST was a great help to me. I learned about my own confused psyche. I learned to accept other people and things just as they are, without conditions or judgments. "Always ride the horse in the direction it is going," Werner Erhard advised. That meant accepting *Guererreses* just as they were. It meant surrendering to the realities of our many differences and learning to live with them without anger or regrets. It was a serious challenge, but it worked.

Problems still materialized out of nowhere. Getting things done still required monumental determination, persistence and patience. Most promises still went unhonored. Nothing really changed except me. I just counted my blessings and refused to worry. Of course, this came at a price. It required four years to do what should have been done in two. But who cared? By 1973 there was a functioning bungalow standing on each of the five lots, just as I had promised Don Carlos. Now that I had fulfilled my promise to him, I felt free to fulfill the promise I had made to myself — to create a Nature Study

Double Murder

While I was still in New York with Becky, I received news of the very untimely shooting death of Arnoldo Veerboonen, our Mexican associate and friend. As Freddy Mohr explained by phone, Arnoldo was walking home from his beach restaurant with a friend one night, when they encountered a *palapa* beach umbrella ablaze with fire. Arnoldo and his friend attempted to smother the blaze with hands full of beach sand. Just then, an armed watchman ran up, brandishing a revolver. *"Alto los manos!"* the guard commanded. "Put your hands up!"

But they did not stop. "The fire is almost out," urged Arnoldo. "Come, give us a hand!"

"No, no!" retorted the excited guard. "Put up your hands, or I'll shoot!"

"Don't be ridiculous!" Arnoldo scoffed. Then he made his fatal error. "I also have a gun." He pulled back his shirt tail to reveal the gun tucked into his belt. At first sight of the gun the watch fired, hitting Arnoldo in the head and the stomach. Arnoldo looked at him with incredulous surprise. As he sagged to the ground, he had withdrew his pistol and shot the watchman three times, killing him instantly. Between them, the two men left behind two grieving widows and eleven fatherless orphans.

It was not the first time that senseless double murders had occurred in Zihuatanejo. In 1988 the Chief of the local Preventive Police encountered the chief of the local Judicial

Police in the parking lot of *El Lobo Cabaret*. In lieu of buying a proper license, the cabaret owner let it be known that he was willing to pay the police for protection, but to only one police force at a time. The two police chiefs got into a heated argument over which police force was the most deserving and ended in a double shoot-out in which both men died. Faster than you can read this sentence, they widowed two wives, impoverished five mistresses and orphaned ten children.

Arnoldo's death was a tragic blow to all of us who knew and loved him. Without Freddy or Arnoldo's presence, Marshall was lost and traumatized. The primitive nature of Zihuatanejo had always intimidated Marshall. Now, it terrified him. All he wanted was to get out of there with his life. I tried to convince him to call Freddy Mohr back to run El Capricho del Rey. However, Rosalin would have none of it. She convinced Marshall to forget about Freddy and turn the hotel over to Sidney Adler, an American lawyer working in Mexico City. Then they left for New York City, never to return.

Marshall's retreat to New York with Rosalin left the door open for Freddy Mohr to return to Zihuatanejo on his own. During his tenure with Marshall, Freddy had become a local legend. His loving presence and sparkling sense of humor spread joy and laughter wherever he went. He had no trouble finding a friendly reception and new employment. He resumed his career by catering the wedding banquet for Joe Cipriano and Patsy Cummings.

Freddy's plans almost went out the window when Joe found Freddy asleep with his wife on their wedding night. With his usual wit and charm, however, Freddy convinced Joe that it was all an innocent mistake. The three of them later collaborated in the creation of the now famous Coconuts Bar & Restaurant.

Largely because of Freddy's presence, Coconuts soon became the most popular restaurant in Zihuatanejo, at least it was among the expatriates. For years, Freddy's unique gifts as a host assured its success. In the year 2000, however, Freddy Mohr succumbed to cancer in Miami, Florida. For me and many other of Zihuatanejo's expatriates, Freddy's departure left a gaping hole that has never been filled.

Enter the Villain!

The Hotel El Capricho del Rey sat vacant and neglected for over a year before Marshall's lawyer came up with a "suitable" tenant. The tenant's name was Alvaro Sanchez Mirus. His business card said he was also a lawyer.

He had ambitious plans for the Hotel El Capricho del Rey. Personally, however, I was not very fond of him, or the idea of him. After participating in the hotel's evolution, I could not imagine it without Freddy and Arnoldo at the helm. The Hotel El Capricho del Rey was their baby, just as the Nature Study Center was now my Baby. We had become synonymous with our creations. Furthermore, Freddy was a professional host who was uniquely qualified to run such a place. I was never sure what Sanchez Mirus was until much later, but I knew for certain that he was no Freddy Mohr.

The Nature Study Center

I conceived the Nature Study Center as a place where students and tourists could learn to reintegrate their lives with nature on a personal level. This required me to work out a curriculum. It was a process that required much more time and introspection than I had ever anticipated, but it forced to crystallize my thoughts on the matter. In the belief that a problem well-defined is a problem half-solved, I looked into our evolutionary past for the reasons that made the present ecological crisis inevitable. This became the theme of my curriculum at the Nature Study Center.

Cousteau convinced me that there was only one world and only one life and that we were all participants in its survival. If the Nature Study Center was to conform to Captain Cousteau's vision, it required my students to recognize Mother Nature as the source and substance of all life. But how do you prepare someone to meet their real maker when it goes against the canons of almost every religious belief system.? That was the challenge that now confronted me. The only way that I could think of to teach this was to let Mother Nature speak for herself. The challenge was to create a process that would reveal what Nature is, how it works and how relates to each person's life.

To recruit students for my Nature Study Center, I placed ads in *The New York Times* and *The Village Voice* and in the *Reforma* and *The News* of Mexico City. My target audience was young people, from their mid-teens to their mid-twenties. Judging from their enthusiastic response, many were ready for just such an experience, but their parents proved more skeptical. In virtually every case, I had to personally convince the parents that their children would return home safely, before they would entrust their children to me for *Camp de Mar* summer sea camp in Mexico,.

Were it not for my past association with Captain Cousteau and the cheap travel provided by Becky's airline passes, the recruitment process would have cost more than it produced. Nevertheless, I managed to recruit thirty students plus the very capable assistance of Mr. and Mrs. Robert Bisom. Both were licensed teachers and certified diving instructors. Doctor Ruth Roman, a vacationing medical doctor from Harvard University also helped, just for the fun of it.

Photo 24: Instruction at the Nature Study Center

Our objective was to give students the opportunity to experience themselves as responsible participants in the global ecosystem through personal participation and experimentation. We taught SCUBA diving as a means of retracing our personal evolution back to its aquatic origins in the sea. In this way they could actually see the marine chain-of-life unfold before their eyes —the microscopic plankton, the tiny fish that feed on them, the larger and larger fish that feed on them, and the ultimate predator of man.

We taught surfing in relation to the dynamics of ocean waves and currents. To demonstrate the latent power in the oceans, we actually built a primitive wave-activated water pump out of PVC tubing. For a few seconds, it produced enough electricity to light up a small flashlight bulb. This stimulated lively discussions about the oceans as a potential source of global energy in the future.

We also taught marine biology in relation to sport fishing and the fisheries industry. We taught sailing in relation to navigation and navigation in relation to sailing.

To sum up what they'd learned, the students and I produced a graphic exhibition explaining ecology, which we mounted on the trunks of the coconut trees near the water. The exhibition addressed three vital questions: What is Ecology? How does it work? How do we each fit into the picture?

My students loved it, and so did I. I think that the experience awakened many of them to their own role in the ecology of life. Over the following three years, the Nature Study Center certified over one hundred students in SCUBA, sailing, surfing, or fishing. Several went on to earn Ph.D.s in the Earth Sciences.

I was very proud of them all. I was also proud of what I attempted to do with the Nature Study Center, though I cannot say it was a roaring success. In creating the Center, I learned much more about human nature than I really wanted to know. Take, for example, the lack of support from the locals.

Educational Vacations

During the hot summer months, tourism to Zihuatanejo-Ixtapa dropped to almost nothing. Thousands of hotel rooms stood vacant. Merchants went broke. Restaurants were empty.

Meanwhile, summer was when thousands of students and teachers were looking for a place to spend their vacation. I proposed to Armando Federico, Zihuatanejo's mayor, that the City tap into the scholastic market by offering a package of "educational vacations" such as my own. I argued that by offering accredited summer school courses in the local culture and language as well as water sports, the City could generate badly needed summer revenues on behalf of the entire community. I even volunteered to produce the brochure.

"If the City will pay the mailing costs, I will pay for the printing," I offered. Armando agreed and I proceeded to print five thousand brochures and deliver them to City Hall. Unfortunately, the City failed to comply and the brochures were never posted. This was the first of many disappointments.

I learned that the Teachers Union protested to the Secretary of Education because I employed non-union English-speaking teachers. The Secretary of Education notified me to "cease and desist" until my school was fully licensed, a process that could take years. Even though none of their members could teach the courses we offered, they chose to hinder rather than help us.

The local Taxi Boat Union also protested to the Port Captain because I used my own boats for diving instead of renting theirs. The coup de grâce came when Jaime Silvestre, one of my local students, showed up at the Municipal Pier with his parents and a group of religious protesters. One of them waved a makeshift sign reading, *"Di No Al Diablo!"* Say No to the Devil!

I couldn't believe my eyes. "Is that sign addressed to me?"

Young Jaime Silvestre was obviously embarrassed. When my questioning gaze met his, he looked up at the sky, raised his open palms and shrugged in resignation.

"Say no to the word of the devil!" commanded one of the three ladies in the group. I think she was Jaime's sister.

"We are here to shield our children from the words of devil," announced the father. He was an adult version of his young son.

"We are withdrawing our son from your school for blasphemy," announced the boy's mother. "And we protest your teachings of the words of the devil."

"Who? Me? The words of the devil?"

I learned that Jaime's father was one of the numerous evangelistic missionaries in the area. On his visits home, young Jaime had informed his parents that I taught biological evolution.

This was true. At the Nature Study Center, I taught that most religions' belief systems offered gods as mere metaphors for Mother Nature, for that is what I sincerely believed. That this should incur the wrath of "true believers" in creationism did not surprise me. That they should to deny me the same privilege of dissent did.

Needless to say, such distractions were discouraging. They robbed much of the creative joy from the project. Desperate, I tried to enlist the support of Armando and Jorge Allec, the leader of the ruling political party, the *Partido Revolutionario Institucional* (PRI). They denied support on the basis that political and budgetary restrictions prevented them from getting involved. I suspected that it was old-fashioned prejudice.

At that time, Mexico was riding the crest of a petroleum boom. A wave of Mexican nationalism accompanied the boom and inspired its leaders to become arrogantly independent. In an egomaniacal spasm of hate and defiance, both President Luis Echavarria and his successor, Jorge Lopez Portillo, proclaimed Mexico to be independent from the rest of the world and the new "leader of the Third-World Block."

To me, that sounded like the creation of an "International Losers Club." Under their banner, anti-Americanism was rampant. It was a bad time for a *gringo* to promote anything that was not one hundred percent by and for Mexicans. It all harkened back to fundamental differences in perspective.

Unfortunately, such differences brought the Nature Study Center to a premature end. After closing the school in 1980, I committed my teaching curriculum to a book titled *Nature's Rebellion.*

Tarascan Indian Village

The untimely demise of the Nature Study Center left my beach bungalows empty but no less costly to maintain. Therefore, I remodeled the student bungalows to accommodate the growing number of nature-seeking tourists. Still, I did not abandon my idea for a Nature Study Center. I simply revised my strategy. Having failed to win support of the local community, I decided that I was thinking too small, too locally, if you will. To attract the kind of high-level support I needed, I decided to expand my idea for a small Nature Study Center into a National Nature Park and seek the support of the National Institute of Sports and Recreation (INDE).

Over time, I developed a plan to convert the entire Las Gatas Beach area into an international tourist attraction of grand proportions. My idea was not original. I was inspired by the Polynesian Cultural Center, which I had once seen on the Island of Oahu in Hawaii. As I remembered it, the Polynesian Cultural Center featured all that was unique about the culture, lifestyle and products of the Polynesian people. The Center included the usual tourist shops, restaurants, and souvenirs stands, but the heart of it was a small Polynesian village featuring the homes, gardens, arts, crafts, clothing, food, music, and dance of the Polynesian Islands. It also promoted environmental harmony and produced handsome dividends for the locale. It was a clean and classy win-win operation that helped make the Hawaiian Islands the tourist mecca that it is.

My "Plan B" was to propose the creation of a similar kind of attraction on Las Gatas Beach. The unique environmental gifts of Las Gatas Beach included the culture, art and products of the Tarascan Indians who are indigenous to the states of Michoacan and Guererro.

Las Gatas Beach was an ideal setting for such a project.

Only three other families occupied the entire beach, so it was still relatively empty and pristine, yet only ten minutes by boat from the heart of Zihuatanejo. Furthermore, it boasted a unique barrier reef. By closing off the two openings in the reef with simple fishing nets and stocking the lagoon with fish, the lagoon could become a unique kind of "Captive Aquarium." The flat area behind the beach provided ample space for a typical "Tarascan Indian Village" that could rival the Polynesian Cultural Center of Hawaii. The existing trail through the jungle to the Point Gorobo Lighthouse could easily become an attractive "Botanical Garden and Nature Trail."

I argued that such an attraction could produce the same dividends for Zihuatanejo-Ixtapa that the Polynesian Cultural Center produced for Hawaii. Moreover, the time was ripe. The new high-rise hotels in Ixtapa boasted over three thousand hotel rooms that were waiting for tourists. The new Zihuatanejo-Ixtapa Airport was already open and receiving international flights from five different gateway cities. Meanwhile, Las Gatas Beach was still relatively empty and waiting. It seemed like an idea whose time had come.

And what did I hope to get out of it? Legitimacy, that's what! If I could convince the Federal government to back my tourist attraction, the chances were that I could also convince them to hire me as one of its directors. That would not only please my ego, it would also legalize my immigration status and give me the stature I needed to be accepted as a land owner in the local community. Otherwise, I feared I would always remain a foreign outsider.

I knew that such collaboration would not be easy. Such a project would create thousands of problems, and there were sure to be many differences to overcome. Still, as a former advertising man, it all made promotional sense. Even if we were not quite ready for each other, I felt that Zihuatanejo and I needed each other. Therefore, I outlined a proposal, much like what you just read, and took it to New York City.

I tried to convince myself that I needed to get the kind of professional help, from my many friends in New York still in the promotion business, such a project warranted. The result was an elaborate twenty-page presentation detailing the design and construction of the Tarascan India Village and Nature Study Center on Las Gatas Beach. But looking back on the trip, my real motive was to see Becky.

Eastern Airlines had stopped flying to Acapulco some time before, and I had not seen Becky for more than two months. Without Freddy or Marshall there, her interest in Zihuatanejo dropped sharply. She no longer shared my obsession with Las Gatas Beach. I sensed that we had drifted apart, not only in body but in spirit as well. Although I loved Becky, I was no longer certain that I wanted to spend the rest of my life with her. On the other hand, I was not certain that I wanted to go on without her.

As Becky became more integrated with life in the Big Apple and more involved with her own projects, she also became more distant. Her work at the Children's Puppet Theatre demanded an ever growing portion of her free time. Her work at the New York Buddhist Center was also demanding, though less rigorous. I also suspected that she was seeing other men.

When I questioned her about it, she neither affirmed nor denied it. Instead, she became defensive. "Well, why shouldn't I be with other men?" she demanded. "What good are you? I hardly ever see you!" She paced in a little circle, then started again. "You want to fritter your time away in Mexico? Go ahead! But don't count on me. If you want to be my man, you have to live with me and care for me."

"What about my Nature Study Center in Zihuatanejo?"

"Forget about your Nature Study Center. You're not married to it. You're married to me!"

"I thought it was a marriage of convenience, for both of us."

"Yes, it was. But it's become something else. Now I want a real marriage. Or else, none at all!"

"You don't want to live with me in Mexico?"

She shook her head. "There is nothing for me there."

"You mean for me to move back to New York and get a job?" I questioned.

She nodded her head. "Yes, and why not? Millions do it, why not you?"

I thought about it all that night, but I simply could not give up all the dreams, all the blood, sweat and tears that I had invested in Mexico. I had dedicated my inheritance, all my energy, and almost twenty years of my life to it. I could not simply walk away in defeat. I had to see it through to some kind of worthy completion.

I was anxious to submit my proposal for the Tarascan Indian Village as well. When the presentation was finished, at last, I phoned the National Parks Department for an appointment and departed for Mexico City.

The man in charge of Parks and Recreation at INDE was Guillermo Lopez Portillo, the younger brother of the current President. When I arrived at his office, a fat receptionist told me that he was not available, but one of his assistants would receive me instead. After waiting about an hour, three well-groomed men appeared and ushered me into an empty conference room. They courteously listened to my pitch and promised that they would recommend my proposal to the Director himself. I said that would wait, but they deferred. Instead, they promised to convey his reaction by telephone. I did not believe them, but what could I do? Reluctantly, I entrusted my expensive presentation to them and returned to

Zihuatanejo.

Months passed and no word came. Not that I was surprised. I understood that an elaborate and costly proposal from a visiting *gringo* had to be among the Director's lowest priorities. Nevertheless, I could not restrain my growing anxiety. In fact, my impatient phone calls may have offended the three men for I never again got past the fat receptionist. To make matters worse, I was now desperately low on funds and without prospects to survive the coming season. I had to create some kind of income on my own.

The New Year's Eve Party

It was Becky who came up with the idea of how to solve my financial crisis. "Considering that the Christmas holidays are just around the corner," she said, "Why don't you throw a Gala New Year's Eve Party on Las Gatas Beach?"

I slapped my thighs and snapped my fingers. "Brilliant!" I cried. I knew the idea was a winner the instant I heard it. Imagine a New Year's Eve party to end all New Year's Eve parties in the world's most romantic setting. Yesssssss! Of course!

I took my idea to Freddy Mohr at the Coconuts Restaurant. He would know just where to go and what to do. When it came to making fun, there was nobody better. If Freddy recommended it, his friends alone could make it a success.

When I told him my idea, he reacted just as I had. "Great idea!" he exclaimed. "It might be a little late, but if you get the tour agents in Ixtapa to sell it for you, it's worth a try."

"Can you help me out on this?"

"I can't help you on New Year's Eve. I have to work Coconuts that night. But maybe I can line you up with some important people," he promised. "Maybe even some movie stars!"

"And how about some entertainment, maybe even a show of some kind? Got any ideas?"

"Yeah, on New Year's Eve you gotta offer some kind of show. But I'm afraid you won't find much talent in Zih." Then, he snapped his fingers. "Wait! Come to think of it, I've got just the man for you. My good friend Ron Rivera produces shows for those big cruise ships that stop in Acapulco. He is a great choreographer. I think he works with two or three different musical and dance groups. If anyone can help you, he's the man!"

Freddy called Ron by phone and we drove to Acapulco to meet him. Ron and I hit it off well. We even got to see one of his shows. It consisted of four salsa dancers and a trio of musicians. For $1,600 plus expenses, Ron promised that he could bring a similar group to work in Zihuatanejo on New Year's Eve. We shook on the deal and I gave Ron a $500 deposit. Since Ron was a close friend of Freddy's, I did not insist on a written contract.

But just in case they might not show up, I also looked into whatever local talent I could find. I managed to locate both a Mariachi trio and a torch juggler who lived in Zihuatanejo. I also found a guitarist who also played a nose flute in nearby Petetlan. And there was one more possibility, a stilt walker who lived right in Zihuatanejo. He made his living by walking on stilts in front of various stores, dressed like Uncle Sam in red, white and blue tails with a tall top hat to match. Rumor had it that one day his top had accidentally got entangled in some hot wires. They say that he lost his memory and couldn't remember his own name.

I hastily printed a one-page flyer and then distributed them to every tour seller in every hotel in the new high-rise hotels of Ixtapa. If I could convince those tour agents to sell my New Year's Eve Party, I felt that I could convince them to sell my Ecology Tours throughout the entire tourist season. Such a move would solve all my financial problems, so I was very anxious to do a good job.

To promote my New Year's Eve Party, I spent every penny I could muster. Throughout Christmas week, I ran ads in the local newspapers and announcements on the radio. I hired boys to hand out flyers on the streets. Later found most of them had been stuffed into a trash can.

I phoned Ron Rivera every few days in Acapulco. He always assured me that he would have his group of entertainers there to perform for me on New Year's Eve. Finally, I went to the Restaurant Workers Union. I hired a team of professional cooks and waiters and loaded up on funny hats, confetti and noisemakers with which to usher in the New Year.

The day before the big event everything seemed to be working. True to his word, Freddy Mohr came to tell me that Lauren Hutton and George Hamilton, two movie stars, were planning to attend my party. The tour sellers in Ixtapa happily informed me that they had already sold 62 tickets and were expecting to sell more. I fully expected that this party would establish my place as one of the prime tour destinations in the area, and thereby assure my economic future.

By ten o'clock on the morning of New Year's Eve day, all was going as planned. The drinks were already on ice and the chef was at work in the kitchen. In addition to appetizers, salads and desserts, he prepared two fresh hams, two roast turkeys with dressing, and a giant rock bass. My only concern was that Ron's entertainment from Acapulco had not yet shown up. I sent a note to Freddy and asked him to call Acapulco to make sure they were coming.

About four-thirty that afternoon, however, things began to change. About that time, a young boy of about ten or twelve came running into the kitchen. "*Señor Owen! Señor Owen!*"

he called breathlessly. "*Vienen el senor Presidente y sus amigos para comer.*" The President is coming here to eat. "Vienen el Presidente!" he repeated.

He pointed his finger towards the opposite end of the beach, but I was busy removing a large baked ham from the oven. He was an annoyance. *"Que? De que hablas*? Can't you see we're busy? *Largate de aqui!"* I commanded. "Get the hell out of here!"

But the kid stood his ground. He continued pointing his finger down the beach. "*Mira! Aqui vienen*!" he exclaimed, still pointing. Here they come!

I looked up from my ham and did a double take. Half way down the beach, a scattered group of perhaps eighty people was moving slowly up the beach toward me. I gazed for a moment in stunned silence. I could not believe my eyes. The kid was right.

As the group approached, I recognized Armando Federico, our local mayor. He was leading a well-dressed group over the soft sand. They walked well above the waterline, because they were all wearing shoes. Close behind Armando, a small family, followed awkwardly over the sand. Behind them came a large, motley crowd that included a contingent of men in uniform.

I was furious with Armando. I knew he was well aware of my New Year's Even Party, because I, myself, had invited him. How could he even think of bringing such a crowd at a time like this?

As they came closer, I saw the answer. Leading the small family group that followed Armando was none other than Luis Echevarria, the outgoing President of Mexico. It was the President's wife and three children that followed. Next came a mixed cadre of local politicians with their small children, followed by friends, bodyguards and anonymous cronies. A uniformed cadre of about ten policemen and twice as many soldiers brought up the rear. I gazed, mouth agape, too dumbstruck to speak.

Try to imagine my anguish, a young illegal immigrant suddenly having to host the leader of the country. Within Mexico, Presidents and most really wealthy people live like European royalty. Their mere appearance can strike ordinary people quite speechless with awe. In fact, that is what President Echevarria's appearance did to me.

As our mayor introduced us, I should have protested. Instead, I spread my arms open in welcome and barely managed to utter, "*Mi Senor y Senora Presidente, bienvennidos*! Welcome!" Smiling broadly, I grasped the President's hand in both of mind, as if he were the second coming. I bowed from the waist as I had learned to do in Europe and kissed the hand of the President's wife. They responded with practiced grace and charm, and then continued to follow Armando. Armando led them into the pavilion of the restaurant and seated them at a large table.

"The *Presidente* would like to eat lunch here," he said matter-of-factly. "And these are his guests," he added with sweep of his hand towards the crowd. He did not ask for a menu. Nor did he mention payment or credit. Like a dummy, I just stood there working my jaws, but nothing came out.

It was a moment of decision I would never forget. Whatever my reply, I knew that the rest of my life in Mexico was on the line. The hard reality was that I could not honestly offer them anything. It had already been sold to the tourists who were coming in from Ixtapa. It was no longer mine to sell. On the other hand, my answer could determine both the quality and the duration of my entire life in Mexico. It was a unique opportunity to curry favor with the leader of my community and the leader of the nation at the same time. Furthermore, if I did not take advantage of this opportunity, it might bring on negative repercussions later on.

There was outside chance that I could manage to do both. Even if the President's party consumed everything we had prepared for the New Year's Eve party, there might still be time, after they left, to replenish the food and drink before the bulk of the New Year's Party patrons arrived. Despite the ringing in my ears, I decided to go for it. I regretted that decision ever since.

In the first place, I really did not like the President or his party. He was accused of being the one who ordered the student massacre in 1968. In the second place, I really did not like what I was doing. No matter who they were, it was morally wrong of me to offer food and drink that had already been sold to others. I knew it. Yet I did it anyway. That I might feed the President, then zip into town, restock the food and bar, and prepare a new party before the paying guests arrived was an excursion in wishful thinking. Yet, stranger things had happened. And one of strangest happened that New Year's Eve.

First, the President insisted that I join him at his family table. Then he commanded, "Tell us all about your diving adventures with Captain Cousteau."

Still intimidated, I took his invitation as an offer that I could not refuse. But neither could I find any joy in it. Sitting with the President's family, I was totally out of control of my temporary staff. I was so distraught over what was happening that it became difficult for me to speak, much less make any sense in Spanish. So I said very little.

Instead, I surveyed the bacchanal that was unfolding all around us. With great gusto, the President's entourage proceeded to drink every drop of liquid in the bar and devour every morsel of food that we had prepared. For good measure, they polished off two gallons of vanilla ice cream for dessert, some of which wound up on the floor.

With a painted grin on my face, I stared at my neighbor's

dog as it finished off a fallen scoop of ice cream that was melting on the floor. Undetected the dog then pissed on the pant leg of some unsuspecting politician, and that brought the faint flicker of a smile to my face.

I no longer knew nor cared who sat beside me. I felt myself sinking into a catatonic state of hopeless resignation. Taking my gaze from the dog, I noticed in the distance a boat load of people heading in our direction. In as much as the sun was now sinking below the horizon, it could mean only one thing—they were the early arrivals for the Gala New Year's Eve Party!!

As the boat approached our little pier, a half dozen of the President's security guards rushed out to confront them with drawn pistols. Terrified and bewildered, the newcomers reluctantly raised their hands. I ran out to the pier to intervene on their behalf. A hasty explanation and a hundred peso bill convinced the chief of the security guards to lower their firearms and allow the newcomers to enter. They were obviously mystified to find a full-scale party already in progress. With no place to sit down, they began milling around and asking the waiters for drinks that no longer existed.

Having eaten his fill, President Echevarria now saw the empty boat at our pier as his means of escape. He sent a body guard to hold the boat for him and hurriedly advised his family that they were leaving. When the President stood, an expectant hush fell over the crowd, and they all stood up as well. The President acknowledged them with a smile and a wave of hands. Then, turning to me, he scooped me up in the traditional Mexican *abrazo* and slapped me heartily on the back.

"We will never forget your kindness", he said sincerely. "Happy New Year!"

His wife graciously thanked me for the delicious lunch

and told me what a pleasure it was to know me. I kissed her hand again. *Feliz Años Nuevos* were exchanged all around. Then he led his family towards the waiting boat. When his entourage began to follow, the President paused and turned to blow kisses to the crowd. He motioned for them to remain seated and continue with the party. Then he thanked them for coming, as if it had been his party all along.

Armando assisted the President's family onto the waiting boat and then swung aboard himself. As the boat eased away from the pier, I managed to catch Armando's eye. "Di-Ner-O!" I mouthed the words silently. I pantomimed by rubbing my thumbs and forefingers together. "*La Cuenta!*" I finally called out loud. "Who's going to pay the bill?" I shouted in English.

Armando acknowledged with his best political smile and a nod of his head. As if to calm my anxiety, he softly patted the air with his hands. "*Estaremos en contacto*." He assured me. He gave me another smile and a reassuring nod of his head. "We will be in contact."

"When?" With a questioning hunch of my shoulders, I opened my palms to the sky. "When?" I was pleading for a miracle. "*Cuando*?"

But he never answered. With another smile and a final wave, Armando sat down and the boat set off across the Bay.

No sooner had it left then the rest of the President's party swarmed onto the tiny pier, demanding transportation back to the village. Fortunately, they did not have to wait very long. As the President's boat departed, more boats full of early party goers were pulling alongside the pier. As each new load disembarked, those departing from the President's party scrambled on board. Others walked down the beach to the taxi boat landing or continued on over the rocky foot trail to the taxi stand at the end of La Ropa Beach. Those left behind were either too drunk to walk or part of the growing throng of bewildered party patrons.

I watched the incoming boats become the out-going boats with dreadful foreboding. Anticipating what lay ahead, I could see no way out of my dilemma. There was no exit. No hope. Had I the money, I would have gladly refunded their money and simply canceled the party. But I could not. More party patrons were already on their way. The entertainment was due to arrive at any moment. Freddy was sending some movie stars. I was too broke and too deeply involved to pull out.

I considered my few alternatives when I suddenly remembered that good old inspirational slogan, "When the going gets tough, the tough get going!" In a feeble attempt to reassure myself that I could survive the experience, I drove a fist into the open palm of my hand and set out to conquer my adversity.

The Tough Get Going

First, I checked my wallet. A quick count of my money revealed that I had just over $400 in pesos. Then, I hastily gathered my entire crew into the kitchen.

"Listen," I said. "You guys are probably thinking, just as I was a little while ago, 'Boy, are we fucked!' But that's negative thinking! That's a defeatist attitude!" I scolded. "I'm telling you, if we all work together we can still pull this nightmare out the fire and make it a success. With your help, I know we can do it! Are you with me?"

Even if not wildly enthusiastic, my crew gamely nodded their heads and mumbled acquiescence. I sprang into action. As the boatman stood by, I gave half the money to Chucho, the cook. "Go to town and buy whatever food you can find," I told him. Then, I gave the other half to the barman. "You, please go buy all the booze and ice until you run out of money."

As they set off for the village in our boat, I tried to placate the gathering crowd, by telling them what had just happened, but many were not amused. While some lolled glumly amidst the debris from the President's party, others paced nervously around the grounds, wondering where to go and what to do next. I searched desperately for the answers, but both pantry and the refrigerator were completely empty, and so was my head.

I suddenly remembered a gallon jug of bootleg mescal that I had hid in the pantry. Since it was bootleg mescal, you could never be sure of how people might react to it. I did not want to risk poisoning anyone in the President's family, so I hid out of sight. Now, I felt my economic survival might depend on it. The staff and I dug it out of the pantry and began handing out paper cups of mescal to our New Year's Eve patrons.

Now, mescal is a potent alcoholic beverage. It is made from the same *agave* cactus that is used to make tequila. It is made by a different process, however, so the results are quite different. tequila may produce some rowdy behavior, but it is usually socially acceptable behavior. On the other hand, mescal has been known to send people off on a hallucinogenic trip said to rival LSD.

The problem with bootleg mescal is that no two batches are ever the same. If a bad batch goes in, bad results come out. Such was the behavior that it produced in some loudmouth drunk from Texas named, appropriately enough, Tex.

He had paid fifty dollars to come to my party and now he grumbled loudly, "Ah want my money back! Don't you, too?"

As the waiters scurried to placate the crowd with mescal, I stood on a chair and tried to apologize and perhaps win their cooperation. I tried to tell them what had happened that afternoon and to tell them how sorry I was, but the drunken Texan continued to heckle me. He stood on a chair of his own and addressed the crowd. "Y'all call this a New Year's Eve Party? Looks more like a New Year's Eve rip-off to me! Don't it to you? No food. No booze. Ah say give us back our money! Don't you?"

I pleaded in vain for their understanding and compassion. "Please!" I begged. "More food and booze is on the way. Really! And the entertainment should be here at any moment. If we make it through tonight, you can come back anytime this year for a free drink whenever you like."

The arrival of Freddy Mohr with George Hamilton and Lauren Hutton brought some timely relief from the Texan tension. It also imbued the place with a badly needed touch of glamour. They were true celebrities, just as Freddy Mohr had promised. Tanned and dressed in white, both looked appropriately Hollywood, yet both were friendly and unpretentious. They smiled and waved to the crowd. A waiter hastily arranged a table and chairs for them in the middle of the pavilion, but they demurred. Freddy told the waiter they'd sit out near the water instead.

As they sat, the drunk from Texas intruded once again. "Come on, y'all. Ain't y'all gonna sing us a song or somthin'?" He was already staggering.

The agent and guide from Apple Vacations pulled me aside. He had brought most of the party patrons who had come from Ixtapa. He whispered hoarsely into my ear, "Owen, where the hell is all the all the food and entertainment you promised? You have got to give these people something more than this or they will all want their money back. They might even lynch us!"

Apple Vacations controls about ninety percent of all the package tour business in Ixtapa. If I could win their support, I knew that my economic future as a tour destination would be assured. Without it, I had no future.

I turned to Danny Fernandez, my number one man, and

pleaded. "Any sign of the musicians and dancers from Acapulco?"

Danny shook his head forlornly. "I doubt they are coming or they would already be here."

At that moment, the cook and the barman returned from the village in our boat. The cook disembarked with two boxes containing two large cans of baked ham, five packages of hot dogs and four boxes of soda crackers. "This is all I could find," he moaned plaintively. "No bread, no *tortillas*, nothing!" He hurried into the kitchen and began to unpack.

Meanwhile Francisco, the barman, disembarked with his cargo of booze. It comprised three cardboard boxes filled with two half-gallons of Ron Baccarat, two half-gallons of Presidente brandy, two boxes of Coca Cola in cans, and one bag of melting ice cubes. "Is this all the ice you could find?" I asked.

"This is all I could find," he repeated. As he came closer, he directed my attention to a telegram tucked in between the bottles with a nod of his head. "This telegram was in the mail box at the Captain of the Port's office," he said. "Look at the date."

I extracted the telegram from between the bottles of rum and tore it open. "Sorry must cancel New Year Eve Party in Zih due to unforeseen circumstances," the telegraph said. "Happy New Year!" Ron Rivera signed it, "The showman from Acapulco."

I turned it over and looked at the date, "Jesus Christ!" I exclaimed. "This wire has been sitting in the Port Captain's office for almost a week. That means NO entertainment!" I could feel the panic welling up inside me.

"The fire juggler just arrived from Zihuatanejo," Danny offered. "Should I put him on?"

"Yes, yes, put him on! Put on anybody you can find! Is there anyone on our staff who can sing or dance? Maybe play the spoons? Anything! We have to give them something or they might lynch us!"

"How about little Vidal next door? He can do all kinds of rope tricks. I saw him sing a song while twirling a lasso. And what about Lalo? He walks on stilts for Hollanda Ice Cream stores. And they live right here, down the beach!"

"Yes, yes. Send somebody after them," I ordered. "Tell them I'll pay him 500 pesos, but they have to come right now, you understand? Within a half-hour! Thirty minutes! Ready to do their thing!"

"And what about that kid next door, Sylviano Lara? He sings pretty well and plays the guitar."

"Yes, go get him! Quick! Explain what happened and then ask him to come play and sing for us. Tell him, I'll pay him 1,000 pesos if he comes back with you *ahora mismo*. Make sure he brings his guitar!"

As I turned back towards the kitchen, I thought of another possibility and called back to Danny. "Hey, Danny! Before you do that, phone up Rosy Galvez. You know Rosy Galvez? She is the local dance teacher. Rosy told me that she had a professional dance team that could appear for shows and events at a moment's notice. Phone her up right now. Her number is in my phone book. Ask her if she can come with her dancers and do a little impromptu show for us for 500 pesos for each dancer. Tell her a boat is waiting for them at the pier."

As Danny went to the phone to do my bidding, I flexed my muscles. I felt like an athlete who had just scored a winning goal. A flash of appreciation for Danny warmed my heart. Danny had worked with me off and on since he was sixteen years old. We knew each other and liked each other. Danny always came through in a pinch. If anybody could do it, he could. My appreciation for Danny turned into a warm flicker of hope.

As Danny set off on his mission, I handed out *Cuba Libres* in plastic cups. I frantically rummaged through my mind for what to do next. In the desperate hope that I could salvage the day from disaster, I was ready to try anything. I was determined to see it through.

When I saw Sylviano Lara approach with his guitar, I almost jumped for joy. I turned the bar over to one of the waiters and rushed off to set up the microphone for him. I found the mike alright, only I could not find the microphone stand. While waiters scurried about searching for the stand, I used the microphone once more to explain what had happened, but once more the loudmouth drunk from Texas interrupted. So I simply introduced Sylviano and his guitar. Scattered applause greeted the news that he would play and sing.

Lacking the mike stand, I hand-held the microphone to his mouth while he sang and played. It was Sylviano's first performance in public and the uncertain tremor in his voice revealed some first-time jitters. But he soon conquered his fear and began to belt it out. I could feel a change come over the crowd. The ambiance seemed to molt and mellow.

After hand-holding the microphone throughout five songs, my arm felt as heavy as lead. When at last someone came forward with the missing stand to relieve me, I felt my arm involuntarily rising as if it had a mind of its own.

Meanwhile, I noticed that Gustavo, the fire juggler, had arrived from Zihuatanejo and was already setting up his act out on the point. To avoid endangering the audience, he carried a can of gasoline and six torches out to the water's edge and set them in a line on the wet sand. The torches consisted of regular kitchen rolling pins. The cylinders of the rolling pins, but not the two handles, were covered with a soft absorbent cloth. He poured gasoline over the entire line of torches on the sand. Then, to my surprise, he took a drink from the gasoline can.

Setting the can aside, he came forward, withdrew a cigarette lighter from his pocket and spewed a huge tongue of flames into the air. He repeated this procedure several times until he had the attention of the entire audience. Then he let fly a tongue of flames at his torches on the sand. The line of torches exploded into cauldron of flames. When the flames subsided somewhat, he grabbed the end torch and threw it into the air. He added torches, catching and juggling, until all six of the flaming torches were twirling in the air. It was truly an amazing display of dexterity and concentration.

Later he combined his fire juggling with fire eating and fire spouting. Punctuating his act by frequent fuel stops, he was good enough to elicit the enthusiastic attention of the crowd.

On the other side of the fire juggler-eater's audience, Lalo was already getting into his in stilt-walking costume. While standing on his stilts and leaning on a branch of a mangle tree, Dolores, his wife, wrapped Lalo's legs and their wooden extensions in long pants bearing the red, white and green colors of the Mexican flag. She closed the openings with Velcro.

Meanwhile, little Vidal showed up in a store-bought cowboy outfit. Twirling a lasso over his head, he sang *La Cucaracha*, then circled casually around the crowd like a real pro.

By some magic stroke of luck, an old friend, Lorenzo, showed up with a guitar. Lorenzo was a handsome Italian American ski instructor whom I had not seen in years. He brought along a friend who carried a set of bongo drums on his back. It was as if God had heard my prayers.

After a quick greeting, I begged Lorenzo and his friend to help me. They joined Silviano and Vidal in singing a reprise of *La Cucaracha* while Vidal danced in and out of his twirling lasso. When they finished, the audience responded with applause, hoots and hollers.

The guests were beginning to warm up to the occasion. One couple started to dance. Others then joined them and I could have kissed them. In spite of everything that had happened, the crowd seemed willing to make the best of a bad situation and have as much fun as possible. It looked like we would make it through the night, after all. But then something strange happened.

Just after Lorenzo and his bongo partner decided to take a short break, Rosy Galvez showed up with her troupe of dancers. After a brief greeting, she set up an old wind-up phonograph. "*Voila*!" she exclaimed. "We're ready to dance."

"But Rosy," I said, "where are your dancers?"

She turned and motioned behind her. "*Voila*!" Behind Rosy, a bevy of eight little girls, all dressed in pink leotards, were wiggling into little homemade tutus made with elastic waistbands.

"But Rosy, be reasonable! Are these little girls the professional dance group you told me about?"

"That's right," she said, bristling. "*Asia es!* These are my dancers and they are really very good."

"But Rosy, this is a drunken New Year's Eve Party. If their parents find out, we could be arrested. I thought you were going to bring a troupe of professional dancers," I pantomimed a mature woman's breasts, "not a troop of Girl Scout Brownies!"

Rosy went ballistic. "You can't send these dancers away without letting them do their act. They are all so excited. You just can't disappoint them like that." She wiped a glistening tear from her eye, then continued. "I'll tell you what," she said, "We will charge you only half price. Instead of paying 4,000 pesos, you only pay two. How do you like that?"

"That is very generous of you, Rosy, but I really don't

think this is the kind of entertainment that they had in mind."

"No, it's much better," Rosy proclaimed. I shook my head and shrugged my shoulders. "Then it's all settled."

Turning away from me, she took matters into her own hands. First, she cleared the chairs from the area in front of the bar. She shooed the people off the floor like chickens. "Shoo! Shoo!" she commanded. "Please, give us some space to perform!" She called to her girls, "All right my darling dancers, places please! Please take your places!"

As the children moved into the clearing, Rosy went to the portable wind-up Victrola she had placed on the bar and frantically wound the crank. Then she released the break on an old 78-rpm record that had seen better days. As the turntable picked up speed, it emitted a rasping prelude of scratches and clicks before the music of Swan Lake came through. Intertwining their little arms, the four stepped out into an infantile version of the famous *pax des quatre* in Swan Lake.

I could not believe my eyes. Apparently neither could the drunken Texan. He staggered up to the microphone and hollered, "Is this what y'all paid fifty bucks to do on New Year's Eve?" he demanded. "Ah don't know 'bout y'all, but Ah want my money back! How 'bout you? If y'all want your money back, join in with me." And he began to clap his hands and chant, "We want our money back! We want our money back!"

Thankfully, only a few others joined him. Then my old friend, Lorenzo, walked up and grabbed the microphone from his hand. When the Texan resisted, Lorenzo pushed him away. The drunken Texan stumbled, recovered and then lunged at Lorenzo to take a swing at him. Quick and nimble, Lorenzo simply stepped aside and brought his knee up to the Texan's groin. With that, the Texan's wife started pounding on Lorenzo with both fists, as Rosy herded her child-dancers out of harm's way.

When friends rushed in to restrain the Texan's wife from beating on Lorenzo, the fight was essentially over. And, thank heaven, so was my Gala New Year's Eve Party. The party-goers left as fast as the two boats could shuttle them back to Zihuatanejo.

As for me, no one could find me. When I heard the drunken Texan lead a chorus of angry customers singing, "We want our money back," I panicked. In my state of utter destitution, the mere thought of having to reimburse everybody, drove me to dive under a kitchen table. I rearranged the overhanging tablecloth so that it effectively hid me from view. There I cowered in fear of discovery. I don't know how long.

I heard the sweet voice of my friend, Natalia Krebbs, softly call my name. "Owen, are you there?"

Timidly, I peeked out from under the tablecloth. "Natalia, is that you?" I answered in a hoarse whisper.

"Owen! What on earth are you doing down there? Did you lose something?"

"I'm hiding, Natalia. They want their money back and I don't have a penny. I am worse than broke. I'm afraid they might lynch me!"

"Well, you can come out now. The Texan has gone. Most of the others have also gone."

Natalia offered me her hand and helped pull me up from under the table. She brushed some cobwebs from my back, and I gave her my thanks. Then I saw Lorenzo. "Hey Lorenzo! Thanks for coming to my rescue, pal. God sent you just when I needed you!"

"Glad I could help," he answered. "I just talked to your tour agent from Apple Vacations," he added. "Boy is he pissed! He wanted to see you, but I told him that you would not be available before Tuesday morning. That will give you a few days to think of something."

"Think of what?" I moaned. "What's to think about?"

"You'll think of something," he assured me.

At the meeting on Tuesday, Apple Vacations announced that they were able to cancel all the tickets that had been charged to the hotel rooms. However, I would still have to pay the commissions for the lobby salesmen. Then they offered me a deal—if I would pay the flat sum of $1,000 they would cover all other repercussions. In my state, that sounded more reasonable than I expected.

As I returned home to Las Gatas Beach, I remembered what my Mother had warned during her one and only visit. "Son," she said, "Some day you're going to pay for all this. And pay and pay and pay!" As always, Mother was right.

Mexico on Stage

Mexico is a uniquely gifted country. With over four thousand-three hundred miles of tropical coastline, Mexico shares the richest fishing grounds of both the Atlantic and the Pacific Oceans. Its verdant hills and mountains are rich in lumber and mineral deposits. Its fields and valleys yield two to four harvests every year. Its benign climate ranges from snow-covered covered peaks to tropical rain forests. Beneath its continental shelf lies one of the world's richest deposits of petroleum.

To this trove of natural treasures, add its richest treasure of all — its population of sweet, loving, hard-working people. Among its more than sixty-two ethnic groups and dialects reside some of the world's most talented and creative people.

Yet despite all its natural gifts, Mexico seems to be unable to pull itself up by its bootstraps to offer the same standards and amenities as first-world countries. In fact, Mexico seems mired down in its turbulent past to the extent that it hampers its journey into the future.

When Hernan Cortez defeated Moctezuma and the entire Aztec Empire, he needed little help. This humiliating defeat left an indelible mark on the national psyche. Mexico's entire history is infused with intrigue, suspicion, deception, broken promises, betrayals, mysticism, fantasy, and fatalism. From its beginning, Mexico's history has unfolded like one of its many popular soap operas. The disparity between the haves and have-nots, the rich and the poor, the Mestizos and the Indians has been the classic theme throughout its history.

With the notable exceptions of Benito Juarez and Lazaro Cardenas, few of Mexico's past presidents were more concerned with the well-being of their country than with their own personal well-being. By the middle of the nineteenth century, Mexico's self-serving politicians had practically sold out the entire country to foreign interests. It was not until 1867 that President Benito Juarez, with the explicit backing of Abraham Lincoln, managed to retrieve Mexico from the greedy hands of foreign capitalists. He did so by defeating the Emperor Maximilliano, a French puppet, and standing him before a firing squad.

After the death of Benito Juarez, Mexican politicians resumed the wholesale sell-out of their country. In 1928 Lazaro Cardenas, at the age of only thirty nine, became the youngest president in the history of Mexico. A democratic populist of inflexible integrity, Lazaro Cardenas was an exception among Mexican politicians in that he was more interested in promoting true social progress and justice than he was in promoting his personal fortune. As Governor of the state of Michoacan, Cardenas worked hard to unite farmers, workers, students, and Indians in demanding needed social and political reforms. As President, he retrieved Mexico's burgeoning petroleum industry expropriating the assets of seventeen foreign oil companies in 1938 and paying them over $140 million in compensation.

Despite the noble efforts of a few honest men like Benito Juarez and Lazaro Cardenas, true social justice is still a long way off for most Mexicans, especially for the indigenous population. Some economists claim that ninety percent of Mexico's wealth belonged to only ten percent of Mexico's people.

When I first arrived in Mexico, the recent discovery of rich new oil deposits under the Campeche Banks produced an unprecedented windfall of wealth. From being one of the world's poorest and most backward nations in the world, Mexico quickly became one of its richest. Oil lubricated the wheels of Mexico's industry. Businesses thrived and the economy boomed. In a single decade, a substantial middle class evolved. The social fabric of the entire nation took a giant leap forward. Opportunity seemed within reach of most of the population, and Mexico was beginning to look like the first-world country that it aspired to be.

True to Mexico's melodramatic history, however, the euphoria did not last. Inept leadership, a series of sordid political scandals and three disastrous devaluations of the Mexican peso plunged the country into demoralizing debts and virtual bankruptcy.

Mexico's brief incursion onto the world stage seemed to have gone to the heads of its leaders. Still drunk on oil, President Luis Echevarria announced that Mexico no longer needed the help or approval of first world countries. "Mexico can now go it alone," he declared.

Mexico's withdrawal from the political realities of the world stage was now complete. Their arrogance alienated almost all those countries that might otherwise have helped them. International trade and social progress ground to a halt. The rising middle class dissolved in a soup of disillusionment. Graft and corruption permeated almost every level of Mexican government and society. Cronyism and legal impunity made the Mexican political structure a mockery, a kind of "good old boys club" who virtually rode to riches on the backs of cheap indigenous labor. Instead of buying a washing machine, it was much cheaper to simply hire an Indian maid. It was the kind of atmosphere that made the excesses of General Arturo Duraso and Raul Salinas de Gotori almost inevitable.

Blacky Duraso

Atop the highest hill between La Madera Beach and La Ropa Beach, overlooking the entire sweep of Zihuatanejo Bay, sat a pillared replica of a the famous Parthenon of Rome. It contained a high ceiling atrium that opened onto two enormous wings of marble pillars that rise from marble floors, all imported from Italy. With ten bedrooms, many with Romanesque paintings and some with mirrored ceilings, twelve baths with golden swan-like faucet handles, an Olympic-sized swimming pool with wet bar, a ten-car garage, an air-conditioned wine cellar, and a private underground casino and discothèque, Caesar himself might have envied it. But the "Parthenon" was not intended as a tribute to the cultural splendors of Rome. It was intended solely as a monument to General Duraso's ostentatious bad taste.

When President Jorge Lopez Portillo came into power, he appointed Arturo Duraso to be his supreme Commander–in-Chief of all the Police throughout Mexico. But it was not because of his experience or expertise, or his qualifications as a policeman. He had never been a policeman. It was because they had gone to school together. That was enough to win him the enviable position of power and influence that was second only to the President himself.

When General Duraso came into power, organized crime was running rampant throughout the nation. The General knew that crime confronted him with an enormous challenge. He was equally aware that Mexico's corrupt law enforcement system could never stop it. After all, many of Mexico's most notorious criminals were on the police payroll.

Armed with his exalted rank and station in life, and the almost total impunity to the law that came along with it, Duraso saw his job as a unique opportunity for personal advancement. Therefore, instead fighting crime and injustice, he opted to join it. That way, he could cut himself in on crime's enormous profits.

To be the Chief of Police in Mexico was a very responsible and powerful position. Yet, Mexico's law enforcement system was notorious for its low wages. Many police got no paycheck at all. They kicked it back to their Chief in return for the privilege of harvesting bribes on the streets.

The official salary of General Duraso was the equivalent of less than $500 per month. However, General Duraso saw the reality differently. He received a small cut from every illicit business transaction in the country.

While his wife flirted openly with a platoon of handsome young men from the local community, his young nephew directed drug traffic from his lair on the as-yet undeveloped Island of Ixtapa. Meanwhile, hundreds of policemen were now moon-lighting as construction workers in Zihuatanejo, and the General himself shuttled back and fourth from in the police helicopter to supervise them. It was said that he brought their salaries in a trunk filled with cash. It was also noted that he had built another retreat in Cuernavaca, a suburb of Mexico City, and yet a third one in Cancun, a new resort city on the east coast.

David Frost, a British television host, was so impressed

with his ostentatious bad taste that he invited the General to appear on his television program. After admiring the scope of the General's accomplishments, Mr. Frost asked the General an embarrassing question. "General, we were amazed to discover that your official salary is the equivalent of less than $500 per month," he said. "Please tell us, how did you manage to build those three palatial mansions on your meager salary?"

The General may have been shameless and unethical, but he was never at a loss for words. "Well, my wife and I did most of the work ourselves on weekends," he replied blatantly.

Shortly after the administration of President Jose Lopez Portillo ended, the country suffered a disastrous monetary devaluation. Lopez Portillo retired to a castle in Spain and General Duraso's impunity to the law abruptly ended. He soon became the subject of a book that exposed his nefarious dealings. The book was titled The Black of Blacky Duraso. As a result, he was sentenced to eleven years in prison, but was released in 1986 after serving just seven years. He lived in isolated luxury and, a few years later, he died in Los Angeles. Blacky Duraso's "Parthenon" is now up for sale by the State. For more information, please contact FIBAZI, El Fidecomiso de la Bahia de Zihuatanejo, telephone 011 52 75555 4 2472.

Mexico's next three presidential administrations under the PRI ruling party were equally scandalous. Shortly after each term ended, the country suffered another disastrous devaluation of the Mexican peso.

Under the administration of President Salinas de Gottori, political corruption got out of hand. When the wife of Raul Salinas, the president's younger brother, attempted to cash a personal check for $83 million, Swiss Bankers became suspicious. Investigative reporters soon uncovered the full extent of the corruption. As a result, Mexico's economy went into another tailspin. The unpredictable peso destroyed world confidence in Mexico's economy, and foreign investment ground to a halt. Once again, the resurgent middle class all but vanished, and Mexico polarized into a two-class country of the extremes — the extremely rich and the extremely poor.

With the election of President Vicente Fox, the leader of the National Action Party (PAN) in the year 2000, Mexico elected the first president ever to oppose PRI. However, the PRI continued to control both houses of the Mexican Legislature. Therefore, Vicente Fox's administration was largely ineffective in passing new legislation. Nevertheless, it set a democratic precedent that has continued to moderate the seventy-six-year monopoly of the PRI.

In January of 1994 Mexico became a member of the North American Free Trade Association (NAFTA), together with the United States and Canada. This ushered Mexico onto the first-world stage at last. As a first-world trading partner in the electronic age, Mexico's political scandals now became instant news around the world. Shady practices that were once routine were now no longer tolerated. The economic repercussions were too destructive to too many people. Mexico's political elite now had to play by a different set of rules or risk being ostracized from the community.

Mexico's debut on the world stage produced some profound changes in the national psyche. Electoral reforms and governmental policy changes made the Mexican government much more transparent and much more accountable to the people Under the latest laws of the land, Mexican land was now available for development and exploitation by foreigners. Fraudulent land deals, which were once common, were now almost a thing of the past. Title guarantees were now common, and investors could be confident on a fair return from their money.

Meanwhile, Mexico's human resources also changed with the times. Not all its cops were crooks and not all its crooks were cops. Not all politicians were liars and not all liars were politicians. In this day of instant communication, there were no longer any secrets. There was a vast difference between today's post-NAFTA Mexico and the pre-NAFTA Mexico that I came to know in the 1960s. What happened to me back then could not happen in present-day Mexico. Having said that, I beg your leave to return to my own story in old Zihuatanejo.

Depression

The New Year's Eve Party blew both my mind and my bankbook. After having to close the Nature Study Center, and after my brush off by the Institute of Sports, the New Year's Eve fiasco was the coup de grâce. It took all the nerve I could muster to ask Marshall for more money to pay off my New Year's Eve debts. Worse yet, it made me resolve to never attempt another project within Guererro. Working in Guererro was just too frustrating, too unpredictable, too full of surprises to be fun. It seemed that no one said what they meant or meant what they said. It was so difficult know what to believe and what not to believe, that I found it safer to believe nobody and do nothing. I became a catatonic cynic, too frightened to move.

Despite my perverted love for the place, the dark truth was that I saw no way I could continue to survive in Zihuatanejo. Apparently, I just did not have what it took. I had given up on myself as well as the place. However fate works in strange ways. I had already sent my resume to several companies, looking for work and already planning my return to New York City. Then fate delivered Colonel Alvaro Sanchez Mirus to my door.

"*Señor Owen! Señor Owen!* I have a letter for you from INDE. That is the *Instituto Nacional de Deportes* in Mexico City." Delighted that my efforts had at last garnered some kind of response, I invited the gentleman inside for coffee.

At six feet four inches tall, Colonel Alvaro Sanchez Mirus was an imposing figure of heroic proportions with a booming voice to match. Intense brown eyes peered out from under heavy dark eyebrows framing a strong, ruddy face. He was the epitome of a military officer in both bearing and presentation — erect, confident and slightly pedantic. He wore a reluctant smile and laughed in a falsetto staccato that sounded like a toy machine gun. The Colonel informed me that he was a fighter jet pilot in the Mexican Air Force, but was now on loan to the Department of National Parks, which was part of INDE.

He handed me a sealed envelope, which I opened with my breakfast knife. It contained a letter, written on INDE stationary, introducing me to Colonel Alvaro Sanchez Mirus as an official representative of the National Parks Department. It was signed by Guillermo Lopez Portillo, whose brother Jorge had recently been elected President of Mexico. I had no reason to doubt its veracity.

Sanchez Mirus informed me that he had come to talk about the proposals I had submitted to INDE. Of course, I was ecstatically happy. I escorted him around the property and elaborated on my ecological curriculum. I showed him the rooms and the various water sports that we could offer.

Later, over a beer on my veranda, I was surprised to learn that he was the very same person who had leased the Hotel El Capricho Del Rey from Marshall Allen and Sarita Veerboonen, Arnoldo's widow. Personally, I was very disappointed. As I mentioned previously, the idea that Sanchez Mirus could ever fill Freddy's shoes was ridiculous. Nevertheless, he obviously had some good contacts within the PRI government. In order to advance my projects, I needed such contacts, so I did my best to make him feel welcomed.

Sanchez Mirus listened politely but seemed oddly distracted. He seemed much more interested in the going price of the surrounding real estate, the local tax rates and the possibility of a road connecting to the beach, than he was in my Nature Study Center.

"Did you see my presentation for the Tarascan Indian Village that I left with *Liensiado* Moldonado at the INDE?" I asked him.

"No. I have not yet seen it," he answered, "but I will certainly do so as soon as possible."

"Then you have no idea of what I've been talking about, do you?" I asked incredulously.

"Well no," he confessed. "But I really don't work directly for INDE. I am a pilot in the Mexican Air Force. I am only on loan to INDE as a consultant. Guillermo Lopez Portillo, the Director of INDE is a friend of mine. When he heard I was living in Zihuatanejo, he asked me to investigate how you and INDE might work together."

When he said, "work together" my heart leapt with joy! Those words seemed to promise the fulfillment of my dream for the Nature Study Center, and I was ecstatic.

"How can I help?" I asked him. "This is very exciting!"

"You can help by telling me how I can help you," he answered.

By now, Sanchez Mirus was a prince charming on a prancing white charger. "God must have sent you!" I exclaimed. I shook his hand heartily and almost kissed it. I invited him to sit and poured more coffee for him. "How can you help me?" I asked rhetorically. I drew a deep breath and let loose. "You can help me by convincing your friends at INDE to collaborate with me transforming Las Gatas Beach into a Tarascan Indian Village and Nature Study Center," I declared. "My idea is to transform Las Gatas Beach into an international tourist attraction, like the Polynesian Cultural Center in Hawaii. But it has to be done soon, while the beach is still relatively empty and pristine."

"What's the hurry?" he asked.

"If we wait much longer, the beach will fill up with cheap restaurants and souvenir shops," I predicted. "In my opinion, it deserves better. Las Gatas Beach could become a rich source of income for the entire community."

"And what do you want out of it, for yourself?"

"Legitimacy!" I answered. "It's my idea, and it's a good idea, so the least they should do is make me one of the directors, if not *the* Director, then legalize my immigration status and pay me a living wage. There, I said it all! Do you think you can help?"

Sanchez Mirus acknowledged by gravely nodding his head. He seemed impressed by my sincerity. "I will help you all I can," he promised, "but first you must help me help you."

"Just tell me what can I do."

"As you probably know, you can't get anything done here at the local level. They'll have you going around in circles. I need to go to Mexico City and talk directly to my friends in the Parks Department. Therefore, there will be travel and living expenses."

"I will be happy to pay your expenses," I assured him. "I just want some action! How much do you think you will need?"

"Well, let's see, the air fare and the hotel; about $3,000 should do it."

"Wow! $3,000? How long are you planning on staying?"

"Well, it can't be done overnight," he protested.

"I agree," I said. "But $3,000 seems like a lot."

"Well, if you would rather not, we don't have to. However, I can't promise results."

"No, no! I mean yes, yes, OK. I'll go along with that."

"If I don't get started recruiting students soon, there won't be any summer tuitions, so we can't waste time."

"What do you have to do?"

"I'll have to fly to New York City. New Yorkers are big on summer camps, but most parents think that Mexico is full of banditos and kidnappers, so I have to convince the parents in person."

"They also think that Taco Bell is the Mexican telephone company, no?"

I laughed. "I wouldn't be surprised."

"While you are recruiting students in New York, I will be working things out with INDE in Mexico City," he promised.

"When can you start?"

"When can you give me the expense money?"

I went to get my checkbook out of its drawer. "All right, but remember, I don't have that kind of money to fritter away on nothing. I want results."

"Think of it as a loan, Owen. This is a loan, not a gift. You can deduct it from my share of the summer tuitions."

"OK." I tore the check from the book and handed it to him. "Try to get INDE's approval before the end of June. *Camp de Mar* runs from July 15th through August, but I will arrive a few days early to help prepare everything."

"Who will look after your place while you are gone?" Alvaro inquired.

"Chucho, the cook. He will look after it for me."

"Are you sure you can trust him?" he asked with concern.

"I can't trust anybody around here," I complained. "But I no longer let it bother me. I learned that at EST. They taught me to always swim with the current."

"Well, you can trust me," Alvaro confided. "I will look after it for you."

"Didn't we just decide that you would be in Mexico City dealing with INDE?" I asked.

"Yes, but not all the time."

"Well, I do trust Chucho. He has been with me a long time. He is a great guy and an excellent cook. However, he knows nothing about the maintenance of buildings or boats. It would be a nice if you could look in on him from time to time."

"I'll be happy to do what I can," Alvaro assured me. "All I need is your signed power of attorney and your phone in New York."

"I'll pick up the power of attorney forms and bring them to you tomorrow," I promised.

The following day, I delivered the power of attorney to Sanchez Mirus at the Hotel El Capricho del Rey, and I was puzzled by what I found. The last time I had been inside, the place was all shiny and new. The garden architecture of the six hillside bungalows blended into the verdant hillside like part of the shrubbery. Luxurious sheets and spreads covered all the beds, fluffy new towels awaited on the racks, the copper sheathed lighting of sculptor Jordan Steko bathed the tasteful furnishings in mellow light.

By contrast, it now looked like a typical bachelor's apartment. Alvaro's clothing lay strewn all over the luxurious furniture and floors. The sink was full of dirty dishes and the trash baskets were overflowing. The luxurious sheets, spreads and towels were missing. So was some of the teak furniture. I should have known then that something was wrong, but I suppose that I was so anxious to proceed that I let it pass without comment.

"Have a look inside my clothes closet," Alvaro invited. When I obeyed, I could not believe my eyes. The closet was filled with military firearms. It included two World War II .30-caliber carbines, two AK47 assault rifles, a double-barreled shotgun, a .30-caliber hunting rifle with telescopic sights, two 45-caliber automatic pistols, and an old-fashioned Thompson submachine gun with a round cartridge container, like the one that made famous by Dick Tracy, the comic-book detective.

"Wow!" I exclaimed "Is this standard issue for all jet pilots in Mexico?"

He fired off a staccato burst of machine-gun laughter. "No, no, that's my private collection," he boasted.

"Do you ever use them?"

"Yes, of course. They all work."

"Who did they work on? Anybody I know? Or knew?"

He responded with another burst of staccato laughter. "Nobody so far," he said," but you never know!"

A heavy tripod with a large telescope stood in the seaward corner of the open room. Only instead of looking up at the sky, the telescope was aimed towards my house on Las Gatas Beach.

"May I have a peek through your telescope?" I inquired.

"No, no, but please don't move it. I have it all focused in for you, so you can see what I see."

Peering into the eyepiece, I was shocked to find the familiar patterns of the pillow on my bed. I might have surmised right then that this guy was into a kind of psychological game. However, I preferred to take it as a simple joke between us two *machos.* I simply chuckled. "I'll have to remember to pull my window shades," I said.

He responded with another burst of machine-gun laughter. Two days later, I departed for New York City to recruit my summer school students.

Camp de Mar IV

Thanks to Becky's airline passes and my rent-controlled apartment, recruiting students in New York City proved to be much easier and cheaper than it had been in Mexico City. It also proved to be more fun. Greenwich Village was then at its ebullient, springtime best. A festive air seemed to permeate the streets of Manhattan. The spring sunshine brought people out in droves, and the usual pedestrian traffic seemed strangely invigorated.

By placing ads in *The New York Times* and *The Village Voice*, I managed to interest a number of parents in my summer *Camp de Mar* program. Again, most were reluctant to consign their beloved teenage kids to me in Mexico without a personal meeting and my assurance that their kids would return. As before, photos and stories of me with Captain Cousteau were usually enough to convince them. Meanwhile, my ads in Mexico City had attracted a half dozen more campers from Mexico City.

I hired my two favorite pros, Robert Bisome and his wife, to come help me with *Camp de Mar*, as they had before. When I had successfully signed up twenty-five campers, I stopped recruiting. Legally, I could carry only ten students and one instructor in each boat. So, twenty-five students plus crew was the maximum I could carry in three boats.

Throughout my stay in New York City, I saw Becky only a few times. She was extremely busy, trying to do two jobs at the same time, flight attendant and puppeteer. Not to mention she was still volunteering at the local Buddhist Center. Becky dearly loved her job at the Children's Puppet Theatre, but her heavy work schedule began to affect her health. It soon became clear that two jobs were one too many. When the theater offered Becky a permanent position, she opted to quit her job with the airlines in spite of a big drop in salary.

I applauded her decision to follow her passion. I believed then, as I do now, that is the most direct route to happiness and self-fulfillment. As I saw it, if you followed your dreams, it would always lead you to self-fulfillment, even if not to success. In that immeasurable realm of the spirit, passions rarely justified all the time, energy and money one put into them. However, they created a divine synergy that always returns more than the sum of its parts. To me, the pursuit of your dreams was the fulfillment of your purpose and the essence of our being. It was living life creatively.

However, Becky's decision did not work to my favor. Her resignation from Eastern Airlines clipped the wings of my flights-of-fancy by ending my access to free airline passes. No longer could I fly any place any time I chose. Consequently, from that day to this, my meager income has kept me a virtual prisoner in paradise.

Becky and I had been separated for much longer than we had intended. However it was done with the same spirit of mutual love and respect that prevailed throughout our entire relationship. Each of us became intensely involved with what we were doing, she in New York City and I three thousand miles away in Zihuatanejo. Without our usual access to free travel, we both became products of our local environments, and our different environments led us in different directions, to different circumstances and to different friends. In time, we each found a different lover, but our love and respect for each other never ended. It simply changed its context.

With twenty-five students lined up for my summer *Camp de Mar*, my prospects for the summer seemed brighter than ever. I returned to Zihuatanejo a week before the camp was to begin in order to prepare for their impending arrival. I took a taxi boat from the pier to Las Gatas Beach, and as I was lugging my baggage up the beach, I noticed that some kind of strange activity was going on around my restaurant. As I came closer, I could see that the kitchen of my restaurant was boarded up, and the place was littered with construction debris. Some workers were mixing cement on the sand.

Mystified, I called out for Chucho, whom I had left in charge. "Chucho? Chucho!" But there was no answer.

"Chucho is no longer with us," came a voice from behind me. It was Alvaro Sanchez Mirus. He had emerged from my house with two armed men behind him.

"Alvaro!" I exclaimed. I shook his hand. "What the hell is going on around here? Where is Chucho?"

"I had to let Chucho go," he explained. "I found out that he was stealing from you."

"What do you mean?" I demanded. "There was nothing to steal! He was probably just doing his job."

"He was robbing you in many ways, Owen. I had to let him go."

I heard that high-pitched ringing in my ears that often accompanies my anger. "How dare you? He is my man. I left him in charge."

"I assure you, we are better off without him."

"No, we are not!" I exploded. "Chucho is my man. He was the one I left in charge, not you! Where is he? I want to see him."

"He and his family have moved to Patzcuoro. I don't have his address, but I know that they are there."

"You had no right to fire Chucho, no right at all. And what is all this construction work going on? Don't you know that *Camp de Mar* starts in a few days? I have twenty-five students arriving in a few days, and look at it! What the hell is going on here?"

"Oh that's our new swimming pool. Our new partners — *your* new partners — decided that we needed a swimming pool. I'm sorry that it's a little late. It should be finished in a couple of weeks."

"Wait a minute! New partner? New swimming pool? What the hell are you talking about?" I demanded.

"Yes, our new partners want to put in a swimming pool. All you have to do is pay your share of the expenses."

"Expenses? What expenses?"

"$90,000," he answered. "That's the cost of the improvements, and your share comes to $30,000."

The ringing in my ears rose to a pitch. "Have you lost your mind? I'm not paying anything to anybody. I've been traveling all day, so I'm tired and I want to go home."

I grabbed my bag and pushed past him. Alvaro signaled to his two armed henchmen with a toss of his head. The two men drew their pistols and blocked the path to my house. I recognized the pistols from having seen them in Alvaro's gun collection. I stopped short and turned back to Alvaro. "Is this, some kind of joke?"

"It's no joke, Owen. You are not going to enter this property until you agree to pay your share."

"What do you mean?" I protested. "This is my home! I built it myself and I've lived here for sixteen years. Are you telling me I can't go into my own home?"

He shook his head. "Not until you agree to pay your share of the bill."

"What right do you have to tell me what to do?"

He reached inside his shirt and extracted a folded letter. "This is what right I have, right here." He fluttered the letter in front of my eyes. From the letter, I assumed that he had planned for this confrontation before hand. "Don't you remember the agreement you signed? You signed it before leaving for New York."

He offered me the paper, and I took it. By now my hands were trembling so violently that I could not read the text. I had to pause, take a deep breath and try again. In one sentence, the letter ceded all rights to the Nature Study Center and Las Gatas Beach Club properties to Alvaro Sanchez Mirus. "By means of this document, I, Owen M. Lee, hereby cede all my rights to the properties known as the Nature Study Center or Las Gatas Beach Club located on Las Gatas Beach, Zihuatanejo, Guererro to Alvaro Sanchez Mirus." The letter was signed "Owen M. Lee," an uncanny likeness, but it was not my signature.

The ringing in my ears rose to a crescendo. "I never signed this document! I never saw this letter in my life!"

"Is that not your signature?" he demanded.

Like an obedient chump, I took the letter back and examined it closely. The signature looked like mine, all right, but it could not be. "I may be dumb, but I am not crazy. That can't be my signature, because I have never seen this letter in my life." I protested.

"Can you prove that in a court of law?" Alvaro asked gravely. "Come. Let's sit down and talk." He turned to lead me to a table under the *palapa* roof of my restaurant.

I very nearly followed, but then stopped short. I could hardly believe what was happening, but I could no longer deny it. "Let me get this straight. You are making blatant move on my property on the basis of this ridiculous letter. Is that right?" I asked rhetorically. "As far as I'm concerned, I'm finished talking. I'm tired and…" I picked up my bag and headed back down the beach toward the taxi boat landing. "If you want to contact me, you can talk to my lawyer. He will be in touch with you shortly."

Alvaro turned to his armed henchmen, "See that he goes and does not come back," Alvaro said in Spanish. The two men slipped their pistols back into their holsters and escorted me off the property.

Once back on the village pier, I took a taxi to see Arthur

Agin. He was an old friend from Greenwich Village and a long-time snowbird living in Zihuatanejo between Christmas and Easter. He lived in a modest *palapa*-roof cabana hidden always in a cove near the *Playa Almacen*, (where La Calla Restaurant now stands).

Arthur was kind enough to let me to live in his guest room until I could make my next move. It was comforting to have Arthur's advice and companionship. I really needed both. Besides, I really loved the cove's exotic setting.

Thanks to its dramatic rock formations and the hypnotic ebb and flow of its waves, *La Calla* was one of the most enchanting little coves in the Bay. It offered the same kind of natural beauty as Las Gatas Beach, but none of its headaches. Although Arthur Agin was a typical Greenwich Village hippy, he was also a successful, hard-headed businessman. He regarded money with a respect that bordered on reverence, whereas I simply took money for granted until it was gone. Of course such reckless behavior often led to moments of crisis, such as the present.

With students due to arrive within ten days for my *Camp de Mar*, I now had no place to put them and no alternatives. Not to mention that when Sanchez Mirus brought firearms into the picture, he changed the fundamental context of our relationship. From one of mutual trust and cooperation, our relatoinship had suddenly become one of fear and open conflict.

This kind of thing was all new to me. I had never been threatened with a gun in my life. Until I enlisted in the Army at eighteen, I had never seen a gun that was not locked in a case or on the hip of a policeman. I had spent two years in the military and never fired a shot. The appearance of a real firearm scared the hell out of me. I was not willing to expose the lives of my students to the possibility of violence. The dangers of diving and surfing are predictable, but the dangers of confronting a mad man with a loaded gun is downright scary.

When I told Artie about it, I asked," What would you do?"

"If I were you, I'd cancel," he said flatly.

"Yes, I'd like to cancel, but gee, I can't. I've already spent a lot of the money. And some of the parents are off to Europe."

"If you don't cancel, he will find some way to use those kids against you. He could even take them hostage!"

"Some of the parents are counting on me to take care of their kids during their vacation. They already have their tickets and reservations."

"Then find some other place to take them. Take them to Acapulco or Cozumel. But I would not bring them here."

"Gee, do I really have to disappoint all those people because of Sanchez Mirus?"

"Go get yourself a good lawyer," Artie urged. "This is a legal matter and you need a good lawyer. But not one from here. Get one from Mexico City." He snapped his fingers. "In fact there is one already here! His name is Federico Samaniego. He is Hector Aguillar's nephew and he's staying at Hector's house right now. Go see him. Get him to help you."

"You're right. I'll go see him tomorrow. Meantime, what should I do about the kids? I can't disappoint them."

"Then better that you take them someplace else, far enough away to be safe from Sanchez Mirus." It was good advice, which I followed to the letter.

The next morning, around eleven, I took a taxi boat to Las Gatas Beach and then walked the rocky trail to Hector's house at the end of La Ropa Beach. When I arrived, Hector and Lois, his American wife, were seated at a cocktail table on a wide veranda in front of their home. They were sipping their first tequilas of the day and invited me to join them. I declined, asking to see his nephew instead.

Federico proved to be quite pleasant and refined. When I told him my story, Federico also advised me cancel. He suggested I take all those students that I could not cancel to some other destination, just as Artie had advised.

He readily agreed to handle my case and we all drank a tequila to our success. I agreed to pay him a retainer of $1,000, and he promised to talk to Sanchez Mirus before returning to Mexico City. Then I returned to Artie's house to plan my next move.

Despite my anxiety over the hostile takeover of my property, I determined that it was now a legal matter that demanded a legal solution. There was nothing I could gain by staying in Zihuatanejo and bickering with Sanchez Mirus. Therefore, I decided to go ahead with the summer camp, but to reduce its size and move the location to Cozumel, an island off the coast of Yucatan.

For reasons of mobility and economics, I had to reduce the number of campers to one that I could handle alone. First I canceled all those who had not yet paid the full tuition and refunded their deposits. That cut the number of students in half. By appealing to other parents by phone, I managed to cut the number down to eleven. All were teenage boys, half Americans and half Mexicans. Twelve was the number of passengers allowed in one *panga* boat. With six campers each in two rented Mini Vans, twelve was a convenient number for ground transportation as well.

Convincing the parents to change their child's camp destination from Zihuatanejo to Cozumel by long distance telephone was a challenge, but somehow I got it all together. On June 20, 1979 we all met at the Hertz rent-a-car desk in the international airport of Cancun, Mexico. Considering the degree of improvisation that had prevailed until now, the remainder of the trip was comparatively easy.

Since we were only twelve, we all fit comfortably into two rental vans and were free to go and do as we pleased. We did everything spontaneously and by consensus. We began each day by reading the *Lonely Planet Guide* to determine our choices. If we liked where we were, we voted to stay another day. If we did not, we voted to move on. Our preferences proved to be remarkably similar, so we rarely lacked unanimous consensus.

Diving in the warm transparent waters of the Mexican Caribbean was a lot different than diving in the Mexican Pacific. The colorful coral reefs made every dive a new adventure in beauty, form and movement. The students could never have had such adventures in Mexico's tropical Pacific. Whereas the Pacific waters were heavy with plankton from the cold nutrient-rich water, moving from north to south, the crystalline waters of Mexico's Caribbean moved from south to north. The water was so clear that you could see bottom over a hundred feet below. It was an enchanted wonder world where you could witness the entire evolutionary cycle unfold before your eyes. Evolution became something you could actually experience as well as see. That was the real value of diving. You could actually see how you fit into the picture.

After a week in Cozumel, we moved our *Camp de Mar* to Isla Mujeres, a smaller island just thirty miles away. Here the diving was not so good, but the ambiance was much more fun. Isla Mujeres was loaded with young Europeans, mostly from France and Germany. It reminded me of St. Tropez on the French Riviera. Outdoor activities and sidewalk cafes were alive with the friendly chatter and smiling faces of people from around the world. Isla Mujeres was the ideal place to hang out. But this was the heart of the Mayan Empire and there was still a lot to see and learn.

In our rented VW vans, we drove south to explore the

ancient ruins of Tulum, a Mayan Temple on the beach near Cancun. Our drive down the Mayan causeway towards Chetumal revealed miles of deserted, palm-lined beaches and clean white sand. Dozens of places along the road offered dreamy seaside shelters with a cot for $15 or a hammock under the stars for $10.

On our return, we spent three days in *Playa* del Carmen, then a mere pueblo of perhaps two thousand people. Today it is a busy resort community of perhaps forty thousand.

Whenever someplace offered SCUBA diving, we usually stopped to do another open water dive. By diving each day in a different location, I managed to certify each camper in open water SCUBA diving. In the process, we dived some of the best locations in the Mexican Caribbean including *Cozumel*, *Playa Del Carmen*, *Xcaret*, *Chel Hal*, *Tulum*, *Isla Mujeres*, and *Isla Contoy*.

We also learned a lot about Mexico, about ourselves and about each other. In short, we managed to snatch the entire summer from the jaws of disaster and make it an adventure we will never forget. That summer's *Camp de Mar* was one of the most gratifying experiences of my life.

The night before we disbanded, I awarded their PADI diving certifications at a farewell ceremony at the Arrecife Inn, a rustic beach bungalow complex about thirty kilometers south of Tulum. The next morning, we drove to the airport at Cancun. After a final and emotional round of *abrazos* and goodbyes, we all went our separate ways. We had become quite close during the past month and it was an emotional farewell for all of us.

Even today my former students show up to visit with me and reminisce. They all tell me what an important experience that *Camp de Mar* had been in their lives. All of them are now responsible parents of their own families. I am proud to say that most are still trying to live as responsible participants in the global ecosystem. I am gratified, for that is all that I had ever hoped to teach them.

We all learned a great deal during that *Camp de Mar*, but as usual, I think it was I who learned the most. Above all, I learned that time is a human concept. We humans have no alternative than to live in a human context of time, while our planet lives in some other time that we can not seem to fathom.

Capital Showdown

Despite the positive experiences of that summer's *Camp de Mar*, the idea that Sanchez Mirus was sleeping, uninvited, in my bed, in my home, haunted me and poisoned my soul. Of course, my primary concern was always the welfare of my students, but I could not get Sanchez Mirus out of my mind. He followed me throughout the day like a dark shadow. Now that camp was over, it was time to confront him and flush him out my mind and out of my life.

I caught the next plane to Mexico City and then taxied directly to INDE's headquarters. My plan was to confront Guillermo Lopez Portillo, the Director of Parks and Recreation, regarding the role of Alvaro Sanchez Mirus. Instead, I ran headlong into Mexican bureaucracy in the guise of the fat receptionist who presided over the lobby like a mother hen. When I asked to see the Director, she curtly informed me that he was not available, so I asked to see the Sub-director.

"Regarding what matter? *Sobre que asunto?*" she demanded primly.

"I would like to verify the activity of one of your employees," I answered in Spanish.

"The personnel department is on the third floor," she informed me.

I gave her a copy of the letter of introduction that Sanchez Mirus had first given to me when he introduced himself. "I need to know if this gentleman is a legitimate employee of the Parks Department," I told her, "because it might involve INDE in a serious law suit."

She read the short letter and acknowledged with a nod of her head. "One of our legal will come to help you," she assured me. She rose from behind her desk and, with letter in hand, marched down the empty corridor, her high heels chattering on marble floor and vanishing through an open doorway. After a few minutes, she reappeared without the letter.

"Our Deputy Director will be out to help you," she announced.

After an hour had passed, I inquired after the Deputy Director and got the same reply. After a second hour passed, I asked again, this time perhaps a bit too brusquely. With obvious irritation, she marched down the corridor once more and soon returned with a young man. She introduced the man as *Licensiado* Luis Maldonado. Then she returned to her roost behind the reception desk.

After greetings, the young man took one of my bags and said, "Please follow me." He led me into an empty conference room, parked my luggage in a corner and motioned to me to sit.

"How did you come by this letter?" he asked gravely.

"I need to know if this Colonel Alvaro Sanchez Mirus is on your payroll."

"Why do you ask?"

"On the basis of this letter, this man has taken over my only home and threatened my life," I told him. "He prevented me from entering my home at gun point and I want to verify if this man is real or not."

"I'll ask the Director's secretary to check the signature,"

he said. He rose and vanished through the door. While he was gone, I looked around the room. One entire wall was devoted to trophies and sports memorabilia from Mexico's past. I nodded my head in approval of the exhibition. It spoke of the pride and passion of this beautiful country, so full of gifts and contradictions, so full of sugar and spice. Beneath all the challenges and frustrations of trying to work in Mexico, I truly loved it.

Licensiado Maldonado suddenly reappeared. An older-looking man followed, carrying my copy of the letter. After shaking hands, he returned the letter to me. "The Director's secretary said that this looks like the Director's signature all right. However, she has no record of the letter in her files. Who gave you that letter?"

I repeated the story about Sanchez Mirus. As background, I also told him about Captain Cousteau and inquired about my presentation for the Tarascan Indian Village on Las Gatas Beach. He denied knowing anything about my projects, or about Sanchez Mirus. However, he promised he would investigate and requested that I come back *mañana*.

"Come back tomorrow around noon," he said, "and I will try to have some answers for you." Despite my impatience to return to Zihuatanejo, I reluctantly agreed and rented a room at the Hotel Maria Christina.

I spent a restless night, trying to make sense of it all. Was Sanchez Mirus for real? If so, what was his role in the Parks Department of INDE? Why did nobody there seem to know who he was? Or care?

The next day, I returned to INDE's headquarters expecting to get some answers. The young *Licenciado* Moldonado was the only representative present. "The others were called to an important meeting in Veracruz," he explained. "But they will return in three days. Would you like to make an appointment?"

It was useless to protest, but I was not inclined to hang around for another three days. I had little money and I was anxious to see if I still had a home. I took their phone number and promised I would call. I doubted then that I would never get a straight answer out of them, and despite many attempts, I never succeeded.

I rode the night bus back to Zihuatanejo and taxied to Arthur's house on the *Playa* Almacen. As houses go, Arthur's house was not much—a locked cement bunker in which to store things and a palm-thatched shelter with two hammocks and a bed. What it lacked in amenities, it more than made up for with a spectacular display of spiraling rocks, crashing waves and lush vegetation. It did, however, have a telephone, which I used to call my lawyer.

"I have good news for you!" exclaimed Federico. "I've made an arrangement on your behalf with Colonel Sanchez Mirus."

"Wonderful!" I exclaimed. "When can I move into my house?"

"First, we must meet to clarify some things. Why don't we all meet at the Hotel El Capricho Del Rey, say tomorrow at noon?"

"But what is there to talk about? This guy has taken over my house without my permission. I built it and lived in for sixteen years. All I want to do is go back home!"

"I wouldn't do that if I were you," Federico said gravely. "The Colonel told me that he has an armed guard there with orders to shoot if you attempt to return without his agreement."

"Are you serious? You think he would actually shoot me if I moved into my own home?"

"If a man is a paid to do that, he is just doing his job."

"But it's my home!"

"Well, that's what we've got to talk about, tomorrow at

noon at El Capricho Del Rey."

"Bullshit! I'm not going there until you tell me what you two have been talking about. After all, it's my home and you are my lawyer!"

"Well, then meet me here at Hector's house around eleven. We can talk privately before we see him."

By now, the new scenic road around the harbor went completely through the coconut plantations behind La Ropa Beach, passed in front of Lois and Hector Aguilar's house where Federico was visiting, and ended at the Hotel El Capricho Del Rey. From there, a rustic trail of uneven rocks skirted the waters edge and emerged at the boat landing at the head of Las Gatas Beach. Normally, I would have thought nothing of walking the rocky trail, but on this occasion I took taxi around the entire bay.

Don Hector Aguilar greeted me on the front veranda. He was a distinguished-looking, silver-haired gentleman who had been a silversmith with William Spratling in the nearby mountain village of Taxco. Don Hector liked his tequila. He and Lois were having their first of the day when I arrived. Hector invited me to join them, but once again I declined and asked to see Federico.

"Feddy tells me that you have a new partner over on Las Gatas Beach," he said, raising his glass. "Let's drink to your success." He raised his glass, and then sipped.

I said, "Well that's news to me! In fact, that's why I want to talk with Feddy. Is he here?"

"Feddy!" he called. A voice answered from the second-story window. Then he turned to me, "He's coming. He's coming. You're in good hands with Feddy," he assured me.

Feddy appeared looking tanned and dapper. He wore white slacks and a blue shirt. Declining Hector's offer of tequila, Feddy sat facing me across the cocktail table and got straight to the point.

"I think that I've made a pretty good deal for you," he said. "There are a lot of details to be worked out, but all in all I think he's being fair. He's waiting to talk to us."

"Being fair in what?" I asked. "Would you kindly tell me what you are talking about before we see him?"

"Well, he's waiting to talk to us right now."

"Then let him wait a few minutes more. Give me the gist of it. Tell me what he has in mind."

"Well, the gist of the deal is that he has incorporated the place, and he's willing to take you in as a minority partner because the majority stockholder has to be a Mexican national. That's the law."

"Wait a minute!" I exclaimed. "First tell me who told you that I wanted a partner? I've been there for sixteen years. Why should I suddenly need a partner?"

"Because of the agreement you signed with him."

"I signed an agreement to turn the land over to Parks and Recreation at INDE for a trial period of three months. I signed nothing over to Sanchez Mirus!"

"He showed me a document you signed. It ceded the property over him."

"I signed it over to the National Institute of Sports, which he pretends to represent. Meanwhile, nobody there seems to know who he is. Do you know who he is?"

"People say he is very important and very well-connected. Anyway, he has a legal document signed by you stating that you turned it over to him."

"Then that document is a lie!"

"It has your signature on it."

"It looks very much like my signature, but I did not sign that document."

"Can you prove that in a Mexican court?"

I heard that familiar ringing in my ears. "Wait a minute, Federico. Whose lawyer are you? Mine or Sanchez Mirus?"

"You'd best listen to Feddy," Hector put in. "Feddy knows what he's doing."

"I'm only trying to help you," Federico assured me. "Foreigners don't have an easy time in Mexican courts."

I could not believe what was happening. I felt trapped in a web of conspiracy and deceit. My intuition told me that Feddy was conspiring with Sanchez Mirus to usurp my property. In my confusion and anxiety, I could not think straight. I refused to accompany Federico to El Capricho Del Rey. I certainly did not want to talk with Sanchez Mirus. Instead, I returned by foot to Artie's house. I needed to talk to somebody I could trust. By talking to Artie about it, perhaps it would help make sense to myself.

When I arrived, Arthur was not there, so I went to see my friend and confidant Helena Krebs. Helena was a fellow Saint Louisian who had lived here for years. She was suffering through a similar struggle to recuperate her home from a local family who had rented it but refused to move or pay rent. If nothing more, we could certainly empathize with each other.

Helena was a wise woman with a big, big heart. Though already a single mother of two, she adopted three local orphans and raised them as her own.

When I told her what had happened, she did indeed empathize. "I know what you are going through, but all I can offer is a little compassion and the name of an honest lawyer."

"May I use your phone to call him?" I asked.

Helen's lawyer turned out to be a very sweet and humble man of perhaps fifty. His sincere and honest demeanor reflected the kind of noble spirit and honesty that Feddy lacked. He explained that he had once been a judge in the nearby village of *La Union,* but was now a practicing lawyer. He agreed to take on my case for a retainer of only $800. That was already twenty percent less than Federico de

Samaniego had charged. He suggested that we file a criminal complaint of usurpation against Sanchez Mirus. Thus I plunged into the boiling caldron of graft and corruption that was Mexico's justice system. My new lawyer lost no time in filing the criminal complaint, but, alas, an entire year passed and nothing happened.

Meanwhile, though all work had stopped long before, Alvaro's armed guard was still in my house. So I was still living in Artie's little house in La Calla, while Artie himself now occupied my apartment in New York City.

I had got world from Becky that she was going off to live in a Buddhist *ashram* in Tibet. Aware of her devotion to Buddhism, I was sad but not surprised. By chance, her move vacated my apartment just when Artie Agin needed to return to New York. It was a fair and symbiotic interchange.

Meanwhile, I sought support from Jorge Allec, Zihuatanejo's three-time Mayor and, not just by coincidence, its richest resident. I also sought support from Armando Federico, the former mayor who now worked in the state governor's local office. Unfortunately, both refused to help. I suspect that Sanchez Mirus was as much of a mystery to them as he was to me. However, his self- avowed friendship with the rich and powerful in Mexico City was enough to make them wary of getting involved. In the absence of evidence to the contrary, they were not willing to risk the possibility of offending anybody of importance.

My nightmare soon won me a measure of fame and a new nickname. I became known as "Owen Lios," which was a play on Spanish words meaning "mess of problems." People greeted me in the streets, "*Hola*, Owen Lios!" meaning "Hi, Owen of the Problems!"

This was not the kind of image that I wanted to project, and I tried to correct them, "Owen Lee si, but Owen Lios, no," I answered.

To make matters worse, the last of my family inheritance was now long gone. In order to survive, I resorted to what few carpentry skills I had to make folding deck chairs out of the beautiful rosewood that grew around the Bay. I managed to sell a few chairs to my sympathetic friends, but that left me with more time than money so I looked for other ways to survival.

As far as I could see, my problem was part cultural, part social, part political, and part greed. Try as I might, I could not seem to accomplish anything positive in Zihuatanejo. It was like spinning wheels in the mud without going anywhere.

Photo 25: Zorro's Executioner with Lauren Hutton

When long-time resident Lauren Hutton offered me a job as an extra in a movie, I jumped at the chance. The movie co-starred George Hamilton and was titled *Zorro, the Gay Blade*. I was delighted to be in the movies! I even managed to convince Peter Wier, the director, to cast me at Zorro's executioner.

No executioner could have ever been happier than this one, for it gave me gainful employment for almost a month in a heady, showbiz ambiance that I had not known since I left New York. It was great fun. Furthermore, it allowed me to escape the nagging presence of my homeless predicament. At last, I could think of other things and other ways to survive. In fact, it led to a new career as an interior decorator.

After seeing my own house on Las Gatas Beach, Loyce Millbank offered to hire me to redecorate her residence in Acapulco, and I was quick to accept. Loyce Millbank was a beautiful, urbane, blue-eyed brunette who hailed from Oklahoma. She was very tall, shapely and sophisticated and spoke three languages. Having been married and widowed three times over, she now divided her time between her three luxurious homes in New York, Paris and Acapulco.

I met Loyce at a party in Acapulco through Freddy Mohr, who was very fond of her. Because of my close friendship with Freddy, Loyce insisted that I was gay. She kept trying to put me in touch with her gay friends, and I kept trying to avoid them. It took the appearance of Lillia Martinez to convince her that I was not gay.

One evening at Loyce's home, I received a bizarre telephone call from a woman I had never met. She introduced herself over the phone as Lillia Martinez.

"Hello, Meester Lee," Lillia said in her heavily accented

Spanglish. "You don' know me, but I know all 'bout you from mi *dentista*, Yollanda Perez. She tell me your whole story, and dats why I tenk we should talk".

"Who is Yollanda Perez, may I ask?"

"Yollanda Perez, she is my *dentista*. She tells me dat she be your *dentista* too!"

I vaguely remembered having had a bothersome cavity filled by a woman dentist named Yollanda several years previously. I said, "Yes. Yollanda, *la dentista*. Please go on."

"Well, Yollanda, she tell me your *problema* wid di property in *Playa Las Gatas*. And den she say to me, 'Because you be *una* single mudder of tree Mexican childrens, why you don' call Meester Owen on de telephone and say to heem, 'why don' we get married' and dat make heem a legitimate Mexicano so he can own hees own land! No? As di fodder of tree Mexican childrens, he becomes a real *Mexicano* and he no have *mas problemas* wid di land.' You see?"

"Yes, yes. I see what you are saying."

The audacity of Lillia's proposal startled but amused me. It also made a lot of sense. As the father of three Mexican children, I could get Mexican citizenship and actually own the land that I bought from Don Carlos Barnard. Besides, any woman who had the audacity to make such a proposal over the telephone, sight unseen, intrigued me. How could she possibly know what she was getting into? For that matter, how could I? Such a person was unusual, to say the least.

Furthermore, Becky had gone off to an *ashram* in Tibet, probably with a new lover, and I had been celibate far too long. I yearned for a new sexual relationship and Lillia seemed to offer the possibility of one without all the hassles of courtship. "I think we should meet," I said, "but I'm working in Acapulco now."

"I can come see you in Acapulco," she offered.

Was she serious? "When?" I asked.

"*Mañana*?" she replied.

"OK then, yes, I'll see you *mañana*."

By sunset the next day, Lillia was knocking at the door. She was surprisingly short in stature, but she had a pretty face and a happy talkative disposition. I invited her to dinner and we talked late into the night about our respective pasts. It turned out that Lillia was the divorced mother of three teenage boys. All of them had been born in the city of Patzcuaro in the state of Michoacan, where they sometimes lived with their father. Lillia, herself, lived in an apartment she owned in INFORAVIT, a low-cost government housing development built for the workers of Ixtapa. She divorced from the father of her children and had been living in Zihuatanejo for the past three years. Before the end of dinner, I invited her to spend the night and she agreed.

Photo 26: Lillia Martinez

I slept in a servant's room that was separate from the main house. It had a private entrance from the street. Therefore, it was an easy matter for Lillia to spend the night with me undetected. In the morning, however, all foot traffic both in and out of the main house had to pass in front of my window, which was always open.

Unfortunately, Loyce had the habit of peeking through the window whenever she passed, singing, "Buenos dias!" When she did so that morning, she discovered Lillian in bed with me and blew her top.

"Get that whore out of my house," Loyce commanded. I tried to explain the circumstances to Loyce, but she would not listen. "How could you do this to me?" she demanded. Her jealous demeanor mystified me. As Loyce thought me gay, we had never had any kind of relationship other professional. We certainly had never been romantically involved. "Out!" Loyce cried. "Both of you, out of my house!"

So that was the end of my relationship with Loyce. With mixed feelings of relief and regret, I packed my bags and returned with Lillia to Zihuatanejo.

As a homeless person, at least for the moment, one of the most alluring aspects of Lillia was the fact that she owned her own apartment with all the amenities. Arthur Agin's house, although a beautiful setting, was little better than camping out. I gathered up my meager belongings and moved into Lillia's apartment in INFONAVIT.

After living for so many years in the garden paradise of Las Gatas Beach, I found life inside the barren walls of INFONAVIT severely depressing. As far as I could see, the low-cost housing was no more than a prefabricated ghetto for the underprivileged. To me, the stark, barren lines of its architecture was cruel and unnecessary punishment for simply being poor. Most of the buildings were merely boxes of cold, hard cement. Not one curve or embellishment broke the stark monotony of angular lines. There was no sign of creativity or imagination to please the eye or refresh the soul.

The boxes were divided into multiple living units that were then subdivided into small, cell-like rooms. Tiny windows offered little light or ventilation. Close the windows and the apartment became a Turkish bath. Open the windows for fresh air and it became a cacophony of sounds that numbed the brain—a hundred radios blaring, a dozen babies crying and several couples quarreling. Now add the shrieks of hundreds of darling children at play, a few shots and screams now and then, and you have some idea of what it is like to live in an apartment in INFONAVIT.

To me, it seemed like a conspiracy to make the less fortunate feel even less fortunate than they really were. For many, such housing became a prison from which there was scant opportunity to escape—not by actual physical confinement, but by the economic, moral and psychological incarceration that comes with it. I was one of them.

Return to Paradise

After a couple of weeks inside INFONAVIT, I was already planning my escape. Then I ran into Leonardo Castillo, my former neighbor on Las Gatas Beach. His house adjoined my property, but he had left the house abandoned for almost two years, and I had not seen him. When the *abrazos* were done, he explained that a sudden illness in his family had forced him to abandon the house and move to Acapulco. "Would you know of somebody who might like to rent my house?" he inquired.

I did not hesitate a second. "Yes," I said, "me!"

Within a week, I moved Lillia and the whole damned family into Leonardo's house. It was a scant sixty yards from my own beloved home, still far out of my reach. It was taboo for me to enter. Sanchez Mirus had left his armed guard living in it, with orders to shoot me should I attempt to enter. By renting his house next door, I could keep my eye on the place while still avoiding confrontation. No sooner had we moved in, then destiny called upon me to save my place from destruction by fire.

One day, for some vague reason, I was leaning against the half-fence that separated the two properties, just as Florensio, the armed guard, was setting fire to a pile of dry leaves that had fallen from the false almond tree behind the *Escondito* bungalow. Having lit the fire, he then abandoned it for some other chore. As I watched, one of the burning leaves rose aloft on the currents of hot air and lit on the dry *palapa* leaves of the roof.

I had witnessed such a fire consume an entire wooden house in less than twenty minutes, so I acted quickly. Marveling at the timeliness of my arrival, I leaped over the fence, climbed up onto the *palapas* roof, removed and disposed of the burning *palapa* leaves, and returned to my original place behind the fence just as the guard returned. He never knew what happened. It was surreal, as though the whole event had been timed and predestined by some omniscient force. I wondered what other surprises my destiny held in store for me.

In order for Lillia's kids to go back and fourth to school, they had to cross through the property that Sanchez Mirus now controlled. This enabled me to approach Florensio and arrive at a friendly understanding. In person, Florensio seemed a quite reasonable but basic *campesino*, somewhat tired and weathered, trying to survive. I made it clear to him that I had no intention of invading the "Colonel's property" without permission. I also offered free boat rides to town. He made it clear that he had no intention of shooting me or my family, so long as we were only just passing through. In other words, we agreed to respect each other's presence without violence.

Unfortunately, I was unable to expand our agreement to include the eradication of Florensio's rooster. Florensio let a whole flock of chickens run free on the property. Chicken shit was everywhere, but for Florensio I guess it was worth it. So long as his rooster did his job, it assured Florensio of an endless supply of fresh eggs, which were the mainstay of his meager diet.

The problem was that the rooster had a peculiarly irritating and piercing kind of crow, which he exercised at all hours, precluding any possibility of sleep. He was indefatigueable. He normally started crowing only shortly after midnight and often did not stop until well after sunup.

It was not long, therefore, before I was plotting how to make it shut up. One night, I dressed up in my black rubber wetsuit, got out my trusty spear fishing gun, snuck up on the offending crow under cover of darkness, and let him have an arrow through the heart. A few anxious moments of loud squawking threatened the success of the mission before I could manage to ring its neck, but all in all the mission was a success. As a bonus, the meat, though tough, was very tasty.

Florensio lost no time in finding a replacement rooster for his hens, but it was great improvement over the last one. It crowed much less frequently and with much less pizzazz. I could actually sleep through it. Halleluya! Mission accomplished.

The Check Bounced

By this time, Florensio and I had become friendly neighbors. He complained bitterly that the Colonel owed him over five months in back wages. He assured me that even if I tried to take back my house, he would not shoot me, unless he had been paid in full. Meanwhile, he complained that nothing worked. The place had been ravaged by storms. There had been no money for maintenance or repairs for months. Furthermore, the Colonel had not shown up for over two months, and he wondered if he was still alive. Sarah Veerboonen, now the widowed owner of El Capricho del Rey, had also complained about the Colonel's disappearance. He had not paid the rent for over a year. She said that she was taking him to court for usurpation.

Quite by accident, I discovered why the Colonel had dropped out of sight. The check for $3,000 that I had given him over a year ago to finance the legalities of our arrangement with INDE had come back to me for insufficient funds. Given the current state of our relationship, I notified the bank that it was not my signature on the check, that it had been forged. The bank then referred the matter to INTERPOL, the international police organization.

Unbeknownst to me, Sanchez Mirus had a record as forger and confidence man. He had already served time in prison for forgery and fraud. Consequently, when his name came up again as a result of the forged check, INTERPOL came and locked him up. By using his many contacts, he was able to get off with a much-reduced sentence. However, he was livid with rage and, when at last he did get out, he came after me seeking vengeance.

I discovered his intentions one day while passing in front of El Capricho Del Rey on my way from La Ropa Beach to *Las Gatas* by foot. As I treaded over the uneven rocks near the water, a shot suddenly rang out behind me. The bullet ricocheted off a rock near my feet with a loud "Zinngggg!" Spinning around, I saw Sanchez Mirus standing on the balcony of his hillside bungalow. He aimed at me with his telescopic rifle, and a second shot rang out. I scrambled across the rocks and hid behind a tree, frozen with fear. Collecting my wits, I cautiously peeked out from behind the tree. When he saw me, the Colonel brought his rifle back to his shoulder. I ducked back behind the tree.

"Have you gone crazy?!" I shouted loud enough for him to hear. "What's the big idea?"

"You sonofabitch!" he shouted. "You know that check was real. You gave me that check! That was your signature! You signed it!"

"Is that any reason to shoot at me? Who are you anyway?

Nobody at INDE even knows who you are!"

"You send me to jail? For this, I kill you!" He shot his rifle again and I could feel the impact as the bullet hit the tree.

"I just want go home" I called. "So get out my house and get out of my life!"

"You send me to jail! I kill you!" he repeated.

For what seemed like an eternity, I hid in fear behind the tree, half expecting him to descend from his hill and flush me out with his rifle. Stealing a quick peek from behind the tree, I saw a group of beach vendors heading toward me. They habitually walked the trail to *Las Gatas* every day in order to sell their wares. As they came nearer, I was relieved to discover that I knew one of them quite well. His name was Mario. He sold silver jewelry from Taxco. Mario prided himself on his ability to swim across the entire bay with one arm tied behind his back. When the group came into my sight behind the tree, I called Mario over.

"Mario! Mario!" I hollered! "Please come help me. I need your help!"

Mario stopped. Then the others stopped. They followed Mario as he approached me

"*Hola,* Owen. *Que pasa? Que haces atrás de este árbol*? Why are hiding behind this tree?"

"Some madman is shooting at me with a rifle," I told him. "Please help!"

"Somebody is shooting at you? Who? Why?"

I motioned towards Alvaro with my head and eyes. "You see that guy on the balcony of El Capricho del Rey?" I asked, "It's that asshole, Sanchez Mirus, the same guy who has my house. He wants to kill me!"

When Mario looked up at the balcony of El Capricho Del Rey, the others followed his gaze. From the blank expression on their faces, I surmised that the Colonel had vanished inside and was no longer there.

"Well, come with us", Mario said. "You can walk in front of us. He can't shoot everybody!"

"Is he still there?" I inquired.

"We don't see anybody," Mario answered.

I scrambled down from my hiding place behind the tree and hustled gingerly to join Mario's group. We walked the rest of the journey to *Las Gatas* without further incident.

My mind was buzzing with fear and paranoia. When I saw Lillia and the kids, the stress must have shown on my face. "*Que pasa?*" she demanded. "You are as white as a ghost."

"Quick," I commanded. "Pack your things. We've got to get out of here!"

"But why? What's happened? Where are we going?"

"It looks like Sanchez Mirus is out to kill us," I told them. "He's been taking shots at me with his rifle. I think we had best go back to your horrid apartment in INFONAVIT."

The Road to Altamirano

In his desperate attempts to wear me down, Sanchez Mirus resorted to some *macho* madness designed to terrorize me into surrendering my beloved property. Twice more, Sanchez Mirus took shots at me with his rifle. One only narrowly missed and sent me scrambling behind a tree. Once I saw him urge a taxi to run me down in the street. Another time, his friends in the judicial police impounded my car and it took weeks to get it back. Such events served to reinforce my determination to recuperate my precious home.

Meanwhile, still serving time in our neo-prison, INFONAVIT, I gradually sank into a state of paranoiac depression. The thought of returning to my hectic life in New York City grew more appealing every day.

One day I was walking alone down the *Calle Ejidal* in

Zihuatanejo, when a large American car pulled up beside me. Four men piled out of the car and surrounded me. One of them motioned me inside the car with the barrel of his .30-caliber carbine.

Reluctantly I obeyed. "*Que pasa? Que he hecho?* What's the matter? What did I do?" I was more angry than afraid.

"Shut up," the leader snapped. "*Calla te*! And get in the car."

"Where are we going?" the driver asked.

"Take the Road to Altamirano," the leader replied.

Now I was afraid. The road to Altamirao was synonymous to "the road of no return." It was famous as a dumping ground for unclaimed cadavers. The mere mention of its name was enough to instill fear in anyone who knew it. It was a tortured ribbon of curves and cutbacks through dense jungles and some of the most rugged mountains of the Sierra Madres. It was notorious for its many hazards, not the least of which was its roadside bandits. Every summer, torrents of mountain rainwater ate away huge chunks of its thin asphalt veneer, replacing them with gaping holes and huge boulders, some as big as a small VW.

Countless speed bumps challenged every vehicle that dared pass over them. They also provided convenient work stations for roadside pirates, a place where bandits could more easily assault the passing traffic. Back then, you never knew what awaited you around the next curve on the Road to Altamirano. And come to think of it, you still don't.

The four men in the car with me were morosely silent. I figured they were friends of Sanchez Mirus, probably state judicial police, because they all wore civilian clothes, black boots and pistols on their belts. Nobody but the police would dare do that. The state judicial police of Guererro were known to flaunt their impunity to the law. Some claimed that the state judicial police included the state's worst criminals.

Sanchez Mirus was known to cultivate their company. I suspected that it was he who had put them up to this. Numerous cadavers had already been recovered from this remote and rugged area. By now, I was deathly afraid that mine would soon join them.

About an hour into the rugged mountains, the leader tapped the driver on his shoulder and said, "Take the next right." The driver nodded and then turned off the highway, the first opportunity.

The rutted dirt road burrowed through dense stands of towering pines and gigantic oak trees. About a mile into the forest, the leader spoke again and the car ground to a stop. Rivers of sweat dripped off my anxious face and soaked my shirt. The leader got out of the back seat, carrying his carbine. Then he turned to me. With a thrust of his head and a wave of his gun, he motioned me out of the car. "Come on. Get out," he said. "*Muevate!*"

"What for? Where are you taking me?"

I knew that if I got out of that car, I was as good as dead. "I don't want to get out. I am not moving!" I proclaimed. I grasped both knees and hunkered down in the backseat. With that the leader raised his carbine and pointed it at my nose. As I looked into the barrel of his gun, my fear erupted. "*Que pasa?* Why are you doing this to me?" I demanded. "I am not moving!"

With that, the fat policeman on my right gave me a shove through the open door and said, "*Ya! Largate de aqui!*"

The leader caught me by the hair and pulled me the rest of the way out. I landed on all fours, but I did not dare to get up. Rather, I remained on the ground, cringing in anticipation of a bullet through my head. Suddenly I burst into tears. "What have I ever done to you?" I sobbed. "Why are you doing this to me?"

But they did not answer. After what seemed an eternity, I

heard the car door slam shut and the car lock into gear. Looking up from my crouch on the sun-baked dust, I watched with incredulous relief as the car turned around and moved off the way we came until it vanished into the jungle.

"Oh, thank God!" I cried. "Thank God!" I giggled with relief and then burst into gasping sobs. It was as if I had witnessed a miracle. Minutes passed before I could muster the will to get to my feet and collect my wits. Slowly, I started the long, lonely trek back to the notorious Road to Altamirao. It was then I became aware that I had wet my pants.

As I walked, I appraised the shameless tactics of my vicious opponent. If it had been the Colonel's intention to scare the hell out of me, he had mightily succeeded. This was a new kind of hardball that I was not prepared to play. It made me long for the relative peace and tranquility of New York City. By the time I reached the paved Road to Altamirano, the idea of returning to New York City seemed like an idea whose time had come.

The Summons

One evening in early December, I was having dinner with friends when a taxi boat suddenly tied up to the pier and disgorged two disheveled passengers. One was Jorge Camps, an Immigration Inspector whom I had once met at a party in Acapulco. The other man, as it turned out, was also called Jorge. He had a fresh clean cast on his forearm and it was cradled in a sling. They were both inspectors for *Gobernacion*, Mexico's Department of the Interior, and were here on a mission.

The two inspectors had driven all the way from Acapulco in order to serve me with an official summons. The summons ordered me to appear before the Chief of

Immigration in Mexico City within seventy two hours in order to "clarify your immigration status." En route from Acapulco, it seems that their car had run off the road and Jorge #2 had broken his wrist.

I tried to be friendly with them and offered them a drink, but they were in no mood. When I reminded Jorge Camps of our chance meeting in Acapulco, he snapped, "Yes, yes, I know who you are. You are one of those pot-head friends of my sister-in-law." I later discovered that he was married to the daughter of "Buck" and Darby Rogers, close friends of mine who lived in Acapulco.

"We're not here to be friendly," snapped Jorge. "We're here to see that you appear at Immigration in Mexico City on Wednesday morning. You'd better be there, or I'll slam your ass in jail." With that, he turned and headed back to his boat.

With one last accusing look in my direction, Jorge #2 followed, limping slightly. I was left scratching my head. "What next?" I muttered in bewilderment.

Monday I checked with Don Bellasario, the local Immigration agent in Zihuatanejo whom I knew quite well. "Are there any discrepancies in my immigration papers?" I asked him.

He told me that all my papers seemed to be in order, but advised me to comply with my summons. He gave a letter of recommendation and the next day, I took it with me on the early morning flight to Mexico City. Because my papers were in order, I expected to return to Zihuatanejo that same afternoon, so I dressed in my usual tropical attire.

The Department of Immigration was located on *Avenida Juarez,* just off *La Reforma*. When I arrived, it was already bustling with foreigners, all looking slightly mystified and confused. When I presented my summons to the receptionist, he did not know what to do with me. He advised me to have a seat and wait. However, there were no seats empty, so I milled around the crowded corridors, returning now and then to check in with the receptionist.

By one o, clock, the crowd had thinned out a bit, so I finally got to sit down. Another hour passed before somebody called my name. He was a young man in his early twenties. I noticed that he wore a pistol on his belt. "Are you Owen Lee?" he asked.

I confirmed that I was, but instead of taking my papers and leading me to some office as I expected, he simply sat down next to me. He introduced himself as Inspector Galvez. When it became clear that he was not going to do anything, I asked, "Don't you want to see my papers?"

"*No, gracias,*" he answered. "*Este bien.*"

"Then what is this all about?" I inquired.

"I don't know," he said. "I was just told to keep an eye on you. My name is Inspector Galvez."

"What for?" I asked. "Am I being charged with something I don't know about?"

"I don't know," he repeated. "I just do what they tell me."

"And what did they tell you to do?"

"They just told me to keep you in sight."

"What for?"

"I don't know," he repeated.

Another two hours passed, and we two were still sitting there waiting. When I got up to use the men's room, he insisted on going with me. I informed him that I had already learned to do it alone, but he followed me any way. "Why are you following me?" I demanded. "Who put you up to this?"

"My boss."

"And what does your boss do?"

"He is our Chief Inspector."

"And why did he assign you to me?"

"I don't know," he repeated.

"Well, I haven't eaten all day. Can I get something to eat?"

"*Claro que si*. There's a good taco place just around the corner. I'll take you there."

"I can do it alone," I said.

"Sorry. I have to go with you."

"Am I being charged or something?"

He shrugged his shoulders. "I don't know. They told me to keep you in sight."

"Who told you that?"

"My boss," he replied. We were going in circles.

Reluctantly, I allowed him to accompany me and even paid for his lunch. Meanwhile, I tried to get more information from him. He didn't know any more than I did, he said, and used the opportunity to ask for a "loan" of $100.

By the time we returned to the Immigration office, the reception room was empty. We resumed our seats and waited some more. Impatiently, I pleaded with Inspector Galvez to go see if he could expedite my case so I could return home before dark. "I'm not dressed for nights in the big city," I joked.

He agreed to try and vanished into an adjoining office, but all too soon returned and resumed his seat. He exhaled a sigh and shook his head. "Sorry," he said. "We have to wait."

Outside, the sky was already turning dark when at last somebody showed up to take charge of me. He was a burly man with a swarthy complexion and a heavy beard. He also wore a pistol on his hip. Emerging from the office, he dismissed the young Inspector Galvez and then motioned for me to follow. He did not take me into an office, as I had expected, though. Instead, he led me down three flights of stairs and across an interior courtyard that now served as a parking lot. By now, only three cars and a truck were in it.

On the other side of the courtyard, we came to a wooden

door. Standing to one side of the door, my burly escort silently motioned for me to enter with a nod of his head. When I opened the door, I saw that it was a barred jail cell and stopped short. As I realized what was happening, I heard that familiar ringing in my ears. Closing the door, I turned back and confronted my escort. When I did so, however, he had already drawn his revolver. He raised the pistol and pointed it at my nose. With a little flick on the barrel, he motioned me back inside. "*Poor a denture*," he commanded.

"But why?" I demanded. "What have I done? Why are you putting me in jail? I want to talk to my lawyer!"

"Inside!" he snapped. "Move!"

My heart began to pound and the ringing grew louder. Nevertheless, I reluctantly obeyed. He switched on a single-necked light bulb that hung on wires from a hole in the ceiling. Behind me, the barred door slammed shut with a metallic "clank!" Then the man vanished, closing the massive wood door behind him.

With anxiety welling up inside me, I inspected the room. Just four bare walls and a cement floor with a filthy sink and a drain hole in one corner. The smell of stale urine permeated the air and there was no circulation. The only furniture was a flattened cardboard box lying in his middle of the floor. With no possible alternative, I sat down on the cardboard and tried to reason why I was there.

Unable to find an answer, I heaved a sigh of resignation and lay down with exhaustion. I tried to meditate, but my mind was spinning like a top. Eventually I managed to sleep, but at about three o'clock in the morning I started shivering from the cold. I was dressed for the tropics and unaccustomed to the night chill of Mexico City. I tried to sleep with the cardboard box on top of me, instead of underneath me, but I could not get back to sleep. I longed to go home, but what could I do?

The next morning, I drank some water from the tap and relieved myself in the sink. Soon, I heard the cars pulling into the parking lot and the day's activities begin to unwind. I pounded on the wooden door for attention, but nobody opened it until well after noon. It was a new man and he gave me a plastic bottle of water and an order of tacos in a plastic wrapper. I tried to pump some information from the man, but he knew less than I did. Nobody else showed up until the following day.

About three o'clock in the afternoon, the wooden door suddenly burst open and the same burly man ushered into my cell six contrite Indians of humble origin. I soon learned that they had all come from Guatemala or El Salvador. They were all headed for the United States in the hopes of finding work there. Immigration authorities had apprehended them in a bus station in the town of Tuxla Gutierrez. Most of them had been here before. They all expected to spend a couple of days in jail and then be sent back to Guatemala, where they would simply start over. That night, we all cuddled up on the old cardboard box like a bunch of grapes. It was a bit crowded, but much warmer.

About ten the next morning, the burly attendant burst again through the door and gave us a metal pail of water which we drank from our cupped hands. Then he herded us all into a mini van that was waiting in the courtyard parking lot. Accompanied by an armed guard, the chauffer drove us down the Causada de Talapan to an immigration prison somewhere south of the city.

The prison occupied about a square city block. A high cyclone fence topped with coils of razor wire enclosed a dusty recreation field where a perpetual football (soccer) game was always in progress. Around the edge of the field the inmates gathered, mostly in small groups, to chat, shoot dice, play cards, snooze, or just hang out. At the far end of the field, two double-storied brick barracks accommodated about five hundred detainees. Most hailed from Guatemala or El Salvador, but there were also about a dozen Europeans.

A guard led us to the second floor of one of the cell blocks at the end of the field. It had about a hundred double-deck steel cots in it. Each cot had a thin cotton mattress and a single army blanket on it. At the end of the room was a spacious bathroom with multiple toilets but only four showers.

All the meals were alike. Breakfast consisted of coffee-colored water with watery oatmeal porridge. Lunch and dinner always consisted of black beans and white rice.

During the day, we passed the time playing football or simply lazing around in a large open field within the fence. Few of the detainees spent more than a week inside the compound. I watched curiously as groups of forty or fifty at a time were called into an office for processing and then taken away by busses. Most were charged with illegal entry and then simply deported back to the Guatemalan border. I was the only exception.

I had spent ten days in detention without anyone so much as asking my name. This worried me because Don Bellisario had verified that my immigration status was legal. Therefore, I suspected that I was being held for some other reason. The fact that I was still not on record could mean that they had other plans for me besides simple deportation. I could disappear without anyone ever knowing what became of me. Yet, it was useless to try to reason with the prison personnel. They simply did not care. If I were to ever get out of there, I had to find a way to do it myself. On the eleventh day, I got my chance.

When I left the recreation field to go the bathroom, I discovered a high-barred window that opened directly onto a public street outside the prison. As I was standing at the urinal, I heard a voice calling from the street through the window, "Hey, in there! Does anybody in there speak English?"

"Yes, yes. I speak English." I answered through the window.

"I think my brother is in there. His name is Dale Reardon. He's an American. Do you know him?"

"There are four other Americans here," I told him through the window. "They're all in the yard right now. Do you want me to ask them?"

"I'd be much obliged if you could do that," he said. "Can I do anything for you in return?" he asked kindly.

"Yes, yes you can. My name is Owen Lee. You can phone the American Embassy and tell them that I'm here. I've been here for eleven days, held without charges." I said. "Please ask them to help me get out of here."

"With pleasure," he said. "What is your name again?"

I repeated my name and then spelled it out for him. Then I returned to the recreation field to do my mission. Finding Dale was easier than I had anticipated. Since we all spoke the same language, all the English-speaking detainees habitually hung out together. This day was no exception. I found the group and simply asked, "Which one of you is Dale Reardon?"

"That's me," answered one of them.

"Your brother is waiting to talk to you," I told him. "You can talk to him through the window of the field house bathroom."

Satisfied that I had talked to somebody who might actually do something, I relaxed a bit and lay back to wait. When Dale Reardon returned, he assured me that I could count on his brother.

The results were quick in coming. Within two hours, the public address system summoned me to the telephone of the

Administration Office. "This is the United States Consular Service," said a voice on the other end. "We got word that you wanted to speak to us." It was sweet music to my ears.

I tried to explain what had happened, but they weren't interested. They simply asked me if I had a lawyer who could help me. The only one I could think of was Federico de Samaniego. I had his number in my pocket phone book. So even though I no longer trusted him, I gave them his number. Before the day was out, he was calling me to the phone.

"Good news!" he said. "I was able to arrange for your release!"

"Fantastic!" I exclaimed.

"But there is a catch," he cautioned. "You have to leave the country on the first available airplane to the States."

"Am I being deported?"

"No. I don't think that it has come to that. It's just what they told me."

"You mean I can't even go back home?" I protested.

"I'm afraid not," he said. "They will probably escort you to the plane in handcuffs."

"What kind of bullshit is that?" I demanded. "Sounds like I am deported."

"That's *Gobernación* for you. The Federal Government, you know. Do you want me to buy a ticket for you? I can loan you the money and you can repay me when you're settled."

"Yes, yes. Anything, just please get me out of here! Buy me a ticket, to anywhere. Just get me out of here!"

By ten o'clock that same night, young Inspector Galvez was escorting me by taxi to the airport in handcuffs and trying again to get me to loan him $100. I said, "You must be joking!" By the time we arrived at the Airport, he was implying that he might refuse to hand me over to the pilot if

I did not "loan" him the money. When I still refused, he sought vengeance. On arriving at the departure gate, he flashed his badge and insisted on a receipt signed by the Captain of the aircraft before unlocking my handcuffs.

My fellow passengers had reason to regard me with suspicion. I had been living and sleeping in the same filthy clothing for eleven days. My beard resembled an over grown armpit. My hair looked like a haystack and my sneakers smelled like the city dump. I must have looked the perfect picture of an escaped convict. But I did not really care. I was just happy to get out of there and on my way home.

New York Revisited

The flight attendant hid me from view in the last row of seats on the plane, which I had all to myself. When the plane took off, I gave a hearty cheer. "Hooray!"

En route, everyone on the plane seemed able to sleep but me. For me, sleep was impossible. I had too much clutter in my mind. The recent turn of events did not portend well for my future. As far as I knew, I had lost my beloved home in Mexico, and I had no idea of what to expect when I arrived in New York City. My friend Arthur Agin had moved to Hawaii almost a year before and I myself had not been to New York for almost two years. Needless to say, I was very excited.

I retrieved the magnetic hide-a-key box from under the corner mailbox. When I opened the front door to 548 LaGuardia Place, I got a quick preview of what lay ahead. Of the six tiny mailboxes in the building's foyer, all were empty except for mine. My mailbox was stuffed and overflowing with junk mail. The tiny six-by-six foot entry hall was ankle-deep with junk mail, almost all of it written in Chinese or Korean and addressed to "O. Wen Lee." Amidst the mountain of junk mail, I noticed a few legitimate letters. On closer inspection, it turned out that all the letters came from a single address, the New York City Housing Authority.

I ascended the narrow stairway to my third-floor walkup apartment, fearing what news the letters might contain. Nevertheless, as I entered the door, I experienced that warm feeling of homecoming. In spite of standing vacant for almost a year, the apartment appeared just as I had remembered it.

I opened the windows to let in some fresh air. Suddenly the raucous, undulating screeches of my burglar alarm saturated the entire building. I had forgotten to turn it off when I entered. It was one of those things you had to turn off with a key within a certain time of entering or else it would awaken all the devils in hell. Both my Italian neighbors from next door and my gay neighbors from upstairs peeked warily into the narrow hallway. I fought frantically to subdue the screaming monster and finally just ripped it off of the wall. When I did so, I could hear the heavy breathing of my neighbors through the eerie and sudden silence.

"Owen? Is that you?" It was the voice of Tom Martin, my upstairs neighbor.

"Yes. It's me, Tom. I'm back. Please forgive me for the racket. I forgot about the burglar alarm."

"Good God, man, look at you! What's happened to you?"

"I'm just now arriving from Mexico." I said. "Invite me up for a drink, and I'll tell you all about it."

"Yes, yes. Ted is still asleep, but do come up a bit later in the day. We want to hear all about it. But right now, I'm really still asleep."

"I could use some sleep as well," I admitted.

After I closed the door, I noticed the silhouette of New York's skyline just emerging from the predawn darkness. I did a quick tour of the apartment, then I sat at my desk and tore open the letters. They were all the same — copies of an official eviction notice issued by the New York City Housing Authority. They ordered me to vacate the property within ninety days of September 15th, the date of issue. I checked the calendar in my wrist watch. It was October 8th. I had just over two months to go.

Out of curiosity, I looked up my listing in the New York City telephone directory. There, I discovered the cause of my predicament. My name had a typographical error in it. An empty space had been left between the O and the W in my first name and it appeared as "O Wen Lee." I reasoned that this not only precipitated the tell-tale flood of oriental junk mail, it also indicated my absence to the building's new owner.

The New York City Housing Authority was created during World War II to control rents and assure adequate wartime housing. However, the increases in rent that it allowed did not keep pace with the rapid increase in demand for housing. Rent-controlled apartments remained static while the value and maintenance costs of New York real estate spiraled out of control. Therefore, rent-controlled apartments became worth much more to the renter in savings than they were worth to the owners.

As a home owner myself, I could empathize with Frank Conti, the building's new owner. Without question, he deserved more rent. I intended to cooperate with Frank, if he elected to cooperate with me.

Please understand that I truly loved my apartment. For one thing, it was the ideal size for a single person or a couple. For another, it was ideally located in the heart of Greenwich Village. For a third, even although I rarely used it, it had served as my home base for over thirty-three years. My pad and I were synonymous in New York, just as the Nature

Study Center and I were synonymous in Zihuatanejo. Last but not least, it had given me the financial freedom to fly away and do my own thing. By relieving me of the burden of paying high rent, it became my ticket to adventure. Whenever I needed cash, I could always find a friend to sublet my apartment. Without my apartment, I could never have lived the way that I did.

When I first rented it in 1953, my rent was only $30 per month. Over the years, the rents were gradually allowed to rise. At that time, my rent was $250 per month, still only a fraction of its value on the New York City real estate market. I offered to pay Frank Conti $1,000 per month. Frank knew he could get more and so did I, but it was quick and easy and it put another $750 each month into Frank's pocket without any investment on his part.

I had spent over S30,000 remodeling the place, and I still had the receipts prove it. The least Frank should do, I thought, is pay me $10,000 for all my work and improvements. In fact, I would need that much to finance my return trip to Zihuatanejo. However, Frank did not share my sentiments. He was most anxious to get rid of me so he could raise the rent. Meanwhile, I was most anxious to maintain the status quo.

When Frank refused to pay me any "key money," we became competitors, squabbling over territory. I now felt compelled to win just for the sake of winning. On the advice of friends, I hired a lawyer to contest my eviction. My lawyer assured me that he could delay my eviction for at least another year, but not much longer. Eventually I would have to leave, but it would certainly improve my bargaining position with Frank.

I phoned Lillia and told her what had happened. She was relieved to hear that I was safe. When I departed, almost three weeks previously, I had told her that I would return the same day. Since then, she had not heard from me and was understandably worried. I told her that I intended to stay in New York until I resolved the apartment issue. She volunteered to come help. "I can ask my mother to look after the kids."

"I would be very grateful if you would come keep me company," I told her.

Before the week was out, Lillia was there and I don't know what I would have done without her. The year was 1987 and the United States economy was in recession. Prices were high and work was hard to find. I had hoped to find work with some of my old friends in advertising and TV production. Instead, I found myself at the end of a long line of recent graduates from the new NYU Film School. I could find nothing better than to drive a taxicab at night. I also sold lady's shoes at Macy's during the pre-Christmas shopping rush.

Meanwhile, Lillia had no trouble at all. She immediately secured a job through NYU as a housemaid and baby sitter for a couple of professors. They took her in and almost made her part of their family. In the process of teaching Spanish to their kids, Lillia rapidly became proficient in English. Soon, she was spending more time with them than she was spending with me. But that was just as well. I was preoccupied with my own employment problems and not in a very happy frame of mind.

Then, Helmut Liens stopped by to visit on his way from Frankfort back to Zihuatanejo. Helmut was the builder-owner of the *Hotel Villa del Sol* on La Ropa Beach, which is now acknowledged to be among the ten best boutique hotels in the world. In the course of commiserating over our respective projects, we had come to know and respect each other both as friends and colleagues.

When I told Helmut about my eviction from New York,

he kindly offered to loan me the money to return to Zihuatanejo. He also offered me the job as beach boy at his hotel. It was a timely and generous offer. However, I could not accept it.

"Not just yet," I said. "I now have two cases pending in courts and still no place to live. I think it best that I stay put, at least until one of my court cases is settled. If I win my case here in New York, it means I have to stay in New York City and abandon my dreams for a Nature Study Center in Zihuatanejo. If I lose, it means that I have to abandon my only home here in America for an uncertain future in Mexico. Until I resolve one or the other, I think I had better stay where I am. However, I would appreciat a rain check on your kind offer of a job when I get there."

"You've got it," Helmut assured me. Then he left for Zihuatanejo.

The next day I called my lawyer, but the news was not encouraging. "Frankly, your chances of avoiding eviction do not look good," he told me. "Unless you can negotiate a deal, he's going to win this case on the evidence alone. I advise you to negotiate or else proceed with "Plan B."

Mexican Consulate

My Plan B was to return to Zihuatanejo. But I was not even sure if I could legally do so. I understood that anyone deported from Mexico becomes a *persona non grata* and cannot return without first clearing his name. Having been put on an airplane in handcuffs, one would assume that I had been deported from Mexico. On the other hand, no charges had ever been filed against me. I had signed no forms or papers. Therefore, I doubted the validity of my removal. Furthermore, the peculiar behavior of my lawyer, Federico de Samaniego, made me suspect that he was conspiring with

Sanchez Mirus to get rid of me and take over my property. Therefore, I sought the advice of the Mexican Consulate in New York City.

The Mexican Consul was a short, vivacious little man dressed in a grey flannel suit with a burgundy tie on a blue shirt. His shiny bald pate emerged through a halo of silver white hair. He spoke perfect English and wore a pleasant smile as he talked. He seemed friendly and eager to help. As I told him my story, it dawned on me how preposterous it must sound. I feared he might question my veracity. When I mentioned the name of Alvaro Sanchez Mirus, however, his eyes lit up, and he raised his hand to cut me short.

"Wait a minute. What did you say his name was?" he asked.

I repeated the name, "Alvaro Sanchez Mirus."

The Consul drummed his fingers on his desk and said, "I think I know who you are talking about. In fact, I think we have a file on him." He rang for his secretary. "Does he live in Acapulco?"

"Yes, I think he used to," I said, "but right now he is living in Zihuatanejo."

When his secretary appeared, the Consul jotted the name on a note pad and gave it to her. "See if we have file on this man, Alvaro Sanchez Mirus." Then he turned to me. "We keep files on all Mexican citizens involved in cases with Americans. His name rings a bell."

We chatted about Zihuatanejo and Ixtapa. When his secretary reappeared, she gave the Consul a four-page computer printout. The Consul studied the pages intently. Suddenly he stopped and jabbed a forefinger onto one of the pages. "Yes. Yes! Here it is!" Silently, he read a bit more, paused and then turned to me. "He has been involved in three complaints of fraud and forgery, all involving Mexican real estate. According to this, he served time for forgery, but his brother intervened on his behalf. His brother is an inspector with *Gobernación*."

"Wow!" I exclaimed. "Isn't the Immigration Department part of *Gobernación*?" I asked.

"That's right, it is."

It all fell into place like the pieces of a jig saw puzzle. "Then it must have been his brother who issued my summons. That's how he got rid of me!" The Consul nodded and giggled triumphantly. "They took me to the airport in hand cuffs," I told him.

"Sounds like he used his brother's authority to get rid of you."

"Does that mean I was deported? Am I now a *persona non grata* in Mexico?"

"I don't know, but I can find out for you."

"Did you sign any papers when they released you?" he asked.

I shook my head no. "My lawyer arranged everything. But I am beginning to suspect that he and Alvaro worked in cahoots."

"It sounds like you are right."

"It does indeed! But why would he do that?"

"To take over your property, of course. That's big business now."

"Yes. That would explain everything."

"If that is the case," said the Consul, "I am almost certain that you were not officially deported. But I will fax Mexico City and let you know. Just give me a couple of days to investigate," he said.

"Meanwhile, would you permit me to read what they said about Sanchez Mirus?" I asked.

"Not at all," he assured me. "It's a matter of public record. I will give you a copy to take with you. I suggest you publish it in the local newspaper. Those kinds of people should be exposed to the public.

"How can I ever thank you?"

"No need to thank me. That's part of my job." I left the Mexican Consulate believing that there was a God after all.

A couple of days later I phoned the Consul for the results of his investigation. "Just as I thought," he said. "You were not officially deported. There is nothing on record about you anywhere in Mexico, including Immigration. You are now free return to Mexico whenever you please, no problems whatsoever."

The news triggered a rush of adrenalin that reddened my face. I was ecstatic and angry at the same time. I could not wait to tell Marshall Allen what I had learned about Sanchez Mirus so I went directly from the Consulate to his apartment on West 13th Street. I showed him the papers that the Mexican Consulate had given me. "Sanchez Mirus is nothing but a professional con artist," I warned him. "You've got to find somebody else to run El Capricho del Rey. Otherwise, he will find a way to take it from you."

Marshall simply shook his head. "When Arnoldo died, I gave the place back to the Veerboonen family and washed my hands of Mexico. Better that you go tell Sarah."

"But they complained that Sidney Adler, your lawyer, leased the Capricho for five years to Sanchez Mirus. They said he did it without their permission."

"Yes. I told Sidney to lease the hotel so that the family would get some income out of it. I did not screen the prospects."

"But don't you see? Sanchez Mirus is a professional con man. The Veerboonen family will never see a nickel from him!"

"Well, they should talk to Sidney Adler then. I don't want to hear about it. It only upsets me."

"And what about you?" I asked. "If I return to

Zihuatanejo, will I ever see you again?"

Marshall shook his head. "Never!" he said adamantly. "I'm finished with Mexico. If you want to see me, you'll have to come to New York."

I left Marshall feeling sad. For all his eccentricities, Marshall had been very good to me. By inviting me to live on his boat and by financing my down-payment for Las Gatas Beach property, Marshall had actually changed the course of my life. Difficult as he often was, I hated to lose him. Now, I felt that I might never see him again. And I did not.

The Eviction Notice

When I returned to my apartment, Frank Conti was standing outside with a local contractor. They were discussing the possibility of tuck-pointing the brick facade of the building. I saw this as a good opportunity to settle our differences, so I asked to talk to him when he finished. He agreed and so I went upstairs to await his arrival. Meanwhile, I hastily explained to Lillia what I had learned from the Mexican Consul and showed her the papers. Then I invited her to reconsider our options. "If you had your choice of spending the rest of your life here in New York City or on Las Gatas Beach in Zihuatanejo, which would you chose?"

After thinking it over she slowly answered, "Well, I love New York. There is so much going on, it is very exciting. But I don't think I would want to spend the rest of my life here. Maybe it is too much excitement. I think I would prefer to live in Zih and just visit New York."

After pondering her answer, I responded in kind. "I feel the just the same. Needless to say, I adore this little apartment. It has been my base for thirty-three years. But if it comes to having to choose one or the other, I vote for

Zihuatanejo."

On the basis of that short discussion, I had a new proposal ready when Frank later knocked on my door As Lillia served coffee, I got to the point.

"Mr. Conti, you must know by now that my lawyer is contesting your eviction suit against me at the New York City Housing Authority. He assures me that we can legally delay my eviction for up to a year. But I don't want to fight with you. As a landlord myself, I empathize with your position. On the other hand, I have a lot of time and money invested in this place. After thirty-three years here, I need both time and money to pack it all up and move out. Therefore, I have a new proposition for you."

"Good, let's hear it," Frank said.

"Instead of the $10,000 for the key and three months of time that I originally asked for — and deserved — I am willing to cut it right down the middle, to just $5,000 and six weeks."

Frank Conti only laughed. He knew he had me against the wall. "I don't have to pay you a gawddam penny," he bellowed. "The way I see it, both you and your stuff are out of here, and the sooner the better!"

"That's not what my lawyer tells me."

"Well then your lawyer is full of shit! The U.S. Marshals are standing by with a furniture van to take both you and your stuff to storage whenever I say the word."

"Come on!" I pleaded. "The only way you're going to get rid of me is to make it so I can afford to leave."

That seemed to hit home. He sat back in his chair and thought a moment. "I'll tell you what I'll do," he said soberly. "I'll give you $3,000 and a month to get out of my life forever."

I thought it over. "With half in advance," I added. "After all, I have to buy a car. They told me that I could buy a surplus van from Con Edison for $1,500."

"Then I want half in advance as well," he exalted. "$1,500 in advance but only two weeks more instead of four, OK?"

I shrugged my shoulders in defeat. "OK," I said.

"Then it's a deal!" He thrust out his hand and I shook it.

The next morning I picked up Frank's check and cashed it across the street. Then I headed for the garage in New Jersey where Con Edison, the utilities company, auctions off its surplus vans. The auction prices were ridiculously low. I bought a four-year old Dodge utility van for only $1,200, then I drove it to a garage to have it serviced for the long trip back to Zihuatanejo. Once home, I told Lillia to sell everything she could, give away everything she could not, and start packing the rest into the van.

I lost the entire next day and a half to the process of legalizing, insuring and servicing the van. The remainder of those two weeks flew by with record speed. Meanwhile, New York City was never so alluring. Now that I had to leave, it seemed to sparkle with promise, and I loved it as never before. Despite the fact that my Big Apple was now forbidden fruit, I could not bear the idea of leaving it. As the deadline relentlessly approached, I pleaded with Frank for just a few more days. But he stubbornly refused.

"A deal is a deal!" he said, adamantly.

The next morning, I phoned my lawyer again. It was my last-ditch effort to find some legal loophole that could buy me more time. However, he just got annoyed. "I already told you, it's hopeless. You're wasting your time," he scolded. Then I took the subway to 34th Street to pick up my final pay check from Macys.

When I returned to LaGuardia Place, I saw that a huge moving truck was parked in front of my apartment building. Four burly furniture movers sat idly on the open tailgate, smoking cigarettes and chatting. Then, I noticed the seal of the U.S. Marshall's Office on the car parked in front. It did not require a genius to figure out what was happening. I was in the process of being evicted.

I ran to the public telephone on the corner and phoned Lillia. "What's going on?" I asked her. "Are you alone?"

"Some people are out in the hall. They are trying to open the door, but I have it doubled-locked and bolted."

"Open the back window so I can enter from the fire escape," I said. "I will be right there."

I hung up, then dialed 911. "Somebody is trying to break into my apartment at 548 LaGuardia Place," I cried to operator. "Please send the police!"

Then I ran around the block to Sullivan Street and entered an alleyway that gave access to my fire escape. I climbed the filthy iron fire escape and entered my apartment through the rear window of my bathroom. Lillia came and kissed me. She was panting with fright and I tried to calm her down.

"There are some people out in the hallway," she whispered. "They are trying to get in."

I softly pressed my ear to the door. Somebody was tampering with the lock. I had an additional deadbolt lock on the inside of the door, so I knew we were safe. However, the lock picking annoyed me and a stand off was senseless. I chose to confront reality.

"Hello out there!" I called. "This is Owen. If anyone out there tries to break in, I will shoot through door."

I heard a cry and then the unmistakable voice of Frank Conti. "Go call the police." Then I heard footsteps running down the stairs.

"Mr. Owen, this is John Murphy of the U.S. Marshall's Office," came a voice of authority. "You have failed to comply with a U.S. Marshall's order to vacate this property, and I am here with Mr. and Mrs. Conti to take possession of it by order of the U.S. Marshall's Office." He paused to clear this throat, then continued. "Now, we're not looking for any trouble, Mr. Owen. We are just here to uphold the law. I have the order right here in my hand."

"We have a truck and movers here to put your things in safe storage," said Frank Conti through the door."

"Frank, just slide the $1,500 you owe me under the door," I answered, "and you can have your apartment, just as we agreed."

"I don't owe you anything, Owen. You didn't comply with the terms of our agreement, so I don't owe you a thing."

"So I'm two days late! After paying the rent for thirty three years, you won't give me two more days to wrap things up?"

"Mr. Lee, please come out with your hands clasped over your head so we can talk," the U.S. Marshall said through the door.

"That is not necessary. Mr. Conti and I made an agreement, and now he wants to avoid paying because I am a few hours late."

No sooner had I said it, then I heard the foyer door burst open and a clatter of feet come bounding up the narrow stairway. It was a squad car full of police. They were answering my call for help. However, the U.S. Marshall had also called the police. Therefore, he thought that the police were answering his call for help, not mine. The resulting confusion was solved only by the timely arrival of the second squad of police in answer to the Marshall's call for help. All this took some time to sort out. Meanwhile, all this commotion attracted the attention of my next door and upstairs neighbors. Both neighbors owned dogs which now leapt into the fray with frantic barking and baying. As the crowd tried to sort things out, the hallway became a din.

I could not resist the urge to see it for myself so I pounded on the door and shouted, "SILENCE!" It suddenly fell as silent as a morgue, so I continued. "All right!" I said. "I am going to open the door and come out with my hands on my head, so please don't shoot or anything!"

The silence continued as I methodically unbolted the double-locked door. Then I stepped back, clasped my hands on top of my head and motioned for Lillian. As she swung the door open, an expectant hush fell over the crowd. For what seemed an eternity, we confronted each other in tense silence. The scene that greeted me in the narrow hallways was so ludicrous, hoever, that I could not restrain the urge to laugh. Both the hallway and the two stairways were scarcely three feet wide, yet squeezed into these cramped confines were the U.S. Marshall and his young assistant, Mr. and Mrs. Franck Conti, their twenty year-old son Rodney, and his sister Clair. Then came my squad car full of policemen from the sixth precinct, followed by the Marshall's squad car full of policemen from the second precinct. Finally, there were my four Italian neighbors from across the hall and their two howling basset hounds, plus the two gay actors upstairs with their two hysterical toy poodles. It was indeed ridiculous, and I could not stop laughing.

"What's so gawddam funny?" demanded police sergeant in charge.

"It reminds me of the overcrowded stateroom scene in the Marx Brother's film, *A Night at the Opera*."

"Oh, yeah? Well, what's going on here? What's your story?"

"The only reason all you guys are here is because Mr. Conti here refuses to pay me the measly $1,500 he owes me as key money for this apartment, so I can actually afford to leave. Because I am a couple of days late in leaving my home of thirty-three years, Mr. Conti says he doesn't owe me thing. The truth is that we can't leave unless he pays me the $1,500 that he promised. We need the money to buy the gasoline, otherwise, we can't leave!"

"Is dis true?" demanded the sergeant in his New York accent. "Is dis for sure, what he's sayin'?" He glared scornfully at Mr. Conti. "If dats the case, then just pay da man his money and let's all go home." The others grumbled a chorus of approval. Some of the cops began to drift down the stairs and out the door, but the sergeant in charge held Mr. Conti in his accusing glare until he responded.

Frank Conti shook his head in resignation and reached into his jacket. "Oh, all right," he moaned. With obvious reluctance, he withdrew his checkbook from the inside pocket of his blazer and wrote out a check, using the Sergeant as a desk. "Here you go," he said. He ripped the check from the book and handed it to me. I fluttered it overhead like a trophy and the police gave a cheer of approval.

"Now, let's all go home," the leader said, and the crowd began to file down the narrow stairs and out into the street.

"Now I hope I've seen the last of you!" Frank Conti said as he offered his hand.

"While I go to the bank to cash this check, how about asking your furniture movers to help me load what's left into my van," I asked. "That way, we can be gone before nightfall."

Frank Conti complied and so did we. Thus, Lillia and I embarked on our return to Paradise.

Return to Paradise

Ten days of monotonous driving took us through the endless tracts of corn and wheat of the Midwest, through the dry plains of Texas to the border town of Laredo, then down through the twisting turns of the Sierra Madre Mountains and, at last, to the welcoming banks of Zihuatanejo Bay.

However, it was not the same as when I left it. For starters, Hurricane Edna had recently passed by leaving the entire area looking like a war zone. Storm debris and fallen trees still littered the countryside. Loose *palapa* leaves lay everywhere and gaping holes yawned through the roofs.

We arrived at Zihuatanejo's pier well after midnight. We were not really hoping to find transportation to Las Gatas Beach waiting for us, but we were pleasantly surprised. I recognized Jean Claude's dive boat, which was tied to the landing. Somebody was curled up on the deck, fast asleep. I did not hesitate to awaken him. It was Chamino, the instructor for Jean Claude's dive shop on Las Gatas Beach. Chamino explained that Jean Claude had accompanied friends to *El Coyote*, one of the local cabarets just outside of town. I explained that we had just arrived from the New York and needed a ride. Chamino helped us bring aboard a couple of our most important bags, then I parked the car and returned to the boat. It was comforting to be so warmly welcomed.

Jean Claude arrived within twenty minutes and the boat carried us across the Bay on the last leg of our journey. As we motored through the water, it left a luminescent trail in its wake. A three-quarter moon laid down a silvery highway that lit our way. My pulse quickened as the peak of my restaurant emerged into view, silhouetted against the night sky. Once ashore on Las Gatas Beach, Chamino used Jean Claude's flashlight to lead us through the trashed ruins of my bungalows to Leonardo's little brick house next door that Lillia and I had rented. To my great relief it was just as we had left it. We did not even bother to change the sheets. We simply shook them out to dislodge any scorpions, then let them settle down on top of us. It was great to be back home!

The next day we surveyed the damage inflicted by the recent hurricane. The entire roof of both my restaurant and my house had "gone with the wind." Only a few patches of *palapa* still clung to the wooden skeletons of the roofs and loose *palapa* leaves covered much of the ground. The mattresses were all soaking wet from the wind-driven rain. There was still no light or water in the village, however, our brick house was still in tact.

Don Sebastian, the replacement armed guard and his family were hunkered down in the one dry room in the bungalow called the Hotel California. He seemed pleased to see us. He even helped us unload the van and settle back into our rented house. Since none of the houses were functional, his presence seemed almost redundant. He complained bitterly that Sanchez Mirus had not paid him for months, so I paid him fifty dollars to help clean up the grounds and burn the trash.

After a few days rest, I walked the rocks to La Ropa Beach and went to see Helmut Liens at the Hotel Villa del Sol. Helmut kindly repeated his kind offer to let me work off some money he had loaned me back in New York City. Thus, at 65, I became one of the world's oldest beach boys.

My job was to rent and maintain the hotel's water sports equipment. This included thirty life vests, twenty sets of snorkeling gear, two sixteen-foot sailing catamarans, one inboard-outboard water-ski boat, and a half-dozen wind surfs whose fluttering sails served as a colorful billboard.

I loved my job. It kept me near the water and my mind off my frustrations with Sanchez Mirus. However, it was not easy. Helmut had the Germanic penchant for order and perfection, which sometimes butted heads against the local penchant for empty promises.

I learned a lot from Helmut. He was professional in every sense of the word. Starting with just a few rooms and a bar in the middle of La Ropa Beach, Helmut built his Hotel Villa del Sol into one of the ten best luxury hotels in the world. In the process, Helmut revealed a great deal about perfectionism and professionalism. “It’s not only what you do,” he insisted, “it’s also how you do it.”

Months later, when rebuilding my bungalows on Las Gatas Beach, I tried to follow Helmut’s example and discovered how difficult it was to maintain high standards.

For the most part, I loved my job. I loved turning people on to Mother Nature and the ocean. It kept me young in both my mind and body. It also provided me with enough time and money to continue my fight for my beloved center on Las Gatas Beach.

Public Relations

Recalling the advice that the Mexican Consul had given me in New York City, I went to see the owner-editor of *El Diario de Zihuatanejo*, the town’s only newspaper. *El Dario* subsided on muckraking, and every day the editor published some minor scandal to help sell his tabloid. From two enormous loudspeaker horns strapped to the top of his battered old VW Beetle, he broadcast its headlines throughout the entire village. At full volume, there was no escaping its urgent message. *El Diario* was the most effective medium of communications and public relations in Zihuatanejo.

The owner-editor of the paper was fascinated by my story. The information that the Mexican Consulate had furnished was especially enticing. He agreed to run an expose on Sanchez Mirus as a series of front-page news articles but charge me only inside advertising space rates, a journalistic practice that was common among small town newspapers. Like everything else, the news itself was on sale.

Within days, the once-bright image of Colonel Alvaro Sanchez Mirus began to tarnish. People discovered that he had never been a lawyer nor a jet pilot in the Mexican Air Force as he had claimed. He was simply a cheap imposter who been jailed for forgery and fraud. That meant that his confidence game was now a matter of public record, and the entire community was quick to respond. People who once curried his favor now shunned his presence. Police and politicians who once paid him fearful respect, now pretended they never knew him.

Even old Don Sebastian, the armed guard whom Sanchez Mirus had put into my home with orders to shoot me if I tried to return, turned against him. He joined three other unpaid former employees and filed a labor arbitration suit against Sanchez Mirus for many thousands of pesos.

To everyone's surprise, Sanchez Mirus never challenged the veracity of the newspaper stories, which only increased their impact. At the same time, Sarah Veerboonen challenged Sanchez Mirus in court over ownership of the Hotel El Capricho del Rey. Sanchez Mirus claimed ownership of the hotel based on another phony document. Sarah hired a legal hand-writing expert who testified that it was forged. Since Sarah was the popular daughter of Don Salvador Espino, esteemed as one of Zihuatanejo's founding fathers and the town's first elected mayor, the entire community knew Sarah's story and supported her cause. This substantiated my own story and further turned the local residents against Sanchez Mirus.

At first, he simply lost his credibility. Then the local tour operators boycotted his nightly dinner tours to the Hotel El Capricho del Rey. Without any income, his debts mounted. Swarms of debtors hounded him for money.

When the Judge awarded the Hotel El Capricho del Rey back to Sarah Veerboonen, hundreds celebrated her victory. However, Sanchez Mirus proved true to his rotten character to the bitter end. Instead of withdrawing from the scene as gracefully as possible, he armed a gang of laborers with heavy sledge hammers and ordered them to destroy the Hotel El Capricho del Rey. The workmen did their job with such uncharacteristic skill that all six of the elegant bungalows were no longer functional and had to be demolished. That dastardly act of vengeance seemed to seal his fate.

One night, under cover of darkness, Sanchez Mirus simply vanished. Twenty years later, still speculate about what became of him. Some say that he was murdered by one of his many victims. Others claim that he murdered a diver who was filching oysters in from the shallows in front of his seaside home in Acapulco, and that he now languishes in jail. Whatever the truth be, Sanchez Mirus was the closest thing to a nemesis that ever entered my life. For me and for Sarah Veerboonen's family, Sanchez MIrus personified evil in its most cynical form; creating only to destroy, promising only to deceive and helping only to steal. If there is any substance to the idea of divine justice, Sanchez Mirus must be rotting in hell right now. And good riddance!

For both me and for Sarah, the departure of Sanchez Mirus signaled a major turning point in our lives. At last the frustrating nightmare of lies and deception was over. For the first time in almost four years, our respective properties were free of any threat of violence. After years of anguish and frustration, we now had safe access to our own homes and our own lives. Nevertheless, we were both so exhausted by the experience that the consequences lingered long after. While continuing to manage Chez Arnoldo, the family's restaurant on Las Gatas Beach, Sarah Veerboonen seemed able to witness the demolition of the Hotel El Capricho del Rey with calm resignation. For me however, the worst was still to come.

The wounds that Sanchez Mirus had inflicted on my mind continued to fester like an open sore. I felt that Sanchez

Mirus had violated not just me, but my entire family. My parents had saved and sacrificed throughout their entire lives in order to bequeath to me all that they possibly could. Had I followed their advice and invested my inheritance in American real estate, I might possibly have been a millionaire by now. Instead, I squandered it all on the romantic notions of a renegade romantic. My hate for Sanchez Mirus poisoned my mind and corrupted my soul. I could not shake my burden of guilt and resentment. All things Mexican were now suspect to me, even my beloved on Las Gatas Beach.

A Fresh Start

The temptation to move into my house was almost irresistible. However, my new lawyer, Don Ramon Vasquez, strongly advised me against it. “If you attempt to reclaim your house while your case is still pending in the court, you will almost surely lose your case,” he warned.

My heart sank in resignation. “Then what do you suggest I do?”

“Your first goal is to get your case out of the court, win or lose,” he said.

“And what if I lose?”

“Then we appeal your case to a higher court,” he answered. “But you can live in your house while your appeal is pending.”

“After all I have been through, that’s not fair.”

“I know it’s not fair,” Don Ramon conceded, “but that’s the law, and we have to respect it.”

“How much money are we talking about?”

Don Ramon reflected a moment before answering. “My base fee for an appeal is 2,500 pesos plus expenses.”

“And how much time are we talking?”

"It shouldn't take more than a year, maybe two at most."

"Let me think it over and I will let you know," I said.

At this point, I had neither the money nor the patience to enter into an extended legal battle with Sanchez Mirus. My faith in Mexican justice was now shattered beyond redemption. For me, all lawyers were part of a special breed of people who speak a special language and follow a special code of ethics all their own. They seemed to excel in creating work for each other at the expense of their clients.

Personally, I think that if all men were honorable, man-made laws would be useless and superfluous. If a man is not honorable, no amount of *juris prudence* can ever make him otherwise. Man's laws, like his concept of time, often have little to do with reality. Unlike the laws of Nature, man-made laws are often self-serving abstractions and interpretations of consensual ideas. When enough people buy into the same belief or interpretation, even lies can become laws. Nazi Germany evolved out of such illusions. Our current ecological crisis is growing out of such illusions. Thus, man made laws are not always wise or effective. They tend to change from time to time and from place to place, depending on local beliefs and circumstances. I suspect that lawyers evolved for the sole purpose of translating man-made laws into logic and reason.

As lawyers go, Don Ramon seemed as honorable as any. Had I had the money to pay him, I might have hired him on the spot. Unfortunately, however, I was flat-ass broke. Nor could I see any hope for help in the immediate future. In fact, I was still working off my travel debt to Helmut. Therefore, I had to invent some other way to solve my problems.

I was in no big hurry, however. Between the neglect of Sanchez Mirus and the fury of Hurricane Edna, the entire property was now a shambles. It would require thousands of dollars and perhaps years of hard labor to make the place functional again. Meanwhile, the sturdy brick house next door where Lillia and I were now living was comfortable and functional. We were quite content to stay where we were, at least until I could get my case out of court. Since I could not afford to pay a lawyer to do it for me, I had no choice but to do it myself.

Courthouse Caper

The judge presided in a brand new court house located behind the headquarters of the Judicial Police. I went there about ten o'clock one morning, but there was no one there except a single armed guard. I sat down to wait and after a few minutes a male clerk appeared. He carried a stack of dossiers about a foot high. He placed the stack on a cluttered desk and made no acknowledgement of my presence. Fingering through the stack of dossiers, he extracted three folders from the pile and set them aside. Each folder had been clearly marked with a red pencil.

To my surprise, the clerk extracted a sheath of bills from each dossier he had set aside. Then he counted the money and recorded the sum in a mini ledger book. Finally, he placed the money in a metal cash box which he then settled in the middle drawer of his desk. He placed the three marked dossiers on top of the stack. That done, he leaned back in his chair and read a copy of *El Diario*. The clerk was clearly selling priority consideration to those clients who were wise enough and willing enough to pay for it.

This did not bode well for me. If a client could pay the clerk to get top priority on the court's docket, it was reasonable that one could also pay the clerk to keep his case *off* of the court's docket. I concluded that Sanchez Mirus had been paying the clerk to do the latter. What else could account for such a long delay in getting a hearing of my case The idea that I had been duped once more by Mexico's self-serving legal system made me furious. I felt my face flush and heard that familiar ringing in my ears. Since I was already hopelessly destitute, I figured that I had nothing to lose if I confronted the judge directly. Therefore, I introduced myself to the clerk and asked if he could tell me about the status of my case. The clerk pretended to know nothing about it and suggested that I consult my lawyer.

"But I filed the act almost three years ago!" I protested. "You have been accepting money from Alvaro Sanchez Mirus to keep my case off of the court's docket. Is that not so?"

The clerk did not take my accusation lightly. His face flushed and summoned a guard to escort me from the building. I refused to leave and demanded to see the judge. At that moment, as if on cue, the judge suddenly appeared in the doorway behind me.

"This *gringo* is accusing us of accepting bribes," the clerk complained to the judge.

I was astounded to see that the judge was a young woman, perhaps in her late thirties, and a rather good looking one at that. Her name was Virginia Martinez. "Good day," she said tersely. "How can we help you?"

I explained that I had been waiting for a hearing on my case against Sanchez Mirus for almost three years and suspected that my opponent had been paying her court clerk to keep my case off of the court's docket. As I spoke, I saw her face cloud up and feared the storm that was coming.

"I don't know what you are talking about," she assured me, "but I know that you can not come in here, accusing us of taking bribes and expect to win your case."

"*Esta bien*! That's OK," I retorted. "Win or lose, I just want to get my case out of your court. I need to get on with my life."

With that, the judge seemed to mellow a bit. "Do you have the docket number?" she asked.

I gave her the copy of my complaint which she then gave to the clerk. "Go see if you can find this file," she ordered. The clerk grudgingly complied. When he returned with the file, she instructed me to sit while she studied it. Within the hour, the judge dictated her verdict to her secretary and gave me what I wanted. It goes without saying that I lost my case. I had accomplished my mission, however. Having got my case out of the lower court, I could now live in my own home while I appealed the judge's decision to a higher court in the state capital of Chilpancingo.

Alternate Justice

By now I had lived in Mexico over eighteen years, and I had finally learned some of the fundamental requirements of local survival. For one thing, I learned that, as in most other counties of the world, Mexican justice almost always goes to the highest bidder. Therefore, I had little choice but to seek some alternate route to justice. Over the years, for example, I had observed that when all else failed, the right social and political contacts almost always produced positive results. Consequently, I embarked on a quest to find and befriend a Mexican national who had enough power, stature and political contacts to overpower those of my criminal opponent. However, this approach proved to be more than I bargained for. It swept me into the forbidding realm of egos and human values, all of which were subject to the peculiarities of the local environment.

I hung around the local politicians and socialites of Zihuatanejo like a backstage groupie at a rock concert. In spite of feeling very foreign and out of place, I jollied every politician I could corner with tales of my diving adventures with Captain Cousteau. But the results were hardly worth the trouble. The most influential candidate that I could find was Luis Figuerora, the teenage nephew of our state Governor.

Luis was a likeable young man and was duly impressed by my history with Captain Cousteau. I volunteered to teach him to SCUBA dive. Luis was quick to accept my offer and he was quick to learn. He was also quick to respond to my needs, so when at last he agreed to phone his uncle, I listened in on the conversation. Unfortunately, the governor brushed his nephew off with the usual Mexican promise, *mañana!*

Mañana, tomorrow, was hardly the caliber of entrée that I needed to enter into local society. Luis was much too much my junior to become close friends and much too far from his uncle's ear to have much influence. Therefore, I directed my search toward the professional world of my contemporary colleagues.

Jose Luna owned two very successful restaurants in Puerto Vallarta, and our mutual friends, Anna Bella and Francois, brought him to Las Gatas Beach to meet me one day. Jose loved the south sea island ambiance of my place, and we hit it off very well. He strolled among the palm trees and sunbathers, singing love songs to the sea in a resonant baritone voice. He liked my concepts and I liked his style. Before long, Jose made me an offer, just as I had hoped he would. He offered to fix my place up and run it, but he offered to pay me only ten percent of its income.

Had I known then what I know now, I would have instantly accepted his offer. I had since learned that ten percent of a restaurant's gross income often exceeds eighty percent of its net income. However, naive as I was at that time, I found his offer to be impossibly stingy. To my lasting regret, I rejected the offer. Instead, I went to Mexico City to romance the big city folks. To help me in my mission, I enlisted the aid of my longtime friend, Nora Beteta.

Nora was the beautiful blond daughter of Don Ramon Beteta. He had served as the minister of finance during the progressive administration of President Miguel Aleman in the late 1950s. Her uncle Mario Beteta was, even then, the presiding Mayor of Mexico City. Thus, I surmised that the Beteta family was politically correct and very well connected.

And that they were. However, Nora herself was the sole exception. Nora had long ago abandoned the high society of her family for the more "liberated lifestyle" of an eccentric artist. Nora was noble, beautiful, friendly, charming, and most willing to help me any way she could. However, Nora had alienated all those in her family who could possibly have helped me. Because she disowned them, her own family now disowned her and seemed reluctant to have anything to do with her. She was virtually a *persona non grata* within her own family circle, and I soon abandoned the idea of using her as my entrée into Mexican society. However, I did not give up on Nora, herself.

In fact, I found Nora's liberated free-wheeling lifestyle much to my liking, so I joined her bohemian entourage of artistic friends. It was exciting and exhilarating to be around her. She surrounded herself with interesting people and flaunted her independence to the world. She loved to test the limits of other people's tolerance and, though she sometimes exceeded the limits of good taste when drunk, she was always honest, loving and kind.

The results were sometimes for the better and sometimes for the worse, but always fun. For instance, we both loved to dance, so we often danced the night away is some anonymous club or disco. It seemed only natural that we also sleep together, so we did. She sometimes even invited others to join us. So, even though Nora failed to produce the contacts I needed to redeem my Nature Study Center, she fed me, gave me a place to live, did volunteer work for the Nature Study Center, rallied the support of her friends, and even shared with me her gorgeous body. Furthermore, she did it all with love, joy and respect. In short, Nora was not only a true eccentric, she was a true friend and remains so to this day.

Nevertheless, we both knew from the start that our party could not last. Nora was scheduled to depart on a long-planned trip to Egypt with another lover, whom she later married. Meanwhile, I had yet to resolve my unfinished business in Zihuatanejo.

Nora's departure for Egypt left me to face my problems alone, and I did not like what I saw. Without Nora's hospitality and support, I knew I could not last long in Mexico City. I simply could not afford it. Yet, I could not bring myself to return to Zihuatanejo without some hope for a solution to my problems. I moved into the Maria Christina, a cheap but comfortable hotel downtown, to buy some time and plan my next move.

In the solitude of my hotel room, I did a lot of thinking about my life in general and about Sanchez Mirus in particular. As far as I could see, the first was a shambles because of the second. Since the day he entered my life, Sanchez Mirus had occupied virtually all my waking thoughts and energy. In spite of three years of effort to recuperate my beloved property, he was still in possession and control of it.

Now I was broke and desperate. The thought of returning to the same frustrations I had left in Zihuatanejo was repulsive. I remember lying in bed thinking, *If only I could wave a magic wand and make him vanish!*

One night at a party, I found myself in conversation with a

table full of anonymous people. I told them about Captain Cousteau and my Nature Study Center in Zihuatanejo. I also told about my frustrations in dealing with Sanchez Mirus. To my surprise, one of them volunteered the ultimate solution.

"Forget about the Mexican courts," he advised me. "Why don't you just go out and hire a hit man?"

I laughed at the absurdity. "Is there some temporary employment agency that handles killers?" I asked facetiously.

"No, but they are around," he assured me. "Believe me, they are easy to find."

I did not pursue the matter any further while at the table. Later, however, I saw him alone on the terrace and dared to ask him, "If I wanted to find one of those hit men you mentioned, where should I begin to look? Do I run an ad in the Help Wanted section of the newspaper?"

"No. You don't look for them. You let them look for you."

"How does one do that?"

He looked at me askance. "You are serious, aren't you?"

"Well, if there is no other way to justice, it's the court of last resort!"

"If you are serious, I really can't help you. However, I know a guy who can put you in contact with someone."

"Can you give me his name or phone number?"

"No. But if you give me yours, I will ask him to call you."

"Room 203 at the Hotel Maria Christina," I said.

"Write it down and I'll tell him to phone you."

I did as he suggested and immediately regretted it. I had never wished harm on anybody, least of all death. Nevertheless, the possibility of simply erasing Sanchez Mirus from my life was darkly intriguing. Also, I was morbidly curious to meet a professional killer. Outside of the military, I had never met one. What do they look like? What makes them different from the rest of us? How might a meeting effect me? I shuttered to think about it and tried to push it out of my mind. After all, it was only an idea. Even if a killer did call, I did not have to hire him. Until I actually paid the man, I could always say no.

To my great consternation, however, my morbid curiosity did not have to wait long for fulfillment. The very next day I received a phone call from a man who refused to identify himself. When I asked, "Who's calling please?"

He got straight to the point. "*Alguien me dijo que tienes una problema que necessita una solution,*" he said. "Somebody told me that you have a problem that needs a solution."

"Oh yes? Who was that?"

"Somebody. I forget who. Were you not talking about your problem to somebody just yesterday?"

"Well, yes, I was."

"*Pues, resolvando problemas, eso es mi negocio*," he said. "Well, solving problems is my business."

"Do you think you can solve my problem?" I asked.

"I can't tell you on the phone. If you want to solve your problem, you must come and talk to me in person. Bring a picture. Also bring money in cash."

My heart began to pound, but my curiosity got best of me. "Where and when?" I asked.

"Tonight at ten o'clock. I will wait for you in the new commercial center on the corner of *Calle Ignacio* and *Eke Cinco*. It is still under construction. Kiosk number L-20 at ten o'clock. Don't forget the picture and the cash," he added. "Kiosk L-20 at ten."

I hung up the phone, but my heat went on pounding. I looked at my watch. It was 4:30, still plenty of time to change my mind. The mere idea was repulsive. But I was intrigued at the same time. Despite my reluctance to get involved, I determined that I should go. *This might be the only chance you will ever have.* I told myself. *For sure it's scary, but it might be the only opportunity that you will ever have. Better do it while you can!* I steeled myself for the adventure and arrived at the designated commercial center just before ten.

The commercial center was still under construction, just as he had said. There was just enough ambient light to see that it was to be a gigantic shopping mall. The kiosks would soon be filled with merchandise and bustling with shoppers. For now, however, it was a ghostly complex of empty buildings. A foreboding air of melancholia hung over the darkened buildings like a cloak. A brief shower around dusk had left behind large puddles of water, converting the future parking lot into a quagmire of mud There was not another soul in sight.

Rounding a corner of a building marked "L," a single light bulb pierced the darkness from a distant kiosk at the end of a long corridor. I saw the lonely figure of a heavy set man in a dark top coat and a broad-brimmed hat He was hunched over a wooden table, reading a newspaper in dim circle of light from a single-necked bulb that hung from the ceiling.

As I approached, the man looked up from his paper revealing a swarthy, round mustachioed face with fat, sagging jowls. The odorless stench of a rotten soul seem to ooze from his massive body. "*Usted debe ser el hombre con una problema,*" he said as I approached. "You must be the man with a problem."

He extended his right arm and I shook a handful of fat pudgy fingers. Then he motioned me to sit in the single metal folding chair. There was no other furniture in the room.

"Yes," I said. "I guess that's me." I felt sick and apprehensive in his presence. I was afraid I might vomit.

He leaned back in his chair and clasped his hands over his copious belly. "*Pues, te costare tres mill dollars para resolvar tu problema,*" he said flatly. "It will cost you three thousand dollars to resolve your problem."

His directness hit me smack in the face. I was stunned by the stark simplicity of it all. Sanchez Mirus notwithstanding, it was the only time in my life I have ever sensed the presence of pure evil. Frantically I tried to speak, but all I could do is stutter, "You, you, you, you, ma, ma, mean to, to, to…"

"*Te costare tres mil dollars para resolvar tu problema*," he repeated.

I tried once more, but the words refused to leave my mouth. "Ya, yes. You, you, ma, mean tha, tha, that you will ka, ka, ka…"

"*Te costare tres mill dollars para resolvar tu problema*," he said once again.

The stutter was back. "Wa, wa, well, I, I…"

"*Entregaste el foto y el dinero contigo?"* he demanded. "Did you bring the photograph and the money with you?"

Suddenly I saw my way out. My voice returned to normal. "No, no photo. I forgot it." I said crisply. "*No foto*." I repeated. "And no money, *no effectivio*! I need go to a bank. Money *mañana*, tomorrow. *El foto tambien*." I was immensely grateful for the excuse he had loaned me.

The killer shook his head in despair. "*Te dijo para entregarme un foto."* he scolded me. He shook his head with exasperation. "I told you to bring a photograph."

"Wa, wa, wa, well…"

"*Pues como quieres que yo puedo reconoscerle*?" He demanded. "Then, how do you expect me to recognize him?"

"Wa, wa, well…" I was still hopelessly tongued tied. Finally, I hunched my shoulders and lifted the open palms of my hands in helplessness.

"*Pues, buscame el foto y el dinero y te llamare de nuevo mañana,*" he said. "Then find me a photograph of him and I will phone you again tomorrow."

"Right!" I exclaimed. "*De acuerdo*!" I hopped to my feet, shook his pudgy hand and beat a hasty retreat through the door and into the mud. Outside a fresh drizzle permeated the night air, but I felt dirty and ashamed. As soon as I was out of his sight, I vomited on the mud. Then I ran to Ignacio Street and hailed a taxi. I felt as though I had just escaped from the devil himself.

Needles to say, I did not wait for the killer's call. I asked the taxi to wait while I packed my things, then caught a midnight bus to Zihuatanejo. On board the bus, I wondered, *Have I lost my mind?* Looking back on my behavior for the past three months, I honestly questioned my own sanity. Here I was, pushing seventy years old, homeless and broke, and ready to kill somebody! Furthermore, I was returning to a dysfunctional relationship that did not make sense. Is that not truly insane? I determined to seek more therapy as soon as I could afford it.

Return Again

I arrived in Zihuatanejo with mixed emotions. On one hand, I was elated at the prospect of being reunited with my beloved home, even though it was still not livable. On the other hand, I was saddened at the prospect of having to face Lillia and her kids. I had been gone for too long for Lillia to not feel hurt and very neglected. I felt guilty and ashamed for the way I had treated her, or rather ignored her. As with Becky, what had started as a straight-forward relationship of convenience had evolved into a relationship of mutual love and respect. The adventures that Lillia and I had shared in New York and Acapulco served to strengthened our bonds.

Yet, unlike Becky, Lillia was not as sexual or as affectionate as I would have liked. Sex never happened except as an afterthought. Furthermore, she was the mother of three active boys, all mired in the quagmire of the normal teenage neurosis.

When the family was all together, I felt totally foreign and out of place. They talked incessantly regarding mundane trivia in a rapid-fire Spanish that I could not follow. Their diet was heavy with tortillas, meats and beans, none of which I cared for. The A.M. radios worked incessantly at maximum volume. There were many other differences as well. Consequently, I spent most of my time in voluntary isolation. Now I found something new to consider.

During my sojourn in Mexico City, I visited the Department of Immigration and Foreign Relations to investigate my true prospects of acquiring Mexican citizenship and, thus, the legal right to own my property in Zihuatanejo. To my dismay, they informed me that dual nationality was still against the law. Even if I married Lillia, I could not become a Mexican citizen unless I renounced my American Citizenship. That meant that I would also forfeit all my social security and veteran's benefits. This revelation put our relationship into an entirely different context. Considering our differences, such a marriage did not make sense. On the other hand, I truly loved Lillia and I certainly did not want to hurt her. It troubled me that I could not offer her a substantial cash settlement. The least she deserved was the where-with-all to live a decent family life in a place of her own. For days, I anguished over how I could end our relationship without leaving Lillia and her family feeling abandoned. However, I need not have worried. Thankfully, Lillia spared me the necessity of doing so, by ending our relationship herself.

With few other options before me and with the new tourist

season fast approaching, I had decided to return by bus to Zihuatanejo and resume my job at the Hotel Villa del Sol. On arriving on Las Gatas Beach, however, I was dismayed by what I found. Even though I had paid a worker in advance to clean it up, the whole place was still a shambles from Hurricane Edna. On entering our rented house, I was further dismayed to find that Lillia was not even there. In fact, it appeared as if no one had been there for several weeks. On the kitchen table, beneath a plastic bottle of moldy catsup, I found a hand written-note from Lillia that read:

Bienvenido, Owen!
I am staying with a friend in Ixtapa and working in a restaurant. Please phone me at this number when you arrive: 554-3797.
Love, Lillia

Las Gatas Beach had no phones, so I walked the beach back to the public boat landing and caught a taxi boat across the Bay. When I phoned Lillia's number, a man answered. The man was Stanley Tharp, an American commodities broker from Chicago. I had met him before, but I could not remember where. After a brief chat, Stanley called Lillia to the phone, and she seemed pleased hear from me. When the salutations were done, I asked, "Where are you? What's going on?"

"Why don't we meet at the Sirena Gorda Restaurant and I'll tell you all about it." As soon as she sat down at the restaurant, she said, "I guess you are wondering where I have been?"

"I guess you have been wondering the same thing about me," I answered. "I hope you are feeling as good as you look."

"I didn't know what happened to you. I am glad to see

you are all right."

"I am sorry I kept you waiting. I admit that I have neglected you. I am very sorry, but I was surprised to come back to an empty house."

"I was afraid to stay there alone. I have been living at Stanley's house in Ixtapa."

"With or without Stanley in it?"

"With," she replied flatly. A long pause ensued while I digested the implications. Then she continued, "You always said I should get myself a lover," she said defensively, "so I took your advice."

"Yes, true. I sure did. Well, I can't say that I am surprised. I think that we both saw this coming." I saw a tear glistening in the corner of her eye. "Yes, well, we have been together over two years now, and…"

"And nothing!" Lillia interjected. "I think you never want to marry anybody, least of all me. You were always going off looking for somebody else. Well, I hope you find her!"

"But that was for business," I parried. "I was looking for investors for my business."

"What investors? What business?"

"Well, that's just it! You know perfectly well that I don't have the money to put the place back together again. I have to find a partner, an investor or something. I can't possibly do it alone."

"And suppose you find one? What about me?"

"Well, yes, that's right. You know that I love you, and I certainly don't want to hurt you. But I don't think that we are exactly made for each other. Do you?"

"Well, maybe not. But you know I love you, too."

"Yes, but you have your own life with your family. And I learned that even if we got married, I would still have to renounce my American citizenship in order to become a Mexican citizen. Isn't that stupid?"

"And would you actually do that? Renounce your citizenship to marry me?" She shook her head. "I don't think so."

"No." I conceded. "I don't think so either. It would mean giving up my social security pension, my veteran's benefits and everything else."

"Then where does that leave me?"

"Well, where are you now? With Stanley, right? Does Stanley love you?"

"Yes, Owen, I think he does. And I think I love him as well."

"And your children?" I asked. "Does he love them?"

She shrugged her shoulders. "He tolerates them, just like you did. So I sent them to live with my mother in Caretaro."

"They are nice kids," I said. I felt a painful lump growing my in throat. Lillia and I had been through so much together, it was hard to imagine life without her. Still, our relationship had always been more about mutual convenience than about real attraction. We loved each other dearly as friends, but we were not really lovers. Those soft caresses, those long kisses, that divine union of two bodies and souls never happened. Still, our shared adventures bonded our friendship together like mortar. We were fellow travelers on the road to eternity. We had made an honorable pact that could not be honored, but we loved each other nonetheless

"If you and Stanley truly love each other, that is perfect," I said. "I hope you both cherish and nurture your relationship."

"Yes, I think we do," Lilia said. "So far, so good."

"Take good care of him and you can expect him to do the same for you."

"Yes, yes," Lillia smiled through her tears. Then she leaned across the table and we kissed.

A feeling of melancholia enveloped me. I felt both

sadness and relief. All things said and done, it pained me to see it end.

Lillia raised her glass. "Friends always," she said, "to the very end!"

I raised my glass and touched it to hers. "To you!" I said.

"To us!" we said together.

Lilia and I parted company, but we remain the best of friends to this day.

Changes

The next morning I helped Lillia move her things into Stanley's condominium in Ixtapa. Stanley turned out to be a very likeable fellow, and I left feeling confident that Lillia was in good hands. After lunch I returned to my job at the Hotel Villa del Sol, feeling a bit sad but happy that it had worked out so well.

I worked at the Villa del Sol throughout the following season, renting and maintaining the water sports equipment in partnership with Helmut Liens. I touted myself as "The World's Oldest Beach Boy." Meanwhile, I spent every spare minute and peso attempting to repair the damages left by the hurricane. I was lucky to get the help and companionship of three young Germans when I most needed it. They loved surfing the waves as they wrapped around the King's Point, so they spent most of their time in the water. However, they also brought some wonderful changes. Two were apprentice carpenters and the third was a journeyman plumber. In exchange for free lodging, they happily devoted their spare time to the repair and renovation of my buildings. Thus, progress came both quickly and cheaply, while also having fun—my idea of a good job.

As soon as we restored the water system, we moved out of the rental house next door where Lillia and I had lived, and each of us occupied his own bungalow. It was the first time in almost four years that I went to sleep in my own bed and I savored every minute. The move gave us all a warm sense of accomplishment that boosted our sagging spirits. Despite the fact that there were still gaping holes in the roofs that exposed us to the rain and dewfall, we celebrated our move with a party for Freddy Mohr, Isabel, Margot and more. For a couple weeks we flew high on the ethereal wings of our success, but all too soon it had to end.

When my three German friends returned to their homeland, my bubble of bliss broke. Without the buoyant forces of their companionship and their skills, my sense of triumph soon degenerated into a listless state of loneliness and lassitude. In mid-May, Zihuatanejo's tourist season ended and so did my job at the Hotel Villa del Sol. Having spent all the money I had on repairing the hurricane damage, I was quite broke and alone. What followed was one of the loneliest and most frustrating summers in memory.

I was ecstatic to be back in the cozy embrace of my beloved house on the beach, but some hard facts of life polluted my euphoria. The amount of work and money that the place needed before I could hope to open for business was truly depressing. Furthermore, although nearby Ixtapa attracted a few guests on weekends, the Bay area remained virtually deserted. There was no place to go, nothing to do but fish, drink and blow smoke rings in the air. The summer humidity tested the limits of my endurance. Although our summer temperatures only rarely broke one hundred degrees Fahrenheit, the tropical humidity made me feel like I was living in a Turkish bath.

To make matters worse, the property was still not legally mine. So long as my case was pending in the local court, I did not have legal access to my own home. Until I could retrieve it from the jaws of Mexican justice, there was little hope of finding investors who could help me,, I could do nothing but feel sorry for myself.

Meditation

With no income and no prospects, I sank into a catatonic state of frustration and despair. I became a reclusive scavenger, living off coconuts, bananas, papayas and fish that Mother Nature provided. At night, I brooded alone over my misfortunes. During the day, I tried in vain to work off my frustrations with vigorous yard work and long swims to La Ropa Beach. But nothing could silence the whining, self-pitying chatter whirling around in my tortured mind. In desperation, I determined that I had to do something about it, lest I go crazy. I sought the consolation my fellow expatriates, Margo Chipman, Isabel Fortune and Arthur Agin.

"Why don't you join our yoga and meditation group?" suggested Margo. She had fallen in love with Zihuatanejo only shortly after I did and lived here ever since. She built her own household and raised four beautiful daughters as a single, working mother. Charming, bright and beautiful, Margo had known me in Zihuatanejo for over twenty five years before we discovered that we shared a lot more in common than our love for Zihuatanejo. We had grown up on the same block and attended the same schools back in Brentwood, Missouri.

"I didn't know Zih had a meditation group," I responded. "I would love to join you."

"We meet every afternoon on La Ropa Beach. Yoga starts about an hour before sunset. When the sun sinks below the horizon, we start our meditation and continue until dark."

Meditation transformed that summer from what was the most destitute and frustrating summer of my life into one of my most enlightening experiences. Between the long swims to La Ropa Beach and the half hour of yoga, I soon acquired a strong and handsome body.

But my tortured mind continued to harass me. My anger and resentment over Sanchez Mirus continued to commandeer almost all my wakeful moments. He even intruded on my sleep in dreams.

Surreptitiously, I cocked opened one eye and stole a forbidden look at those around me. They sat in the lotus position with apparent ease and comfort, their faces aglow in blissful ecstasy. A pang of jealous envy swept over me. Feeling annoyed and impatient with myself, I closed my eye and tried again.

While all the others in our meditation group seemed able to slip into their trance with graceful ease, my restless mind simply would not shut up. Pictures of my past flashed before my eyes like scenes from an old movie. Instead of slipping into a blissful state of Nirvana, it a conjured up a cornucopia of fears and frustrations out of the past, present and future. It reviewed every mistake I ever made, offered possible corrections and then projected them into future in revised format. Images of me strangling Sanchez Mirus by the throat or punching him in the eye popped up more often than I like to admit, triggering guilt and remorse. Even as all the others seemed to float off on cloud nine, the incessant jabber inside my head was literally driving me to distraction. My mind never rested. When at last it had processed all my personal problems, it gamely proceeded to take on all the urgent problems confronting the world.

The Monk's Largess

Photo 27: Margo Chipman and Chalo with the *Rempoche*

I complained of my dilemma to Grace Ralf, another long-time expatriate and a member of our group. She confessed that she was just as distracted as I was. However, she also offered a note of hope. "There's good news for us tortured souls," she assured me, "because a *Rempoche* is coming!"

"Rempoche? Who's that?" I inquired.

"Haven't you heard? He's a high Buddhist Monk. He lives in a monastery near Rhinesburg, New York. He's supposed to be one of the greatest Buddhist teachers of all time," Grace explained.

Within a week, the *Rempoche* appeared as promised, saffron robes and all. He had been invited to vacation here by several members of our meditation group, all of whom subscribed to the ideas of Buddhism. He was a peculiarly likeable fellow. Even when discussing serious issues, he wore the same benign smile as the Dali Lama. In his presence, my mind seemed to stop babbling enough to listen to what he had to say. I gratefully acknowledged this to him and took the opportunity to invite him to lunch on Las Gatas Beach. To my delight, he accepted my invitation.

The following day, the *Rempoche* and several others from our group showed up as promised. I offered to take them snorkeling over the King's Reef, but the *Rempoche* settled for a tour of my garden. Later, we strolled along the waters edge, listening to the eternal music of the waves. I told him about my frustrating experiments with meditation, and asked for his advice.

"Maybe we suffer, because we choose to suffer," he suggested.

"No one consciously chooses to suffer, do they?" I inquired.

"Oh yes, they do," the Monk corrected. "Few people actually live in their right mind simply because they are not aware that they have the option to do so. People who needlessly suffer are not living in their right mind. You must not be in your right mind or you would not suffer, especially in a setting like this."

"You make it sound simple. But I know that it's not."

"You simply have to choose well. Choose to walk in the light, instead of the shadows. Choose to focus on the good instead of the bad. Life is a matter of choice."

"Well, what happens when you did not choose for things to happen?" I asked. Then I proceeded to tell him about Sanchez Mirus and my problem with the land. "That was certainly not a matter of choice," I protested. "I never expected anyone like Sanchez Mirus to show up in my life, but he did."

"Well, look around you. Did he make off with some of it? Do you see anything disagreeable, anything ugly or repulsive?"

"Well, no, but I see all the work it still needs."

The *Rempoche* chuckled softly. "Is there anything worth having that doesn't require work and frustration?" he asked rhetorically. "Possessions create their own problems. Desires exact a heavy price. Whether they are realized or not, the price is dear."

"That is precisely my problem," I complained. "I don't even have possession of my own house. It's still tied up in litigation. I can't get it out of the courts."

"That is why it is always easier to want what you already have. It seems to me that you already have everything you need to be happy, everything except your right mind that is. Just look around you. Do you see any law courts or villain's lurking about?"

"Well no, not at the present moment."

"The present moment is all you will ever have," he assured me. "All the rest, the past and the future, don't exist. They never did. The present is the only true reality."

"Then why am I so miserable and broke? Why can't I sleep in my own bed tonight? Why does somebody else control where and how I live?"

"Look around you again. Do you see anything you don't like?"

"No, don't get me wrong. I love this place."

"So here you are, alive and well and, may I say, living in paradise."

"Well, the property is not really mine. It's tied up in court and it needs a lot of work that I can't pay for."

"Do you want to know my humble opinion?" he interjected.

"Yes, of course," I answered.

"I think that you may be living in your right body, but I question if you are living in your "right mind." Your mind is not living here in Paradise with you. It is living someplace else, which is not so nice. It has trapped you in some other place, either in your real past or your imaginary future or both. One thing is certain, however. It is not real. It is not here right now or you would not be suffering, for this is truly paradise. You are missing out on the only thing that is real and true. That is, being here now, at this instant."

He paused and I thought it over. I could see the logic of what he said, but I did not feel it conformed to my view.

"Have you ever done or thought anything other than in the present?" he asked. "Nothing ever happens in the past or the future. It always happens in the present. When you dwell in the past or the future, you are living in an illusion, for neither exists outside the mind. The only thing that is real is the present, so why choose to live in the past or in fear of the future? Why not enjoy the present for all that it is worth?"

"I admit, that makes sense." I said.

"When the future becomes the present, the solution to your problem will show up on its own."

"So what can I do about it right now?"

"Do nothing," he said. "Enjoy life and give thanks. This property has been here a long, long time. I think it will stay here a while longer without you fretting about it. Don't you?"

"In that case I guess I should worry about me worrying about it so much!"

The *Rempoche* laughed. "Now you are catching on! It's just a trick. Your noisy mind wants you to believe that you and this property are one and the same, but you are not."

"I often feel that we are mere extensions of each other."

"Synonymous, perhaps, but otherwise, not related. You each have your own survival agenda and your own separate life to live."

"So what can I do about it?"

"Live and let live. Just acknowledge your mind for what it

is and what it is doing. Its selfish, self-centered obsession with itself is nothing personal. It is simply doing its job. It is part of the price we pay for being human. But you don't have to buy into it. Just recognize it for what it is. Let it know that you are on to its tricks and know what it is doing. Humor it as you might humor a child. You will be surprised at what a difference it will make."

"How do you do that?" I asked. "Can you show me?"

"I can't show you, but I can guide you," said the Monk. He motioned me to sit down on a chair. "Now, close your eyes," he said, and I obeyed. "Now, erase all thoughts from your mind. When your mind is completely blank, ask yourself this simple question, 'I wonder what my mind will think of next?' If some random thoughts intrude, just acknowledge them and let them pass. Then repeat the question, "I wonder what my mind with think of next?'"

I followed his instructions, expecting the usual barrage of senseless jabber. However, much to my amazement, I didn't think of anything! In a few minutes, the *Rempoche* said, "Now, open your eyes."

"Amazing!" I exclaimed. "For the first time in my life, my mind remained a total blank. It didn't think of anything at all. It was blank!"

The *Rempoche* giggled. "Now you know how to meditate," he said. "And when you open your eyes and you somehow see things differently. Instead of seeing things in your shadowy past or unknown future, you see things in the true light of the moment. Meditation teaches you that time is a human element. that there is no past and no future. All that exists is what you see before you, right here, and right now. So take a look around you and tell me what you see."

"Yes. It's beautiful!" I said. I felt an overwhelming pang of love for the place.

"If you are alive and well, you can be sure that you are

living in paradise, for that is where we all live. The essence of our planet is paradise. So why not love it now, which is the only time you can?"

I shook my head forlornly. "I wish I could, but I can't. As long as Sanchez Mirus still has legal possession of this place, he also has possession of my life."

"Then where is he? Show him to me! I don't see him."

"I am saying that legally it is still not mine."

"But that is only an idea, an illusion. In reality, it is nobody's property. It simply is."

"Then why all this torment? Why all this fighting?"

"Perhaps because you simply won't let him go."

"Why would I not let him go? I want him out of my life!"

"Probably because you would have nobody to blame for your mistakes but yourself."

"Yes. It's lonely out there."

"If you want that man out of your life, you have to forgive him and let him go. Let him go to be who and whatever he wants to be."

"Only if and when I get my home back, legally as well as in fact," I interjected.

"If you don't choose to let him go, he may haunt you for the rest of your life," he warned. "You will spend your time debating what you should have done, or could have done or would like to do some time in the future."

"But how can I do that? Is there some secret? I'd really like to get rid of him, but he keeps popping up in my mind like a clog."

The Monk chuckled again. "Then simply give in. Surrender to his reality. Accept him as he is, faults and all, without conditions. Let him go out of your life just as he is and he will leave. Just try it," urged the Monk. "When you are ready, go to the beach and shout it out loud, 'Sanchez Mirus, I forgive you. I forgive you and I love you just as you are!' Do it ten times. Do it every day until you actually feel it and believe it in body and soul. Will you do that?"

"Yes, I will try it. I promise."

"No, trying is not enough," the *Rempoche* insisted. "You must actually do it. If not for yourself, then do it for me. Do it for humanity."

The Monk smiled and gently pressed his forehead against mine. "I know you will do it, because you really want to do it. You are in a noble struggle. For that reason I will give you a Buddhist name. I will name you *Tarching,* In my language, *Tarching* means 'Peaceful Warrior' and that is who you are."

That evening at Sunset Beach, what I called the beach directly in front of my house, I went to the water's edge alone and did as the Monk suggested.

Now, I was not a religious person. In fact, I thought most religions and gods were man-made metaphors to explain Mother Nature. The defense of religious gods and beliefs systems resulted in more murder and mayhem than all other crime in the world. However, if the *Rempoche* could convince me that if I forgave and forgot the abuses of someone like Sanchez Mirus, there was still hope for the world at large.

And I managed to do it. I forgave Alvaro Sanchez Mirus and wished him a pleasant departure out of my mind and out of my life. As a result, my environment, my ambiance, my social and political stature, and above all my personal outlook on life took a sudden turn for the better. Without him there, life seemed lighter, my prospects brighter.

Tarching had triumphed where Owen Lee had failed.

Photo 28: The *Rempoche* blesses the NSC Ecology Exhibition

Transformation

As the *Rempoche* had promised, forgiveness worked miracles. Within days of forgiving Sanchez Mirus, my melancholia lifted and miracles began to happen. For example, Blake Mitchell, a casual rental client, showed up out of nowhere and volunteered eight thousand dollars in cash to pay for the most urgently-needed building repairs.

Blake's random act of kindness literally put me back in business. It also inspired me to return to work with the drive and spirit that such a gift warrants. Each new improvement or repair served to lift my spirits and strengthen my self-confidence. Once more, my shaken relationship with my beloved began to blossom. I regarded the place as one might a beautiful mistress whose insatiable appetites constantly tested my limits. I loved her madly and lavished her with gifts. So long as she responded to my advances, I was content to be her willing slave. The only thing left for me to desire was the soft warm body of someone like Becky in my bed.

I must confess that I missed Becky. After years of searching elsewhere, I had finally but belatedly come to realize that Becky had been the kind of all 'round female companion that I had always wanted from the start. In the wistful hope that I might be able to entice her back, I sent her a letter in care of her parents. I asked her to please forgive my past neglect and invited her to come back and join me in Zihuatanejo. Nine months later, to my surprise, I received this answer:

Dear Owen,

Thank you for your kind invitation. I am deeply moved by your thoughtfulness, but, alas, I can not accept it. I am in the process of becoming a Buddhist nun, which requires my vow of celibacy and poverty.

For the past two years, I have been studying and teaching in the Temple of Ten Thousand Buddhas in Tallmadge, California.

I have found happiness here and hope you have found the same in Zihuatanejo. Please convey my love and best wishes to all my old friends.

Namaste,
Becky

Although I personally subscribe to the beliefs of Buddhism more than any other religion, I also believe celibacy and poverty are both dull and stupid even for nuns and priests. Why deny oneself two of nature's most precious gifts just to prove your fidelity to an abstract belief? I resented losing Becky to a religious idea, no matter how benign it be. It was almost as if Becky had died. Suddenly, I felt truly alone. It made me want her back all the more. It drove me to stop and think about who I really was and what I really wanted out of life. I was beginning to feel that my forbidden love for a piece of Mexican real estate had simply made me a lonely prisoner in paradise.

Deliverance

One sunny morning, I was out in the garden weeding when a helicopter circled noisily overhead. At first, I paid little attention. It was not unusual to see choppers belonging to the Judicial Police scanning the surroundings for the tell-tale green of marijuana plants. It was part of Mexico's on-going war on drugs financed by the U.S. Government. This time, however, the flight behavior was different. The chopper hovered low over the roof of my restaurant for several minutes. I could see people inside the aircraft peering down at me. Nervously, I wondered if they suspected me of growing marijuana. Then, to my amazement, the chopper slowly settled onto the flat open surface of Sunset Beach. As the monster settled heavily onto the beach, it stirred up its own little sand storm and drove all the animals berserk. My two cats scrambled under the house and Coco, my dog, ran around in tight circles, barking frantically.

I hastily ditched my cigarette for fear they might think it was a joint. When the doors of the chopper finally opened, I was pleasantly surprised. Instead of police, out stepped a short, baby-faced young man dressed in Bermuda shorts and sandals. Several other young men clamored out of the helicopter behind him, all dressed in shorts or bathing suits. Only one was wearing a uniform. He was Jose Angel Lara, a young officer I knew from the Captain of the Port's office. I knew then that their visit was friendly and casual.

As the rotor wings slowly ground to a stop, the group moved out from under them, gazing about like curious tourists. Finally, their gaze met mine and I haltingly approached them, wearing only my underpants.

"You must be Owen," said the first young man. He smiled and extended his hand.

I shook the hand and said, "*Asi es*. I'm Owen. And with whom do I have the pleasure?"

"My name is Hector Alonso," he said. "These are my friends."

"Hector Alonso Rebaque," interjected Jose Angel, the one in the uniform. He was a familiar sight around the village pier.

"I heard a lot about you," said Hector, "and I thought we should meet."

"And I've heard about you as well," I said. "You are Mexico's most famous race car driver! I like the way you get around. I am pleased to meet you."

Photo 29: Hector "*Rebaque*" & friends arrive on Las Gatas Beach

"Well, I was once a race car driver," he smiled modestly. "But that was years ago."

Two years earlier, Hector "*Rebaque*" had led the Indianapolis 500 Memorial Day Speedway Classic for over an hour. This made him an instant celebrity within Mexico, and everybody except me seemed to know his story. He had inherited the name "*Rebaque*" from his grandfather who had performed the same feat many years earlier. Neither car had ever finished the Classic Memorial Day Race due to mechanical failures, but leading the race was close enough to winning to insure their instant and lasting fame.

Since my restaurant was still a shambles, I invited the group into my house for a drink. To my delight, they made over my little house as if had had been the Taj Mahal. "What will you have?" I asked, "Booze or beer?"

Everyone except Hector asked for beer. Hector wanted water. I was out of water, but I knew there was some in the rental house so I said, "We have to go next door for water, so bring your drinks and I will show you around."

As I led them to the rental house next door, Hector asked, "Do you own this house too?"

"I built the original buildings to house the students for our summer *Camp de Mar* program, but I had to sell it. So now I just rent it."

"I've heard that you had a few problems regarding your property," he said.

"That's putting it mildly," I answered. I poured Hector a glass of water. "Let me tell you about it."

As I escorted them around the grounds, I told them about the Nature Study Center and Alvaro Sanchez Mirus and INDE. Over the following weeks, Hector Rebacque and I met on several occasions and we got along well. I soon learned that Hector was the son of a wealthy architect and real estate developer in Mexico City. He was here to scout out potential investment opportunities, he told me. He had come at the right time.

Hector knew all about the problems pertaining to *ejido* lands in Mexico. He had had to face them himself. Furthermore, he seemed to know a lot about my problems with Sanchez Mirus. Near the end of the week, he asked, "Is there any way I can help you?"

With a tinge of excitement, I took his offer as my long-awaited cue to act. It was the first time that a qualified Mexican had offered any help. "Yes, Hector," I said. "I think we might be able to help each other."

Hector could have coasted through life on the shirt tails of his wealthy father, but he had chosen to make his way on his own. As I got to know him better, it became abundantly clear that Hector intended not only to follow in his fathers footsteps, but also to beat him in his own game.

Like his father, Hector was a real estate speculator and he made no bones about it. He liked to get down to business.

Therefore, he had little time for the idealistic dreams of creating Nature Study Centers or tourist attractions like the Tarascan Indian Village. However, he was quick to recognize its potential as a profitable real estate investment.

Hector's casual display of wealth and power enabled him to open doors and get things done where few others could. He was very ambitious and a fierce competitor, and I liked that. I determined that Hector had just the right degree of social and political stature that I needed in order to get things done and to challenge the ruthless tactics of Sanchez Mirus. At the same time, I recognized what a rare and timely opportunity that I represented for him.

I never doubted that my property was the most desirable in the Bay. As a *gringo*, however, I could never hope to do it justice under the current laws of Mexico without a Mexican partner of some stature. I felt Hector and I would make a symbiotic partnership to mutually benefit both of us, and the community as well. I decided to go for it by revealing to Hector my "Secret Plan."

My Secret Plan

From the beginning of my conflict with Sanchez Mirus, I had been nursing a plan of last resort by which I might legally recuperate my beloved home on Las Gatas Beach. But first I needed to find the right kind of partner with the right kind of money and political connections. Hector was as close to being the right kind of partner as I was going to find, so I decided to make him a proposal. The only problem was that I could never get a moment alone with him. In Zihuatanejo, Hector was always surrounded by an entourage of people who were competing for his attention. This made it difficult to have a private conversation, so I went to see him in Mexico City.

"I am here on the assumption that you are still interested in acquiring a property like mine around Zihuatanejo Bay," I said.

"*Asi es*. That's a valid assumption."

"I have a plan by which I can legally recuperate my property from Sanchez Mirus, but I would need the help of someone like you in order to do it. Would you be interested?"

"Well that depends. What do you have in mind?"

"When I first acquired my property from Don Carlos Barnard in 1967, I knew that the sale of *ejido* land was against the law. Yet I also knew that there ways to get around that law. Marshall Allen and Freddy Mohr had effectively "bought" the land for the Hotel El Capricho del Rey by doing so in the name of Arnoldo Veerboonen, their Mexican partner. Since it worked so well for them, my lawyer advised me to follow their example by buying the property through my three name lenders whom I could trust. These were my three principal building contractors—Manual Almaguer, my general contractor, Francisco Rabollard, my masonry contractor, and Ernesto Lara, my carpentry contractor. I knew and trusted all three of them. They qualified within the local community as legitimate *ejidatarios*. In return for a modest fee, in addition to the building contract, each signed a legal document that ceded all future sales rights exclusively to me. At this stage, all three had long since finished their work and gone their separate ways. However, all three are still living in Zih and still willing to collaborate. However, their willingness comes at a price, as always, and that, my friend, is why I need you."

I took a breath. "Hector, you are here looking for real estate investments. Meanwhile, I am here sitting on the most beautiful piece of land in the Bay. Do you think we can work together?"

Hector nodded his head. "Yes. I think we can work together,"

"These three contractors are the legitimate homesteaders or *ejidatarios* of the property," I assured him. "It is not Sanchez Mirus and it not me. However, they can sell the property only to me. Therefore, if you were to negotiate a price with them, I will authorize them to cede the land over to you or your company. Then you can pay me with stock in the company. That way it is all legal. Sanchez Mirus could never dare to challenge us in court."

Hector had been listening intently. Now he was nodding his head. "How much money do you think they will want?" he asked.

I shrugged my shoulders. "I will have to go ask them."

"Yes. Please find out and let me know. I am definitely interested."

I went to visit my three *ejidatarios,* one-by-one, and I was pleasantly surprised in every case. All three were friendly and eager to help, albeit at twice the price we had originally agreed on some twenty years before. Hector then registered the deeds with the Fidecomiso de la Bahia de Zihuatanejo (FIBAZI). Using these deeds as collateral, he then acquired six additional hectares (14.5 Acres) of adjacent land from FIBAZI at the same bargain price. Then he formed a corporation, the *Imobliaria Punta de Princessa, S.A. de C.V.* and awarded me the stock.

My share of the corporation amounted to less than one percent of the total stock. I questioned Hector regarding the fairness of such a meager portion. Hector assured me that it was a fair exchange. He showed me statistics and computer projections to back up his claim. I finally signed, but many friends think that I was crazy to accept it. "It leaves you at the mercy of Hector's whim," they complained.

Conclusion

Whether my friends were right or wrong remains to be seen. I suppose sometime soon Hector and I must determine what our worth has really been to each other. Meanwhile, he and I have enjoyed a friendly relationship that is its own reward. I prefer to have faith that Hector won't turn against me in my old age. When the big money makes Hector the offer that he cannot refuse, perhaps all my dreams will be shattered. But I don't think so.

Hector's timely arrival released me from the grip of local power politics and enabled me to refocus my attention on my beloved paradise—to work my splendid restaurant on the King's Point while continuing in my quest for a Nature Study Center promoting the ecological views of Captain Cousteau. Meanwhile, our association effectively ended hostile attempts to take over the land by the likes of Sanchez Mirus. Whenever someone challenged my right to live and work on Las Gatas Beach, I simply directed them to Hector, and I never heard from them again.

As the *Rempoche* said, "Why worry about what does not exist?" I choose to leave the past to the past and the future to the future, so that I may fully savor this present moment with my beloved.

Now, as I approach my eightieth year of life, I am thankful for the privilege of having spent over half of it living where I most wanted to live and doing what I most wanted to do when I most wanted to do it. People often ask, "If you had it to do all over again, would you?" To them I answer with an unequivocal "Yes!"

I still believe that it is important to follow your dreams. They may take you to some strange places and confront you with many unexpected challenges, but they will never bore you. I firmly believe that we live in a beneficent world, wherein good dominates bad, right dominates wrong and divine justice ultimately triumphs over adversity. For that is the nature of the universe.

I believe that life is its own reward, and that living it for all it is worth is our sacred duty and our reason for being. For that reason I believe that it is never too late to start over. We all make mistakes, for that is how we learn and evolve. The second time around is always better than the first, if only for having had the experience. For example, I am now in the process of changing my business to something more in keeping with my station in life. I am ready to turn over the more strenuous activities of my restaurant and ecology tours to someone who is as young and energetic as I was when I first arrived, so that I can devote more time to real estate.

I am now in the business of helping others to fulfill their dreams of owning a tropical seaside paradise like mine. It is now legal for foreigners to do so. Times have changed and so has Mexico. Whereas both laws and culture were once against it, owning a piece a tropical paradise in Mexico is now an idea whose time has come.

Thanks to recent reforms in Mexico's Immigration and Real Estate laws, it is now possible to fulfill those dreams of owning a piece of Mexican beach property without having to face the kind of social, political and economic hardships that I had to face. Mexico is now a prominent actor on the world stage. The kind of Mexico that I encountered in 1968 no longer exists. Mexico is now locked into a vital and symbiotic relationship with her two northern neighbors via NAFTA. This treaty binds Mexico together with the United States and Canada in a common market for their common good. Citizens of these countries can now buy, sell and invest in each others life and real estate without the fear of losing it to corrupt citizens or dysfunctional governments.

Today, Mexico, Canada and America not only need each other, they depend on each other for their own survival.

Despite some gargantuan efforts to maintain the ethnic, economic and political barriers that once separated them, the three nations are now united in a contemporary alliance of wills as well as ways. The driving forces behind these changes are the population densities and the economic disparities that exist on both sides of the borders. As the more sophisticated populations move away from a rural labor-based farm economy into an economy based on creative and intellectual services, they need somebody to replace them. Otherwise the entire system will stall and crash. As the old saying goes, "It may be a lousy job, but somebody has to do it."

The same social and economic pressures have brought about massive cross-border migrations throughout the free world. Over thirty-six million foreign-born people now live and work inside the United States alone. Almost half of them come from their Hispanic neighbors south of the border. In the year 2005, Mexican immigrants in the United States sent around $19 billion back home to Mexico, making immigration, whether legal or not, the most profitable source of national income after oil and far more lucrative than even tourism.

As a result of cross-border immigration, the majority of the voting population in the state of California is now of Hispanic origin. Therefore, it was not surprising when, on July 1, 2005, Antonio Villaraigosa, son of Mexican immigrants became the first Hispanic Mayor to preside over America's largest metropolitan area, the City of Los Angeles.

Similar changes have been taking place in many smaller areas throughout the country and throughout world. As poverty, wars, pestilence, natural disasters, and just plain ambition inspire more people to immigrate abroad, other countries will experience the same dynamics until eventually some nation votes to close its doors to immigration. If and when this happens, I fear it might trigger an ecological feeding frenzy of such monstrous proportions that it could test the limits human depravity.

Meanwhile, cross-border immigration is changing not just the face of our planet, it is also changing the face of our species. Immigration serves as an ethnic and cultural homogenizer. As the innate resources of Nature succumb to the demands of our endlessly growing populations, these same pressures are blending the various physical, mental and cultural aspects of humanity into a new homogenized breed. By the end of this century, the typical person will probably look, act, think, and behave quite differently than we do today. So might their governments.

A new international breed of person is already evolving, and I consider myself to be among them. At the turn of this century, over forty million Mexicans — almost fifteen percent of Mexico's total population — were legally living and working in the United States. Nevertheless, most remained more closely tied to their mother land than to their adopted country. In body, mind and spirit, most remained more Mexican than American. Consequently, many demanded the right to vote in Mexican elections. In 2003, the Mexican Congress unanimously granted them that privilege. Thus, Mexicans immigrants living in foreign countries acquired dual nationality. The Mexican government felt obliged to grant the same privileges to foreigners living and working in Mexico. That is why I, like many others, can now claim dual nationality.

As a dual national, I am now legally qualified to live, work and vote in Mexico. I can also buy and sell real estate in both countries. Consequently, I have now acquired a second profession as well as a second nationality. Although I continue to tout the natural wonders of Zihuatanejo on my

Reef and Jungle Tours, I have also become a sentimental old matchmaker. I specialize in matching romantics with the seaside properties of their dreams. As the oldest resident expatriate in Zihuatanejo, I probably know of as many seaside properties as anybody in the area, and I delight in putting them together with the right people.

Postscript

Some of you might wonder what became of my plans to create a Nature Study Center on Las Gatas Beach and to propagate the ideas of Captain Jacques Yves Cousteau.

Regarding the latter, I have embodied Captain Cousteau's philosophy regarding our ecosystem in yet another book titled *Nature's Rebellion*. This book grew of the preface for that one.

As for the Nature Study Center, my dreams for it endure, but on a much smaller scale. My once-elaborate exhibition regarding man's inter-relationship with the global ecosystem was devoured by ubiquitous and insatiable termites. A more modest series of educational posters and paintings has now taken their place among the coconut palms that lead to my restaurant. My dream of converting the reef-protected lagoon into a "Captive Aquarium" were eventually overwhelmed by the beach's own little population explosion. As the children and the grand-children of the three original families grew into adulthood, they opened their own restaurants on the beach next door. The reef-protected lagoon is now chuck full of swimmers and lined with thirteen waterfront restaurants.

The hills behind Las Gatas Beach, where I had once envisioned the Tarascan Indian Village, have succumbed to the march of progress. They have been divided and subdivided into building lots that are now for sale to the highest bidder. The only part of the original proposal I once made to INDE that remains a possibility is the conversion of the paved lighthouse jungle trail into a "Botanical Garden Trail." Nature has already endowed the trail with a tropical splendor that is breath-taking. With a little help from her friends, The Botanical Garden Trail could become of international importance, a valuable tourist attraction and a source of communal income.

The last time I submitted my proposal to convert the Lighthouse Trail into a Botanical Garden, I talked to Licensiada Lilia Rueda and Licensiado Alejando Massa Abascar, Directors of Alternative Tourism for the Secretary of Tourism in Mexico City, once in May and again in November of 2005. As of the end of January 2006, there has been no response, but hope springs eternal and Mother Nature is awesome. After almost forty years of looking at each other, my forbidden love has not waned nor wavered. Her control remains firm and strong. Despite her incessant, often unreasonable demands, I still love her as much as anybody could. And between you and me, I think that she still loves me, too.

We certainly would not be the same without each other, that's for sure! It is a very special relationship, and we delight in sharing it with people like you. We invite you to come share our paradise on your next vacation. For more information and reservations, please visit our websites at www.LasGatasBeachClub.com.

Photo Credits

Made in the USA